"[An] eye-opening history. . . . [A] great reminder of the value of the field, and the importance of these skills for anyone at any age."   —Matthew Wheeland, *Civil Eats*

"There's one important thing you'll fully understand after you've read *The Secret History of Home Economics*: our foremothers were not to be trifled with. . . . Readers of women's history will love this book, as will general historians, feminists and anyone with an interest in domestic arts."

—Terri Schlichenmeyer, *Washington Informer*

"Home ec . . . may conjure up lessons in baking blueberry muffins and sewing dresses, but in her detail-filled and fascinating book, Danielle Dreilinger dynamites that cliché with glee."

—*Air Mail*

"Thoroughly entertaining. . . . As we look toward the future, it's always good to consider where we've been, and *The Secret History of Home Economics* helps us do that."

— Deborah Hopkinson, *BookPage*

"A fascinating work of history, extensively researched, on a subject long ignored: how home economics helped shaped American life. Full of delicious anecdotes, *The Secret History of Home Economics* makes the case that home ec, often maligned and misunderstood, always provided students, regardless of gender, with skills that make life better, and should be revived."

—Nancy Jo Sales, author of *American Girls*

"This book tells the unexpected story of how home economics began as an intellectual haven for smart women—Black as well as white—who were otherwise blocked from studying science, but ended up as a field less rigorous and more conforming. Black women were at the forefront of this history, and their role is a revelation. Danielle Dreilinger makes a convincing case for bringing back the skills that home economics alone could teach."

—Marion Nestle, professor of nutrition, food studies, and public health, emerita, at NYU and author of *Let's Ask Marion*

"This is an extremely interesting and engaging page-turner book. . . . It will stimulate important dialogue among those within and outside the profession about our past and present, and what the future of the profession, education, and society should be."

—Virginia Vincenti, professor emerita at University of Wyoming and coeditor of *Rethinking Home Economics*

"A thorough, delightful, inspiring history of heroines whose stories Danielle Dreilinger gloriously rescues from the compost heap of history." —Gustavo Arellano, author of *Taco USA*

"Danielle Dreilinger's *The Secret History of Home Economics* is a revelation. That secret history is rich with gender and race issues, and opened the eyes of this former home ec student. It will open yours too."

—Ann Hood, author of *The Knitting Circle*

"I took home economics by choice in seventh grade, and I always assumed it was an outdated way to train budding Stepford housewives. This book made me realize that everything I thought I knew about home economics was wrong. It's a career that provided vital scientific and economic inroads for women, and a history that is so relevant today."

—Marisa Meltzer, author of *This Is Big*

"By reading Danielle Dreilinger's biography of this long over-looked and deeply influential field, we come to understand not only the secret history of home economics but the secret history of American feminism. Dreilinger's case for continuing to rein-vent this too oft maligned discipline for the twenty-first century provides a thoughtful—and spot on—road map for how and why schools can teach children not only to manage homes efficiently but to become lifelong advocates for racial, gender, and social equality." —Sarah Carr, author of *Hope Against Hope*

"In an important new work revealing a surprising history, Danielle Dreilinger has rescued women home-economists from the past. . . . Her book will convince you that this field of study should be restored to its proper place in STEAM education for all." —Katherine Sharp Landdeck, author of *The Women with Silver Wings*

"Finally, someone has written a social history of American home economists that is neither patronizing nor hostile. . . . Kudos to Danielle Dreilinger for this very readable and very sophisticated account of the women who had such an enormous impact on American society and culture."
—Ruth S. Cowan, author of *More Work for Mother*

"With lively prose and engrossing portraits of dynamic and accomplished women, this is a vital and inspiring reassessment of an oft-caricatured field." —*Publishers Weekly*, starred review

"Spirited. . . . A fresh contribution to women's history and a resurrection of contributions too often overlooked."
—*Kirkus Reviews*

THE SECRET HISTORY

of

HOME
ECONOMICS

THE SECRET HISTORY

of

HOME ECONOMICS

How Trailblazing Women
Harnessed the Power of Home and Changed
the Way We Live

―――――――――― ⌂ ――――――――――

DANIELLE DREILINGER

W. W. NORTON & COMPANY
Independent Publishers Since 1923

For information about permission to reproduce selections from this book,
write to Permissions, W. W. Norton & Company, Inc.,
500 Fifth Avenue, New York, NY 10110

For information about special discounts for bulk purchases,
please contact W. W. Norton Special Sales at
specialsales@wwnorton.com or 800-233-4830

Manufacturing by Lakeside Book Company
Book design by Lisa Buckley
Production manager: Beth Steidle

Library of Congress Cataloging-in-Publication Data

Names: Dreilinger, Danielle, author.
Title: The secret history of home economics : how trailblazing
women harnessed the power of home and changed the way we live /
Danielle Dreilinger.
Description: First edition. | New York, N.Y. : W. W. Norton & Company,
[2021] | Includes bibliographical references and index.
Identifiers: LCCN 2020054841 | ISBN 9781324004493 (hardcover) |
ISBN 9781324004509 (epub)
Subjects: LCSH: Home economists—United States—Biography. |
Housekeepers—United States—Biography. | Women scientists—United
States—Biography. | Home economics—United States—History.
Classification: LCC TX139 .D74 2021 | DDC 640.92—dc23
LC record available at https://lccn.loc.gov/2020054841

ISBN 978-1-324-02186-5 pbk.

W. W. Norton & Company, Inc., 500 Fifth Avenue, New York, N.Y. 10110
www.wwnorton.com

W. W. Norton & Company Ltd., 15 Carlisle Street, London W1D 3BS

1 2 3 4 5 6 7 8 9 0

This is for Kate.

CONTENTS

Everything You Know
about Home Economics
Is Wrong

When you imagine the founder of home economics, who do you see? Betty Crocker, Donna Reed? A white man with a handlebar moustache glaring at women to stay in their place? A stern, conservative lady teacher with 1950s glasses, teaching girls how to do housework—someone like Dolores Umbridge, only less evil?

Try a white female chemist, Ellen Swallow Richards, the first woman to attend MIT, who believed fervently in the power of science to free women from "drudgery." "My life is to be one of active fighting," she wrote.[1] Try a famous Black woman, Margaret Murray Washington, who thought that improving the home could end racial inequality.

That's all you need to know to realize that everything you thought about home economics is wrong. Home economics was far more than baking lumpy blueberry muffins, sewing throw pillows, or lugging a bag of flour around in a baby sling to learn the perils of parenting. In its purest form, home economics was about changing the world through the household.

Home economists instructed and inspired waves of women who built science careers helping people live better lives. Together, they built an empire of jobs and influence. They originated the food groups, the federal poverty level, the consumer-protection movement, clothing care labels, school lunch, the discipline of women's studies, and the Rice Krispies Treat. They were the first to measure the economic value of housework and the amount of physical effort it took. They enabled millions of people around the world to survive harrowing deprivation. They had the ear of presidents and first ladies and queens. They helped win wars. Their work operated in as large a sphere as battlefields and on as intimate a scale as counting calories. All done with pragmatic empiricism, with an eye on careers. Home economists created tens of thousands of jobs—not just in high school classrooms but in labs, colleges, government agencies, and business departments. For decades, there was always a job for a home economist. For decades, the profession was even respected.

Through home economics, Gladys Gary Vaughn went from segregated Florida to a doctoral degree and a career that included the civil rights office of the US Department of Agriculture and the presidency of a major international volunteer organization. "The nation has benefited. They have laughed at it. But they have benefited," she said.[2]

Home economics has been a back door for women to enter science; part of a surprisingly large government-backed movement; a guilt trip for women left cold by the household arts; a trapdoor or a springboard for women of color; a sometimes ironic, sometimes nostalgic preoccupation of third-wave feminists; a conservative calling card; an aesthetic obsession for the

Instagram set; a feminist battlefield; and the locus for countless anxieties about women's lives.

A revival seems bewilderingly overdue. The last twenty years have seen countless DIY homemaking blogs, the Food Network and *Project Runway*, Instagram and Pinterest, eco-friendly slow fashion and knitted pussyhats. We live amid high-pressure parenting, financial and environmental crises, the return of vo-tech education, stress over "adulting," and women still doing the lion's share of home labor. In response to a global pandemic, people stripped supermarkets of flour and big-box stores of sewing machines. Why *hasn't* home economics come back? Practitioners will tell you: because it never went away. Though most people think it went the way of the eight-track, home economics is, though diminished, still here.

I went to the 2019 convention of the national family and consumer sciences association—that's what the field calls "home ec" now—and saw its members address crucial societal problems with creativity and compassion. A fifty-year-old father, veteran, and prison educator presented his dissertation on how he used self-exploration to gain insights into reducing the chances of prisoners reoffending after release. A fashion student manufactured bags from an upholstery factory's leftovers. A teacher at a Native American boarding school told me about the day each year that she takes the students to fish and then to clean and cook their catch. (It's a very long day.) She hoped her lessons would give them an alternative to the few options in their remote communities besides fast food. A St. Louis housing inspector went back to school for home economics and thought she would change jobs after graduation, only to realize that her new studies fit perfectly into her current job. Now she brings neighborhoods together around reducing blight. And yes, an Idaho community educator talked to a full room about her Instant Pot workshops. Many people who attend get multicookers as presents and then don't use them because they're scared of blowing something up, she said. That session took on extra significance when I visited my mother and we took her new Instant Pot out of the box where it had sat since the holidays.

But, you argue, we can't fix the world one person at a time. Making one's own clothes is an expensive privilege when shirts are cheap at Walmart. Cooking dinner doesn't solve health or family problems, and emphasizing the value of home cooking puts an unnecessary moral burden on people who are already struggling to raise children without enough time or support. Women are still stuck trying to "do it all," while we still don't expect the same of men. You're not the first to air those arguments. Home economists have made all these points, the exact same ones, over and over again. Their foresight has been tremendous. To thumb through the home economics literature is to find our current questions debated decades or longer ago. In 1899 home economists argued for school gardens, STEM education for girls, takeout food, and affordable day care. Forty years ago, under visionary businesswoman Satenig St. Marie, J. C. Penney's home economics magazine—yes, one existed, and it's fascinating, as you'll see—addressed conscious consumption, the impact of screens on children, and racist microaggressions. And yet home economics has been denigrated, over and over and over again, as "just stitching and stirring."

Sewing is actually a perfect example of the field's sophistication. Its place in home economics has been stereotyped, omnipresent—and eternally questioned. The sewing machine, patented in the US in 1846, was a truly revolutionary invention. Nonetheless, Richards and Washington didn't find sewing romantic or soothing, living as they did in the time of textile factory accidents and women taking in piecework to try to keep their families from starving. Even when home sewing appeared to be cheaper than buying, home economists reminded everyone that women's time had value. Simultaneously, they sought to protect garment workers and customers by fighting for better working conditions, nonpoisonous dyes, and accurate labeling of consumer goods. Mass production, they believed, should not free some women from drudgery by exploiting others. Moreover, many home economics teachers insisted that sewing instruction should cohere with intellectual goals, should be carefully designed to lead to real careers and exercise the brain as much as the fingers. "Skill of hand may but multiply our cushions and doilies," a Massachusetts home economics teacher wrote in 1917. "Power of intellect will go further." A college administrator forty years ago advocated to replace sewing machines with chemistry equipment and "study fibers for their endurance and thermal properties; and then study the subsequent fabrics for safety and comfort features for persons of all ages and for consumer aspects of durability."[3] Virginia teacher Angela DeHart carried on that tradition in 2017: she got rid of her classroom's sewing machines, because the only jobs they prepared students for were sweatshops outside the country. Hand-sewing was a different matter, however, and she did teach that: surgeons, she said, have to sew. Yet despite decades of pushback, machine-sewing has endured in home economics. Students and teachers told me that sewing taught spatial relations, geometry, and problem-solving, and helped with stress relief and depression. To everyone's surprise, the coronavirus pandemic even revived its utility, as people clamored for masks.

Home economists were not always paragons of modernity, and they did not all have the best motives. Sometimes they got it wrong. The group of white people that appointed itself the founders of the movement embraced western agricultural universities but ignored Black colleges. Some got in bed with nativists and eugenicists, expressed disgust for people who ate tortillas or garlic, imposed a middle-class vision of the good life no matter how irrelevant, and used immigrant stereotypes to mock servants. Later on, in the 1950s, they got jobs telling other women to stay home. They successfully created a professional domain for women that at first flourished but over the long term painted women into a corner. However, for all their faults, they believed that women—that all people—should be chemists, university deans, and business leaders, and that they should be free to lead fulfilling lives. They thought that homes should foster health, intellectual development, and loving relationships, not show off the perfect set of drapes.

This book does not advocate for homemaking or bring you home-ec life hacks. Ellen Richards and Margaret Murray Washington did not want women to spend their lives cleaning. Richards wanted to update the home to reflect progress. "What are the essentials that must be retained in a house that is a home?" she asked.[4] Was it essential to do your own cooking or wash your own windows? No. If you could afford to pay someone else to do it, great. If you enjoyed a particular chore, also great; she loved to garden. Undoubtedly Richards would have embraced networked thermostats and smart speakers—and fought to protect us against hackers and corporate invasion of privacy.

Six months into writing this book, I remembered that my mother double-majored in home economics and journalism. The year that she graduated from college, more people earned a bachelor's degree in home economics than in math. (That continues to be true today.[5]) When I was a child, she had the kind of job in the General Foods marketing department that home economists used to hold. She ran consumer focus groups, wrote scripts for the Kool-Aid Man, and occasionally brought home test-kitchen samples such as the beta version of

Jell-O 1-2-3. She even belonged to the professional group Home Economists in Business. Yet I'd forgotten all about her connection to home economics, because she never talked about it. She was like many women in the 1970s and '80s who studied home ec to pursue the careers they wanted, but didn't identify as home economists. By the 1980s, majoring in home economics seemed passé and unintelligent. When I brought the topic up, she demurred. What she studied "wasn't *really* home economics," she said.

You will find many baby boomer women who hide their home economics education in the same way. However, you will also find people of all genders today studying home economics in college, and more than three million young people taking the class in public school.[6] The teenagers think it's useful and fun, and don't understand why anyone would ever restrict it to girls. The college students feel passionate about their ability to create change in the world. After I told my mother the stories of Margaret Washington, Ellen Richards, and the other heroines you'll meet in this book, she changed her tune. "I was embarrassed to be a home-ec major," she said. "I'm not embarrassed anymore."

I invite you to join me in learning about home economics and its much-too-hidden history.

THE SECRET HISTORY

of

HOME
ECONOMICS

CHAPTER 1

The Road to Home Economics

I t's almost impossible to imagine now, but in the middle of the 1800s, school was not the central experience of children's lives. It's common knowledge that it was illegal to educate people who were enslaved; less familiar is the fact that close to half the country's whites didn't attend school, and it wasn't until the end of the century that the majority of Americans completed eighth grade. As late as 1870, the average child who was enrolled in school went for less than four months a year.[1] Many girls learned at home, either alone or in small groups called "dame schools"; even education-mad Boston did not allow girls in public high school. College was for wealthy white males, with barely a handful of exceptions. Mt. Holyoke and Georgia Female College (now Wesleyan College) were women only; the Institute for Colored Youth, now Cheyney University, educated Black men and women; Oberlin College admitted women and men, Black and white. As for rights, when white and free Black women married, and nine of ten did, legally it was as if they had died. They lost their right to own property in their own name, sign a contract, or claim wages.

All of which made Catharine Beecher, born in 1800, all the more remarkable.

Beecher was marked for greatness by her father Lyman: The first words he whispered to his newborn were "Thou little immortal!" The oldest child in a family that became famous for abolitionism, education, and Calvinist piety, she grew into a sociable but fierce young woman who debated theology with her beloved father and preened her corkscrew curls. Fortuitously, Lyman received a ministry in Litchfield, Connecticut, home of one of the few secondary schools for girls. Beecher, a quick-witted but lazy student, attended school for about six years before leaving to care for the family after her mother died. By our standards, Beecher was religious. Even so, when her father pressed her to have a deep religious conversion experience and submit to God—else, he believed, she would not be saved—she resisted, deciding that she would follow Christian doctrine but not act excessively humble herself. She refused to sing a hymn with the lyrics "I am nothing, Lord," because, she said, "I am not nothing."[2] Despite the never-resolved doctrinal conflict, the family remained intensely loyal to each other.

At twenty-one, Beecher became engaged to a Yale science professor. Then a tragic accident changed the course of her life: her fiancé's ship crashed on the cliffs of Ireland. Beecher wore his engagement ring until the end of her life. Yet, in mourning, she found her way. While living with her late fiancé's family and tutoring his younger siblings, she read his scientific and mathematics books, and found she enjoyed the mental exercise. She decided to use the $2,000 he had willed her to start a school in Hartford, Connecticut. Hartford Female Seminary rapidly became popular. Within five years it had its own building and eight teachers. The daughters of the city's finest citizens learned geography, grammar, algebra, geometry, philosophy, and composition. Some also took Latin, French, Italian, piano, earth science, and chemistry. Despite her success, Beecher wondered whether she was following the best educational plan for these girls. Too many women were sickly, children's moral development was sadly lacking, and schools paid no attention to the future most women would have: caring for a household. "There was a time when the only object of woman's education seemed to be, to prepare her for an active, economical, and accomplished *housewife*, and no intellectual refinement or erudition was esteemed of any value, but rather a disadvantage," she wrote her trustees in 1829. "Mankind, perhaps, are now urging to the other extreme; and in regarding the *intellect* are beginning to overlook the future duties and employments of domestic life."[3]

In 1832 Beecher moved to Cincinnati, where her father had a new job, to open another school, the Western Female Institute. Her goal was to add "moral education" to the lessons, and to train women to teach on the frontier. Though initially all went well, after several years the Beechers' social position collapsed. The upper crust thought she was domineering, with ill-bred curiosity and appalling manners: "She devoured all before her and *licked her fingers!*" one member of society exclaimed.[4] She put on airs, acting like easterners were better. And though the family were not yet the abolitionist leaders they became, any support for abolitionism was touchy an eyelash away from a slave state. The school failed. Almost forty years old, Beecher now had no school and no home of her own. She stayed with her siblings and former pupils; wrote and tried to publish math and moral-education textbooks; and wrote fiction, though nowhere near as successfully as her sister Harriet Beecher Stowe. She suffered from depression and headaches and brooded over the danger she thought Catholic immigrants posed to the body politic. She also began writing a book on household education, which turned the moment of her deepest failure into her biggest success.

Household guides were nothing new. Many women already read miscellanies of advice and recipes such as Lydia Maria Child's pantry staple *The American Frugal Housewife*. But Beecher's book *A Treatise on Domestic Economy*, published in 1841, was an entirely new animal. The four-hundred-page tome brought together education, cleaning, religion, civics, gender, and morality. It wasn't just about how to care for a house. It was about the power of women to glue together a fragile society.

Beecher's philosophy was unified and pragmatic. Woman's place was in the home, she wrote. That was God's plan. But that seemingly submissive position was in fact the core of democracy. "The mother forms the character of the future man; the sister bends the fibres that are hereafter to be the forest tree; the wife sways the heart, whose energies may turn for good or for evil the destinies of a nation," she wrote. "Educate a woman, and the interests of a whole family are secured." (Her father and brother weren't the only Beechers who could preach a sermon.) That education had to include not only academics but housework. To underline the intelligence of such work, she gave housework education an intellectual-sounding name: "domestic economy." And she made an argument that would create jobs for countless women: domestic economy was too important and complex to be left to amateurs—that is, mothers. It had to be formally taught by professional educators. (To be sure, after two decades in education, Beecher had a somewhat jaundiced view of what happens after graduation. "It may be urged, that, even if it is studied, it will soon be forgotten," she wrote, but "so will much of every thing studied at school."[5]) Some people argued that educating a girl damaged her femininity. Domestic economy most emphatically did not. No one seemed to notice that while seeming to celebrate the home as sanctuary, Beecher politicized and professionalized it.

The rest of the *Treatise* synthesized an enormous amount of information: peristalsis, pimples, calisthenics, manners, charitable giving, time management, servant management, the ways that corsets weakened the spine, and the senselessness of an educated woman doing her own sewing while paying someone else to teach her children instead of teaching the children and farming out the sewing. The *Treatise* included an antidote for cobalt poisoning and precise illustrations of both human and architectural circulatory systems. The Massachusetts state education board soon adopted it, making it the country's first officially recognized home economics textbook. It sold for two generations, as did add-ons Beecher wrote, such as a cookbook. Domestic economy would play a key role as schooling expanded in America, with unmarried, childless Catharine Beecher as the nation's homemaker in chief. A generation later, Ellen Swallow Richards and Margaret Murray Washington picked up her mantle.

Ellen Swallow was the fastest reader in town. She had to be. She was trying to pull off the near impossible for a country girl in the mid-nineteenth century: to become college-educated. Born in 1842, "Nellie" won first prize at the county fair at age thirteen for a loaf of bread and an embroidered hankie. She also ran around the hillsides, kept her own garden, and helped her father do everything but milk the cows—her mother drew the line there, believing it ruined the hands. Her parents, Peter and Fanny, were unusually well educated for the time, having met at New Ipswich Academy in New Hampshire, and thought the village school wasn't good enough for their daughter. They taught her at home, at the kitchen table. Eventually they gave up farming and moved into town so their child could attend West-ford Academy, one of the oldest coed schools in the state, led by a future governor of Massachusetts. Peter Swallow opened a general store on the Westford town green, and his daughter walked to the school, where she made a point of registering not as Nellie but as Ellen. Already she was beginning to have a determined mouth, a strong brow.

At Westford, Swallow studied a range of scholarly subjects, including German, Greek, and logic. Simultaneously she got a hands-on education in business. After waking up in the morning she did the household chores and restocked the store shelves. Then she read while walking across the green, attended school, came home, and staffed the cashier's table while keeping her father's accounts—her math skills outclassed his—and occasionally sassing the customers. Always she kept a book open on the table to study in idle moments. For Ellen Swallow, there was never, nor would there ever be, an idle moment.

Swallow left high school in 1862 and launched her boat into becalmed seas. More than anything she wanted more education, but how? So few colleges accepted women, and none close enough for her to attend—evidently she could not travel outside the region. Mount Holyoke had a college-level curriculum but did not award bachelor's degrees. Her father opened a larger store in a nearby town that doubled as the post office; Swallow advanced her own education by ordering lots of newsy periodicals for him to sell (and for her to read first). For an agonizing six years her life remained frozen in a pattern. She went away and taught to earn money for college, sometimes living on bread and milk to save as much as possible, then bounced home to help her ailing mother; while there she also helped with the store and tutored or nursed to continue building her college fund. Her age-mates began to marry, but Swallow did not. "The young or old gentleman has not yet made his appearance who can entice me away from my free and independent life," she wrote her cousin in 1866. Married women seemed to live in "silent misery." To the outside world, she seemed cheerful and busy. But for the last two years of her purgatory she was wracked with fatigue, what we would today call depression—"thwarted and hedged in on every side," she wrote later. "If I had not had an almost Napoleonic faith in my star I should have yielded." She clung to a strange encounter on the street in Lowell, when she accidentally jostled an old lady. Swallow apologized. The woman stared at her and said, like a prophet, "And *you* . . . you have a great deal of work to do."[6]

At last her effort paid off. In one of the magazines she got for the store, *Godey's Lady's Book*, Swallow learned that a new college for white women was opening just over the state line in New York: Vassar. Tuition and board cost $400; remarkably, at a time when teachers were lucky to earn $15 a month, she had saved and borrowed $300, and there were scholarships. Several thousand women took the Vassar entrance exam for one hundred places. Swallow made the cut. As she unpacked in her dorm room, dusty from the train, she wrote home, "Am delighted even beyond anticipation."[7]

Swallow spent her two years at Vassar in a rapture. Older than her high-society classmates, she tutored to earn money and got a dispensation from the rule that limited study time— books were said to hurt the female brain. While memorizing German verbs or walking up to her fifth-floor dormitory bed-room, she knitted. And especially she threw herself into science. Vassar's first faculty hire was pioneering woman astronomer Maria Mitchell, and its first building was Mitchell's astronomi-cal observatory. One week into school Swallow peered through Mitchell's telescope, the third-largest in the country, and was dazzled to see Jupiter, such a beautiful color, surrounded by bright moons. Soon she was spending night after night in the observatory. Then she began taking chemistry and fell in love with the world under the lens of a microscope, and with the power of that branch of science to help people in their daily lives. She analyzed every substance she could get her steady hands on, from shoe polish to baking powder. The old woman's prophecy, she thought, was being fulfilled.

Swallow graduated in 1870. She was the only graduate who didn't wear a new dress to the ceremony, but she had an offer to teach from the president of Argentina, perhaps as part of his program to have US women set up teacher-training schools. When war in South America canceled the job offer, Swallow decided to pursue further education in chemistry. But where? No school open to women offered more than she already knew. She wrote to two commercial chemist firms, in Boston and Philadelphia, asking to apprentice. Neither had the capacity for a trainee. However, the Boston chemists made an astonishing suggestion: that she apply to the all-male Institute of Technology, now the Massachusetts Institute of Technology, founded five years before in Boston. To call it a long shot would be generous: two women had already been turned down, and the registrar held Swallow's application on his desk for weeks hoping she would withdraw it. Almost miraculously, though, institute president J. D. Runkle believed in women's education. He went to the mat for her with the faculty senate and won.

"You shall have any and all advantages which the Institute has to offer without charge of any kind," Runkle wrote in welcome. She would be a "special student" doing independent study, not registered in any class. Swallow thought the scholarship was due to her inability to pay. No, its purpose was plausible deniability: should a trustee raise a fuss, Runkle could simply say that she was not enrolled. "Had I realized upon what basis I was taken, I would not have gone," she wrote later.[8] Fortunately she had no idea.

The men treated Swallow at first like a dangerous element. They put her at a desk alone behind a wall, with separate lab space, and slipped documents under the door. Even then she was happy, writing, "I have a chance to do what no woman ever did and the glimpse I get of what is held out to me makes me sober and thoughtful." Gradually, Swallow won over the faculty and classmates. It wasn't for nothing that a relative later called her "Ellencyclopedia." She sometimes signed her letters "Keep thinking."[9] Mining-engineering professor Robert Hallowell Richards noted in his diary that he and Swallow had debated coeducation (she was for it). One of the professors who had objected to her presence eventually chose her to do most of the work on his water sanitation project—and gave her credit for it, in public. After studying mineralogy, which wasn't even her primary interest, she wrote a thesis analyzing the chemical composition of mining debris, work that resulted in the discovery of two new elements. She kept all this up while managing a boardinghouse in lieu of paying rent; mourning her father, who had died after a train accident; traveling to Worcester to care for her mother; and sometimes sewing on the male students' torn-off buttons. Swallow earned a second bachelor's degree from MIT in 1872 and, simultaneously, a master's from Vassar, and then became MIT's first female instructor. Against all odds, she had become a working woman in science.

As if Ellen Swallow's odds weren't long enough, Margaret Murray did not have the advantages of educated parents, a peaceful town, or whiteness. She was born in Macon, Mississippi, a town that had no public schools. The way Murray told the story, she was born to a Black washerwoman and an Irish railroad man (the census has no record of him) in March 1865 (the census says 1861), in a family that eventually numbered ten children.[10]

As happened with Swallow, Murray's family must have recognized her unusually keen intelligence, because she stayed home and studied while her siblings worked in the fields. Her education was supervised by the Sanderses, a white, Quaker brother and sister who had come South to educate freedpeople. The day after her father's death, when she was not quite seven years old, she moved in with them. When Murray turned fourteen the Sanderses asked her, "Would thee like to teach?" She would.[11] She borrowed a long skirt and passed the teaching examination, soon leading classes that included children older than herself. Freed African Americans hungered for education, and every teacher mattered.

That was as far as she could go educationally in Macon. The Sanders siblings supported Murray to move 280 miles away to Nashville so she could attend Fisk College, which had been founded in 1866. She started as a part-time high school student, teaching to earn her keep, and eventually moved up to the college course. At Fisk, Murray expanded her knowledge and social life. She wrote for the school newspaper (edited by W. E. B. Du Bois), contributing international news and elegant notes about the Mozart Society. She gained prosperous friends who hosted her for restful vacation stays between summer teaching stints and who became valuable connections for employment. (Probably at least some of those friends were white, as Fisk's faculty was predominantly white.) Along with the classical curriculum, Murray imbibed a sense of social responsibility: she was part of Du Bois's "Talented Tenth," with the obligation to give back to and lift up her race. She was, in short, a model Fisk student. In job recommendations, Fisk administrators praised her scholarship, energy, piety, skill in management, and leadership. She was one of two women graduating in her class, a class "distinguished for its pride and poverty," the *Fisk Herald* reported. (It also called her matrimonial prospects "good.")[12] She woke up on her 1889 graduation day with a job offer from Prairie View College in Texas.

As happened with Swallow, though, Murray's life was about to take a sharp postgraduation turn. She had submitted another job application but never heard back. At the graduation dinner, she happened to be seated across from the college president who had not replied to her letter: Booker T. Washington. He was not yet famous among whites, but he was renowned in African American and education circles for building Tuskegee Institute literally brick by brick: the property had no buildings when he was hired. He had charisma, enormous energy, a strong jaw, powerful oratorical ability, and penetrating gray eyes—and he was still only thirty-three years old. Furthermore, his beloved second wife, Olivia, had died just one month earlier, of smoke inhalation from a fire. Olivia Washington had been Tuskegee's dean of women and chief fundraiser; light enough to pass for white, she had wealthy New England connections thanks to her education at a Massachusetts teachers college. Her death had left Washington with not only a broken heart and three children, one still too young to sit up, but a serious staffing problem. By the time he and Murray rose from dinner, she had a job at Tuskegee.

Hired to teach English, Murray was promoted after a year to "Lady Principal" (a position later called dean of women), and wrote to her employer, while he was on his many fundraising trips, of campus matters great and small. Murray styled herself carefully. She appeared stately, imposing, and perfectly groomed, with hair in a pompadour, glasses, a frill at her throat, a brooch on her chest. But in private she didn't hide her feelings, which were warming. "Dear Mr. Washington, Your letter came one day this week and I can not tell you how much I felt what you said of your Christian life," she wrote in a late-1890 letter he saved. "It is a bright and lovely afternoon and all human souls ought to be perfectly happy but I wonder if I am." She progressed to addressing letters to "my dear Booker," and writing, "You can never guess how much I have thought of you today."[13] In 1891 or 1892, he proposed marriage. She said yes.

Despite being in love, Murray felt intensely ambivalent about the match. Her fiancé traveled so much. Would he have enough time for Murray? Everyone said Olivia had been the love of his life. Was he really in love now? Most pressing, the future champion of the Black home was afraid of becoming a stepmother. Would she have to give up the work she loved? Could she ever get along with his oldest child, Portia? The daddy's girl had lost two mothers—she was not even a year old when Fanny Washington, the educator's first wife, died—and was not happy about getting a third. One moment Murray was writing her fiancé about their future home together, "Will you not get me a bedroom set to match my desk?" and "We can rest so much better if every thing is delicate and refined. I hope you will not think me very extravagant." The next she was writing of her anguish "because I can not feel toward Portia as I should. . . . I wonder Mr. Washington if it is a wise and Christian thing for me to love you feeling as I do? Still I shall be absolutely honest with you and if you feel that you prefer giving me up I should find no fault with you."[14] Soon after that she was criticizing the children's nanny and planning their wardrobes.

"My very nature seems to be one of constant rebellion," she confessed.[15]

No one knows what her fiancé did or did not say, but their betrothal held. On October 10, 1892, Margaret Murray became the third and final Mrs. B. T. Washington.

Vassar, MIT, Fisk, and Tuskegee were part of an unprecedented expansion of education after the Civil War, particularly for

African Americans, women, westerners, and scientists. This is when what are now known as Historically Black Colleges and Universities opened, as well as six of the "Seven Sisters" and other colleges for women. In 1867, President Andrew Johnson established the nation's first federal education office. Seeing the need for scientific progress in agriculture, Congress created the land-grant system in 1862 under the Morrill Act. It funded at least one college per state to build better farms through research and education in the agricultural sciences and "mechanical arts." In the South, the money was supposed to go equally to Black land-grant colleges, but that didn't happen until the second Morrill Act—of 1890—guaranteed it.

New student populations, plus enormous societal changes—not just emancipation but the Industrial Revolution, immigration, and urbanization—called for more and different colleges. What were these new students to learn? Was the classical curriculum for everyone? Was the purpose of school to broaden the mind, or to prepare for a job? The leaders of these new colleges knew that they were reaching beyond the traditional elite, and many thought the curriculum should reflect that fact. They favored what they called "industrial education" or "manual training," what we would later call vo-tech and then career and technical education. Land-grant colleges were coed from the start, as were most Black colleges whether urban or rural, and these colleges typically offered a separate manual-training course for women: "domestic science," the slightly updated term for Beecher's "domestic economy." Hampton Institute, which opened in 1868 to educate Black and Native American students, got there first: it quickly opened a "Women's Labor Department," in which, among other tasks, women students learned to sew clothing that the school sold to support their tuition. Iowa State offered its first domestic science course in 1871, followed by Kansas State in 1873 and the University of Illinois in 1874.[16]

Was it empowering, or repressive, to include housework in a college course? Or, à la Beecher, both at once? Did it keep women in the kitchen? Some proponents of industrial education thought that Black, Native American, immigrant, and women students weren't as smart as white men. Bryn Mawr president M. Carey Thomas rejected domestic science outright, saying, "There are not enough elements of intellectual growth in cooking or housekeeping to nourish a very serious or profound course of training for really intelligent women." Her students would have the same curriculum as men at Harvard. The debate was sharpest in Black communities, where manual labor reeked of slavery. Du Bois was particularly cutting, saying that industrial training could not be the acme if African Americans were to be truly free. "An education that encourages aspiration, that sets the loftiest of ideals and seeks as an end culture and character rather than bread-winning," should not be the exclusive privilege of whites, he wrote.[17]

Arguing the other side, the leaders of these new colleges proclaimed that manual training was not menial labor, but mental work worthy of a bachelor's degree. Speaking specifically of domestic science, they said that everyone with farming experience knew that wives and daughters played a crucial role in agriculture. Besides, women needed respectable professions, Kansas State president Rev. John Anderson said. He derided elite eastern women's colleges as "furnishing intelligent playthings for men possessing exhaustless wealth."[18] (Left unstated was the fact that many of these cash-strapped institutions, unable to afford paid janitors, needed to have students care for the facilities. At Tuskegee, for instance, every female student rotated through the laundry plant.) Booker T. Washington in particular argued that the trades had both practical and spiritual value, that they built both employability and character. "The masses of us are to live by the productions of our hands," he said in his most famous speech, the 1895 "Atlanta Compromise" speech. "No race can prosper till it learns that there is as much dignity in tilling a field as in writing a poem." He often told the story of how his "examination" to enter Hampton consisted of sweeping a classroom floor. He brought over Hampton's "head, hand, and heart" approach when he was hired to run the new Tuskegee Institute in 1881. All Tuskegee students had to take industrial subjects as well as academics. Five years later, the *Christian Recorder* reported favorably on the results, admiring neatly sewn and ironed shirts, embroidered tablecloths, and excellent loaves of bread. At any rate, all the Black colleges eventually established trade programs, because the white institutions supporting African American education in the South—including the General Education Board, the Rosenwald Fund, the Phelps-Stokes Fund, the Slater Fund, and the Jeanes Fund—promoted it. Indeed, Margaret Murray took an early Slater-funded cooking class as a student and was "much delighted with the art," the *Fisk Herald* reported. At Tuskegee, she quickly adopted the prevailing view. The year after she started teaching there, she wrote a flowery, Beecher-esque article for the *Fisk Herald* advocating how best to educate the Black woman. "Practical training of our young girl is fearfully neglected," she wrote. Married or not, a woman must know how to cook, clean, sew, and raise children. And that knowledge would be transformational: "As the homes among the Colored race make progress, so will the race itself advance."[19] She would hold that philosophy to the end of her life.

Washington began running domestic science at Tuskegee, and then took her work outside the traditional classroom. Sitting at Tuskegee's first conference for farmers in 1892, where speakers urged men to raise their standards of living and buy homes, Washington thought they were leaving out something important: their wives and children. "I felt that history was repeating itself," she later wrote. "Women had no rights that were worth mentioning, and, notwithstanding the fact that there were many women present at this first conference, they had little actual place in it."[20] She knew the desperate circumstances in which these families lived. What could these farmers accomplish without their wives? The place to start, Washington thought, was community homemaking education. With trepidation at first, she began holding weekly Mothers' Meetings on Saturdays, when country women came to town to shop and visit. The women gathered above a store, and Washington and her friends advised them on housework. Shortly thereafter, she published a book with contributions from her friends.

Work for the Colored Women of the South was just twenty-one pages, but it may well have been the first household manual for impoverished Black rural women. It had essays on furnishings, cooking, childrearing, dress, and a favorite domestic science topic, ventilation. "Do not hang your clothes all around the house, but make a frame about the size of a door, drive nails in it, and place it in a part of the home that is not often used," Mrs. Nathan B. Young wrote. "Hang a calico curtain across this frame. Thus you have a cheap wardrobe. Put the shoes at the bottom, with toes turned toward the wall." Washington laid out the rules of What Not to Wear—no plaids for the stout! The book was emphatically moralistic and brooked no disagreement that middle-class ways were best. Corporal punishment did more harm than good. Parents should hold Saturday-night sings at home so teenagers would not be tempted to carouse. "Country people eat too much and too little meat. Too much of the wrong and too little of the right kind," Adella Hunt Logan wrote.[21]

Washington thought that the lower classes of African Americans needed what she later called "a cleaner social morality." She thought they were ignorant and intemperate—that is, they drank alcohol. There were too many illegitimate births and young-child deaths. They had unhealthy habits, such as going barefoot and not washing enough. But it was all slavery's fault, not their own. They could learn better ways! All they needed was domestic science education. To her, such instruction had moral, psychological, and deeply political implications. By changing personal habits, women could erase the traces of slavery from the body and house. Washington railed in particular against her lifelong bugbear, "wrapping the hair" in a kerchief, a style that has retained emotional weight and controversy to this day. To her, kerchiefs were a visual symbol of oppression. (She didn't mind Aunt Jemima, she said years later, but why couldn't the food company use a respectable-looking woman?) The practice came from "the days of slavery, when there was not time given by the masters for combing the hair," she wrote, adding, bitterly, "How many women remember how careful was the master, who refused to give them time to comb their hair, to have his horse curried every day."[22]

Sitting on a chair instead of a bed or the floor, even if the chair was just a box covered with calico, built self-respect. Not only was self-respect a political statement in itself, but Washington thought it would lead to respect from whites. That philosophy infused Tuskegee's curriculum as well. By teaching domestic science, which the school called "women's industries," the institute wasn't training maids. It was educating moral leaders who would lift up their communities. Hampton had the same philosophy, expressed in a 1911 booklet whose (possibly pseudonymous) author Virginia Church bid good riddance to a white housewife who visited Hampton looking for a maid. "She decides that education has made them 'too good to work' and complains in irritation that she supposes she'll have to go to an employment bureau in Norfolk, after all.

The unruffled head of the visitors' office agrees calmly that she supposes she will."[23]

Nowadays, we might call Washington's attitude toward poor women condescending or classist. We might say, as Du Bois did at the time, that telling Black sharecroppers to pull themselves up by their bootstraps ignored structural racism and took the blame off whites. A mob had recently destroyed Ida B. Wells's newspaper office in Memphis for reporting on lynchings: in the face of that intensity of racist hatred—both to hang Black people and to keep it from being known—could self-improvement really change society? Even so, Washington genuinely believed that education, moral improvement, and the reform of home life would free African Americans from prejudice.[24] If poor Black families lived in a respectably middle-class way, then whites would have to recognize their full citizenship. And even if that didn't happen, educated African Americans would have gained the knowledge, self-determination, and financial independence to choose their own path as best they could in a deeply unjust world.

In 1895, Washington took her work to a bigger audience. She founded the Tuskegee Woman's Club, which provided an organizing ground for community service along with musical performances, literary discussion, social occasions, and temperance and suffrage campaigns. That July, as the club's representative, she attended the first national conference of African American clubwomen in Boston. Even in that renowned group—attendees included editor Josephine St. Pierre Ruffin, William Lloyd Garrison, missionary society founder Eliza Gardner, suffragist Lucy Stone's husband, and her own husband—Washington took a leading role, with a plum speaking spot. The Black press, *Boston Globe*, and *Chicago Tribune* covered her speech. Standing before a crowd in Berkeley Hall, Washington evoked the one-room cabins around Tuskegee, twelve by ten feet, with just a little hole for a window that had to be kept shut all winter. Children lived their entire lives in these dark and dirty places, she said; she had witnessed pathetic and hopeless scenes. In the thirty years after emancipation, a generation in which Washington had gone from washerwoman's daughter to college dean, her compatriots' living conditions had barely changed. The prospect of intervening in those shacks "was not a very inviting work, but we could not rid ourselves of the recognition of the bond which linked us to these women. We knew that as they were lifted up, so might we rise," she said. How was it going? Well, changing habits took time. "We do not feel discouraged," she told the clubwomen.[25]

At the end of the conference, the new national federation of African American women's clubs voted Washington its president. The attendees waved her to the dais with handkerchiefs in their hands, and sang "'Til We Meet Again."[26]

Ellen Swallow was also taking her work outside the lab. She had made an experiment of her own house. At the Institute of Technology, "Cupid had appeared among the retorts and receivers," a friend quipped.[27] The day Swallow received her degree, Robert Richards, the tall mineralogy professor, whispered a marriage proposal to her in her lab. On the surface, they had many differences: she was quick, he judicially slow; he was handsome, from a prominent family, vain about his curly hair, and she was plain. For two years, she found reasons to refuse him. She wouldn't marry a smoker; he quit. Then she was finishing the water study. *Then* she was setting up evening chemistry classes for women teachers. Her mother thought she was passing up the chance of a lifetime. At last the two married and set out on a joint life of science. For health and ease of care, their home had small rugs, not dusty, dank carpets; plants and flowers, not dust-catching drapes. They designed a ventilator to suck away the combustion of the chandelier, and Ellen Richards moved the gas meter from the basement to the kitchen so she could monitor it. Her measurements showed that the new "vacuum cleaner" took less physical energy and time than sweeping, so she switched. (They also installed a glassblowing works for Robert, who liked to amuse their many dinner guests by making a little on-the-spot lab ware.)

For the next decade, Richards divided her time between analyzing water quality and environmental hazards and helping women in science. She taught chemistry to high school teachers in person and housewives via correspondence; with her own money, she funded a women's laboratory at MIT. (She closed it when the institute began fully including women in doing experimental work a decade later.) Disparagement from men was routine. Walking into her lab, the Boston school superintendent asked, "What good do you expect this will do in the kitchen?"[28] Though he meant it as a sneer, as putting Richards in her place, the question resonated. Like Washington, Richards was beginning to see that her work had broader possibilities. She had chosen chemistry over astronomy in the first place because it was more relevant to everyday life. Testing wallpaper for arsenic for an insurance company and co-analyzing the entire water supply of Massachusetts, she saw the good that science could do in the world.

In 1879, Richards's former astronomy professor Maria Mitchell invited her to speak at Vassar. Afterward Mitchell always said, "I discovered Mrs. Richards." In a speech titled "Chemistry in Relation to Household Economy," Richards laid out a formal argument connecting science and the home. Scientific discoveries had transformed industry, but the home had not kept pace, she said. Cooking schools were opening in

Boston and New York, but did their menus promote health? Even though manufacturers marketed tricks like chemically enhanced dish detergent, the average American home was an unhealthy miasma of damp cellars, stuffy air, and bad cooking, where "labor is wasted . . . in a manner which would ruin any business or workshop." Richards added, "No wonder that living is so expensive."[29] But chemistry could fix all that, if taught properly, not just as an academic exercise. Richards envisioned housekeepers testing the cream of tartar for purity when their biscuits came out yellow and bitter. Such knowledge would protect consumers not only at the mouth but at the source. If merchants knew that women were wise to their tricks, they would stock better products.

Richards had found her life's work: to improve the home, and thus society, through science. She formed a Sanitary Science Club and wrote books on adulterated food and the chemistry of housework. In 1890, she and her business partner Mary Hinman Abel opened a prepared-food shop with a mission. The New England Kitchen offered inexpensive takeout and recipes with the goal of teaching customers how delicious and healthy cheap food could be. Middle-class women ended up more amenable to this message than the working-class immigrants Richards and Abel tried to reach, who rejected the Kitchen's bland offerings, even after the Kitchen added pork and pepper to the pea soup. But the New England Kitchen did begin providing lunch for Boston schools—an innovation at a time most urban schools didn't have cafeterias. It also promoted a proto–Crock-Pot called the Aladdin Oven. A year or two later, while visiting Boston to learn ways to cook economically for a crowd, Booker T. Washington met the Aladdin Oven's creator, a friend of Richards's. He immediately envisioned setting up a battery of Aladdins at Tuskegee. Did he visit the New England Kitchen, or meet Richards? The records do not say.

In 1893, Richards and Abel made the big time: they were offered space at the Chicago World's Fair. Richards turned down the initial offer to exhibit in the women's pavilion—the Kitchen was not just women's work, she said—and opened instead in a freestanding structure outside the anthropology building. That summer, more than twenty-five million people visited the fair to ooh at the Ferris wheel, the ornamented Tiffany Chapel, and Buffalo Bill's Wild West Show. When they got hungry, some ate at Richards's thirty-seat Rumford Kitchen, named for a physicist who had made early investigations into food chemistry and efficient cooking devices. In the wood-frame building, surrounded by charts and apparatus, ten thousand people in all ate perfectly standardized and nutritionally optimized pea soup and apple cake, or escalloped fish and baked apples, or beef broth and gingerbread, accompanied by bread and butter. They wrote down the mottoes on the walls— "Preserve and treat food as you would your body, remembering that in time food will be your body"—and took home leaflets expounding the Kitchen's philosophy and calorie counts.[30]

After Richards's big success, the US agriculture secretary wrote her. The agriculture department had been establishing "experiment stations" to test and circulate findings on plant science. Perhaps she would be interested in helping them establish food laboratories at these stations? Richards, excited, shared the news with Abel, writing, "The whole subject is ready for a boom. We *must be in it*."[31] In fact, she would lead it.

Though home economics wasn't even named yet, its goals were set. For the many differences among Beecher, Richards, and Washington, all three were working women who wanted to empower other women through education. They believed that improving the home could and would improve society. But the field's core tensions were there too. Was the backbone of home economics moral, scientific, or both? Was its purpose practical or intellectual? Would it serve farms or cities? Would Black colleges or MIT take the lead? Was a curriculum that focused on the household empowering or repressive, feminist or sexist? For now, the fledgling home economists were going to have it all ways, to get as many people on board as possible.

CHAPTER 2

The Lake Placid Conference

By the end of the nineteenth century, domestic science seemed to be flourishing. Practically every agricultural college offered it. Schoolchildren studied household arts in the cities of Chicago, Boston, New York City, Toledo, and Los Angeles, to name a few. The National Household Economic Association had chapters across the country. *The American Kitchen Magazine* reported on all the developments in the field, with long lists of domestic science school alumnae who ran institutions or taught in an expanding range of places: hospitals, Native American reservations, city cooking schools, orphanages. The US Senate even held hearings to open a Bureau of Domestic Science.

The problem was, Ellen Richards thought, that they were going about things all wrong. She was examining structures and systems—trying to set an eight-hour workday for household employees, popularize Wilbur Atwater's studies of the calorie, and create healthy people who flourished through the application of science to the home. Meanwhile, cooking schools taught middle-class women fancy menus to pass along to their servants so that guests would be impressed, and schoolchildren learned embroidery, not chemistry. The NHEA members were society women who clung to pointless traditions for the home. "I grant that each family has a weakness for the flavor produced by its own kitchen bacteria, but that is prejudice due to lack of education," Richards wrote.[1] In short, domestic science's other leading lights were insufficiently scientific.

In Albany, New York, Annie Dewey was feeling a similar frustration. In her case, it came from the pressure of running an expensive private Adirondacks resort. Annie Roberts Godfrey Dewey had never planned to be a hotelier. She shared Richards's central Massachusetts upbringing and Vassar education, though Dewey had a private income and elevated social connections, and began her career buried in books as Wellesley's founding librarian. Through work she met the magnetic reformer of library science, Melvil Dewey. He had an unusual combination of traits: a big personality committed to big ideas who was fanatical about detail. You could see it not only in the book-organizing method he invented—the Dewey decimal system—but in his passion for the metric system and simplified spelling (né Melville). Annie fell in love with his vision and energy. Some of her relatives were horrified—they thought Melvil, a shoemaker's son, would never make anything of himself—but in 1878 the two iconoclasts joined their books and lives together and embarked upon a rigorous program of self- and social improvement, including itemized daily time budgets. They moved to New York City so he could run Columbia University's library and open its library school, where he controversially began admitting women, and then to Albany in 1889, where he assumed the directorship of the New York

State library.[2] Behind the scenes she helped her husband found the American Library Association, did bibliographic work, led a dozen committees, and raised their son. Once in Albany, the Deweys began looking for a country getaway, both to alleviate Melvil's severe hay fever and to fulfil their dream of starting a private club for families where they could put their purist ideals into action. It would be a wholesome place, healthy and refined, free from alcohol and tobacco. In 1893 they founded the Lake Placid Club, and Annie gained a new job: hotel management. The Deweys billed the club as demonstrating the latest domestic science principles, including a delicious and healthful table. To live up to the claims, Annie needed help. Soon she was visiting Richards's domestic science projects in Boston, bringing Richards on as a consultant, and taking charge of the New York Household Economic Association. However, when she tried to put domestic science principles into practice, she found herself thwarted by some guests' ignorance. How was she to schedule housekeeping when her uninformed, demanding patrons wanted their beds made up right away during breakfast whereas her enlightened visitors knew that beds had to be thoroughly aired? She complained to Richards, who sympathized. "While women's likes and dislikes outweigh hygienic principles the difficulties of right living will continue," Richards wrote.[3]

Annie Dewey decided it was high time to spread the knowledge of domestic science more broadly. She organized a conference.

The home economics profession remembers the Lake Placid conference as being the brainchild of Melvil and Richards, and perhaps they did float the idea. However, it was Annie who made it happen. In fact, Richards almost didn't come. When Annie sent her an invitation in July 1899, the enthusiasm of the woman now considered the founder of home economics was tempered at best. Richards demurred in a series of letters, each floating a different objection. She had planned to spend the late summer in Boston finally getting work done. There were so few professionals who shared her experience joining science and practice in household matters—why not have two separate meetings, one for the scientists, one for the practical workers? "We are ahead of the times and can afford to wait," Richards wrote. She had other conferences to attend and a book to finish, to be titled *The Cost of Living as Affected by Sanitary Science*. And *then*, having temporized for six weeks, she said it was too late to gather a critical mass of attendees. The surviving correspondence doesn't reveal how Annie won Richards over, beyond offering a prepaid train-ticket voucher and a free room. Perhaps Richards was thinking about a comment that nutrition scientist Wilbur Atwater had made: "The science of household economics is now in what chemists call a state of supersaturated solution which needs to crystallize out. Sometimes the point of a needle will start such crystallization."[1] Richards wanted to be that catalyst.

"All right. I will reserve the time," she wrote Annie just days before the conference. "I dare say you are right and I am glad you are willing to make the effort. I too have a feeling that it is a critical time."

Ten white women and one man gathered in the Lake Placid library on the crisp morning of September 19, 1899, the scent of fir trees in the air. Annie wore white, as she always did. Along with Richards and the Deweys, there was the eternally serene Louisa Nicholass, director of a Massachusetts teachers college household-arts program; pragmatic Alice Peloubet Norton, a public school system domestic science director; Rumford Kitchen assistant Maria Daniell; cooking school chief Maria Parloa; immigrant educator Emily Huntington; and ascetically thin *American Kitchen Magazine* editor Anna Barrows, who gave the lie to the stereotype that domestic science was just about food: she ate only to live.[5] Plus two rich women who were there as funders, recorded in the minutes under their husbands' names, Mrs. William G. Shailer and Mrs. William V. Kellen. As Richards predicted, several key players could not come, including Atwater and Mary Hinman Abel.

Nonetheless, Richards had found her people. She described the connection in terms of electricity: "Each contact of mind with mind flashed out a spark of light."[6] The attendees shared one overriding goal: to convince universities to embrace home science as a serious study in order to create "a new profession commanding adequate compensation." For this, they needed a new, serious name. "Domestic science" wasn't enough. "Household arts," they agreed, "could never expect to be recognized as part of the university curriculum." They decided on "home economics," as a subset of general economics. In that first hour, they renamed the field. In the conference's five days they remade not only domestic science but the world in their image. "Perfect harmony prevailed thruout," Anna Barrows wrote in the notes. It was one of those magical times when every idea seems to build upon the last, when attendees nod and say, Yes, that's exactly what I was thinking. They talked about the preparation of young women for higher leadership, school curricula, the need for further nutrition-science research, and home economics' Dewey decimal number. The last was a bid for respect: they wanted to be shelved with sociology, not needlepoint. Indeed, they wanted to take over 339 from "pauperism," because home economics would eliminate poverty. They created committees and pledged to continue work during the year. Melvil praised the group extravagantly, telling them that "those who can make the home all it should be will get nearer the foundations of life than even teachers, ministers, and editors."

Richards left convinced that they had driven not just a nail into the problem but a spike. "Every day convinces me that you were right and I was unbelieving," she wrote Annie one month later. "I am more and more convinced of the epoch making possibilities of the Lake Placid work."[7]

Over ten years, through annual meetings and voluminous correspondence, the Lake Placid group accomplished a huge amount of work. Their field of thought was as big as the Adirondack forest. They addressed Thorstein Veblen's new theory of conspicuous consumption, shop class for girls, labor relations between maid and mistress, juvenile justice, and the need for a living wage. They were energized, unified, bold. Their favorite least-favorite word was "drudgery." Science, they said, would liberate people from onerous and repetitive household labor, improve health, and provide opportunities for careers. There was nothing sentimental about washing clothes, they said. Send it out to a laundry—and improve training, work conditions, and sanitation for those professional laundresses.

They were pragmatic. "Both boys and girls should have as much wood working as will make them independent in the matter of simple shelves, doors, and bookcases," Richards wrote later. When men wielded the hammer, they "do the work as they please, not always as we would like it done. Closet shelves are always too high."[8] Yet underlying the practical bent, their philosophy was utopian. Home economics, they said, stood for "the ideal home life for today unhampered by the traditions of the past; the utilization of all the resources of modern science to improve the home life; the freedom of the home from the dominance of things and their due subordination to ideals; [and] the simplicity in material surroundings which will most free the spirit for the more important and permanent interests of the home and of society." Everything connected. The home was not a retreat from the world: it *was* the world. "A lecture on the economics of consumption, and a lesson on the making of bread, are they not phases of the same whole?" a housekeeping-school director said. "Are they not all varying expressions of the same conviction: that the home is the organic unit of society, that to raise the standard of living and of life in the home is to elevate the whole social system?" Such elevation would not happen tomorrow, but it would happen: "We shall sow for others to reap."

As for home economics' connection to general economics, it was not an invention. At the base of Richards's analysis was an almost Marxian analysis of labor. The Industrial Revolution had permanently eliminated the home as a site of economic production, relegating the loom to the attic and the soap kettle to the shed, she said. That was good—technology freed time for higher pursuits. As Chicago domestic-economy instructor Caroline Hunt put it, "The woman who today makes her own soap instead of taking advantage of machinery for its production enslaves herself to ignorance by limiting her time for study." However, the advances also made home boring, Richards said, full only of "the dull routine work never done." And it meant that women needed opportunities to earn money—opportunities a career in home economics could offer, whether that be running a cottage industry or becoming a college professor. Richards laid down her dictum most concisely in one of the most passionate speeches of her life, an impromptu retort at an otherwise all-male educational conference whose attendees told her that schools wouldn't have to teach housekeeping if women stayed home. "You cannot make women contented with cooking and cleaning and *you need not try*," she said, beetling her dark brows. "We are not quite idiots, although we have been dumb, because you did not understand our language. We demand a hearing and the help of wise leaders to reorder our lives to the advantage of the country."[9]

Soon the Lake Placid group began to tighten its hold over the discipline and to co-opt it. Close to fifty people attended the third conference; by the eighth, they had about 145 members, the majority of whom did not attend the conference. Linda Hull Larned was president of the rival National Household Economic Association, and later editor of *Good Housekeeping*. First she endorsed the Lake Placid conferences in *American Kitchen*, calling them "unusual gatherings of scientific women." Within a few years Larned was attending Lake Placid and her own group was defunct. The midwestern land-grant colleges jumped on board even though their deans and professors took a back seat to northeasterners. The US Department of Agriculture's nutrition investigations director, C. F. Langworthy, became a key ally starting in 1905, not only connecting the home economists to the federal government but working tirelessly for them. Most of the attendees over the ten years of the Lake Placid conferences subscribed to Richards's vision of home economics, which was by her design: she limited invitations, "more afraid of getting an unwieldy body of people with diverse views and so failing of real accomplishment than of leaving people out," she wrote Annie.[10] She was not immune to the power of celebrity, though, inviting such well-known figures as social-work innovator Jane Addams, cooking school director Fannie Farmer, and cereal baron/health-spa director John Harvey Kellogg. The only target the home economists failed to win over was the classical women's colleges, whose leaders continued to insist that housework was too unimportant to study in higher education.

Despite that rejection, the Lake Placid group's politics were largely what we would call feminist, certainly for the time.

True, Larned was not in that camp. She told the conference in 1902 that "homemaking is the most natural and therefore the most desirable vocation for women"; boys should get minor housekeeping instruction so as not to be complete animals, but "heaven forbid that the threatened emancipation of women should ever make it necessary for men to manage." On the other hand, Charlotte Perkins Gilman, the author famous for her feminist story "The Yellow Wallpaper" and books about revolutionizing housework, was apparently a little too strident for them. However, members such as Caroline Hunt and Canadian freethinker Alice Chown championed women's right to choose their own future and employment regardless of gender. "The final test of the teaching of home economics is freedom," Hunt said at the third conference, in a speech later published as a stand-alone manifesto. "If we have unnecessarily complicated a single life by perpetuating useless conventions or by carrying the values of one age over into the next, just so far have we failed." (Hunt also hated skirts, though sadly there is no sign that she wore trousers.) The Lake Placid attendees consciously constructed home economics as a profession for women. Specifically, for women without husbands. That's who seemed drawn to it, at any rate, either because they needed the income or because it was difficult to have a career if you were married. Paradoxically, the field devoted to the home attracted a disproportionate share of women who bucked societal expectations by remaining single. Isabel Bevier, the new head of household science at the University of Illinois, became a chemist after her fiancé died. Martha Van Rensselaer began working with farmers' wives after losing her bid for reelection as a school commissioner in western New York. Lenna Cooper planned meals for hundreds of health nuts at Kellogg's Battle Creek Sanitarium; she later ran the sanitarium's home economics school, which Kellogg's magazine advertised with headlines such as "Work for Women" and "Women's Independence."

That said, despite the possibilities for female empowerment, they had a blind spot that is glaring to us today. In 1906, the American Library Association quietly evicted its cofounder Melvil Dewey after a number of women complained of unwanted groping, kisses, touching, and other sexual advances dating back many years. Melvil admitted that he was "very unconventional" in his actions but that it meant nothing—"pure women would understand my ways." Annie roared to her husband's defense, echoing that he could behave freely with women because everyone knew he was pure of heart. Had he not been so high-minded when they met that she had hesitated to interrupt his work by becoming his wife? Did they not ban alcohol from their club, and kick out women who smoked? She sent signed letters to ALA members accusing them of conspiring to get him, sneering, "Go to work at some honest occupation and earn your bread by the sweat of your brow."[11]

The home economists did not deal with this development, except obliquely. Richards wrote Annie warm, albeit vague, letters urging her to look after her health (she had been diagnosed with atherosclerosis), to go abroad if necessary—they could always hold the conference somewhere else. But ebullient, undaunted Melvil hosted the next meeting at Lake Placid with Annie as usual. How could the home economists ignore the reports of his sexual predation? It was said that Melvil never got handsy with his social equals. He preyed on women with less money, often those dependent on him for a library or secretarial job, who found it risky to complain about his actions—though clearly some did complain.[12] He simultaneously promoted careers for women. And the home economists depended on him, too: his hospitality, his connections, his influence.

Despite Richards's control over invitations, perfect harmony did not in fact always prevail, at least behind the scenes. Richards wrote of her various annoyances to Mary Hinman Abel and to Annie. Atwater kept trying to hijack the conference, she thought. She found John Harvey Kellogg's religiosity (and possibly his guru-like status in Battle Creek) distasteful, though she accepted a tube of yogurt starter he sent. She needed Larned as a conduit to the mass female audience but always viewed her with minor contempt, writing to Abel, "Mrs. Larned is learning but she is superficial."[13] And there was one group the Lake Placid organizers apparently felt no compunction to include, even though the conferences routinely included a trip to abolitionist John Brown's grave. President Theodore Roosevelt might invite Booker T. Washington to dine at the White House, but Richards and company did not ask his wife to Lake Placid.

The group knew who Margaret Murray Washington was. *American Kitchen* began covering her activities and Tuskegee's domestic science curriculum even before her husband's 1895 "Atlanta Compromise" speech made him the most famous African American man in the country. Lest anyone miss her role, her husband's secretary Emmett Scott wrote a fulsome article in the *Ladies' Home Journal* titled "Mrs. Booker T. Washington's Part in Her Husband's Work." (Margaret edited the piece before publication.)[14]

One reason for the exclusion is plain: the Deweys banned African Americans and Jews from their resort. Melvil Dewey said that was what the club's "big Southern clientele" wanted; "personally, many of my choicest friends are Jews," he wrote a man who unsuccessfully sought membership. In reality he bought up land to keep it away from Jews. The Jewish exclusion drew greater attention than the African American one, especially after a number of powerful New York City Jewish businessmen petitioned for Melvil to be dismissed from state employment. They were offended that a state employee, a person whose salary was supported in part by Jewish residents, owned an overtly anti-Semitic vacation resort. In 1905, Dewey agreed to resign from his state job, under duress, for his club's exclusionary policies and for allegedly handling club matters on the clock. (His laudatory authorized biographer wrote, in simplified spelling, that he resigned because he "preferd originating ideas and having others carry them out" and got tired of people seeking favors.) However, the home economics group held two meetings away from Lake Placid, and no one seems to have suggested inviting any Black home economists to join them there. For that matter, Black colleges hired many white faculty, who could have attended. The Lake Placid conferences simply left Black colleges completely out. Never mind that *American Kitchen* featured Atlanta University's innovative "practice house," possibly the first of these live-in home economics labs.[15] Or that Mary Hinman Abel praised Hampton and Tuskegee at the 1901 conference, saying that they were "showing us the way."

Washington knew who the Lake Placid group was, too. She sent a cooking teacher to study with Anna Barrows and subscribed to Larned's *Good Housekeeping*; her stepdaughter Portia attended the college where Louisa Nicholass ran home economics. Washington, however, possessed dignity and a knowledge of her own value. She may well have felt that with US presidents knocking down the door to visit Tuskegee, these home economists could perfectly well get in touch with her, not the other way around. At any rate, Washington focused primarily on strengthening Black communities, and occasionally on trying to convince all-white national and international associations of women's clubs to integrate. And she had an overpacked schedule without invitations to Lake Placid. As Annie Dewey compiled her initial invitation list in 1899, Washington was sweeping through Europe with her husband meeting ambassadors and having tea with Susan B. Anthony and the "dear old Queen," she wrote a friend.[16] She returned just in time to lecture the National Association of Colored Women's Clubs and the Afro-American Council on education and the home. Then she settled into a new home of her own. The Oaks was a stately Victorian house that Tuskegee students built for the family, where she maintained an enormous network of activity and influence, with herself at the center.

Washington continued to run women's industries at Tuskegee, as she would for the rest of her life. The university's canning plant was preserving an enormous amount of fruit; the steam laundry was constantly breaking down. She ran a de facto employment agency for alumnae. She kept abreast of new techniques, copying Atlanta University's practice cottage and updating the curriculum to include a course on child development and nurture. There were her own stepchildren to nurture: over time she had become a true mother to the boys, who could not remember any other. She also essentially adopted her niece Laura, who went by the name Laura Murray Washington.[17] As for Portia, tension dissolved once she went to the Northeast for school. (The Washingtons sent their children to elite colleges and prep schools, not Tuskegee.) All the while she held down the fort for her husband, who was usually traveling to raise money, sending her constant telegrams.

Then there was her service and activism. On top of the Mothers' Meetings, which drew almost three hundred women per week, Washington established a grade school at a former plantation and founded a chapter of the Women's Christian Temperance Union. She was eternally president of the Tuskegee Woman's Club, which was taking over a boys' detention facility, advocating for women's suffrage, and promoting moral purity; she edited the newsletter of what was now named the National Association of Colored Women's Clubs and served on its executive council with its endless political wrangling. She spoke at university commencements, Black conferences, churches, women's clubs—both integrated and Black—night after night, all over the Northeast and South. In her remaining time, she wrote to newspapers criticizing ads that gave stereotypical depictions of African Americans.[18] Decades before American culture valorized the supermom, Washington had (and did) it all.

Like her white counterparts up north, Washington was optimistic about the powers of home economics. Thanks to education, "the advancement of the women of the Black race of America is assured," she wrote. Alumnae were lifting others as they climbed. By learning to practice thrift in housekeeping, they were helping their husbands buy homes. The ideal educated African American young woman attended school as far as was possible at home, then sacrificed to work her way through New England domestic science schools to prepare for teaching, Washington wrote in *Outlook* magazine, describing an appealing scene in words that echoed those at Lake Placid: "She has a laboratory for her theory classes in cooking. She teaches practical cooking daily to large classes of white-capped, white-aproned girls, with individual towels and holders . . . putting in brain with the would-be drudgery." Through all this effort women were gaining "that wealth of character that will be the means eventually of dispelling the greatest barriers that may confront the race."[19] Even so, perhaps it is telling that Tuskegee held on to the name "domestic science," not "home economics," for more than a decade.

Ironically, at one point Melvil did invite Booker T. Washington to his home in Lake Placid. They ate in his house. The club members wouldn't like it, Melvil said, if the great Tuskegee leader ate in the club dining room.[20]

By the time Lake Placid marked its tenth and final meeting, these white northeasterners were the internationally recognized founders of home economics—no matter that Black and midwestern colleges got there first. Really, they pulled off a coup. How did the Lake Placid group succeed? They had all the advantages. They were white, educated women connected to wealthy and powerful people—indeed, living in the centers of power—in ways their southern and western colleagues were not. They were politically savvy. Their very first resolution thanked the US secretary of agriculture for his prior work in their area and offered their cooperation.[21] Immediately after the first meeting they connected with the National Education Association, not yet a union but already the biggest teachers' organization in the country. Rather than pay attention to individual housewives as the National Household Economic Association did, they focused on setting up home economics teacher-training programs, writing curricula, and gaining government support. They corresponded with the Librarian of Congress, met with US senators, and lobbied for legislation. Those lobbying attempts did have a rough start. Annie's efforts to secure New York State funds to start home economics classes at Cornell provoked an irate response from the university's president, Jacob Schurman: "If, therefore, you push the matter next year, I am compelled to ask [sic] you in the defense of Cornell University itself that the department shall not be established here."[22] Atwater, who was directing the USDA's new agricultural experiment stations, explained to her that educating men took time. They understood the need to investigate irrigation, but not to investigate the home. Even so, he reassured her, behind the scenes many DC government leaders wanted to help the home-science movement. The Cornell agriculture department urged Annie to continue agitating for funding as well.

And they had Richards, who was a true star. At Lake Placid she ran the show, cutting off dead-end discussion without hurting anyone's feelings and poking fun at herself: "Old members of the conference know what to expect," she said at the eighth meeting. "They will be mercilessly held to work till some result is reached, positive or negative, or will be asked to report to the next conference." The rest of the year she taught at MIT, lectured, wrote books, chaired the city's health-education league, consulted on an early version of Merry Maids that included a dorm for the employees, and tested water for corporations—while taking a daily constitutional around Jamaica Pond with her husband, synopsizing German-language engineering-journal articles he could not read, hosting dinners for students, and teaching their parrot, Carmen, to recite hymns. She also continued to refine and expand her thinking about home economics, coining an even more elevated name and vision, "euthenics," in which individual and community action would unite to improve living conditions for all.

Richards was the source of the canny thinking that made the Lake Placid group succeed. She accepted the Lake Placid invitation in the first place, she wrote Abel, because New York State was fertile ground: its K–12 schools and many colleges had domestic science curricula, and the Deweys had influence in education. As the group prepared to become the American Home Economics Association in 1908, Richards made the strategic decision to hold the final "Lake Placid" conference at Chautauqua, home of the adult-education movement that had swept the country. The popular intellectual summer camp would draw attendees, particularly men. "I do not believe we shall get much *constructive* work done at Chautauqua but on the other hand we have a good deal in print which is ahead of the times and it might be well to let the world catch up," she wrote Annie.

With its open-air design, Greek columns, and setting in a grove of trees, Chautauqua's new Hall of Philosophy was a temple to knowledge. "After 48 hours you will probably begin to reorganize Chautauqua as to architecture, gastronomy, and sanitation," the camp president joked to the Lake Placid members, presumably to polite laughter. Richards replied pleasantly, "Our purpose is constructive, not destructive." (In reality, Chautauqua needed no help in gastronomy and sanitation: founding Lake Placid member Alice Peloubet Norton ran the place.) The home economists' spirit was celebratory. Richards ran through their long list of accomplishments. Ten years earlier, women's time was valued at nothing, and to most people, "domestic science" meant cooking and sewing lessons for the poor. But she'd had faith, she said, "that if attention were called to the gaps in knowledge needing to be filled, woman would be quick to take steps towards the desired end." Her followers had fulfilled her faith. Now there were as many as three thousand home economics teachers in the US and Canada, committed to transforming the home. They were linking to other social-change movements in the Progressive Era, pushing forward social work, pure-food and drug laws, and even temperance—home economists theorized that if men ate properly, they would feel no need for alcohol.

Melvil was even more buoyant as he addressed the audience. "We shall see the time when [home economics] will be constantly kept before the mind of the child from the time he first enters school to the day he graduates from college as one of the most vital concerns of life," he proclaimed.

The Lake Placid meetings closed with two hundred members. The American Home Economics Association started with six hundred.[23] Already, they were bounding ahead. In order to accomplish their goals, they would have to expand further, far beyond the people who shared their mutual vision of home economics. Some of those people, such as the men who ran public school systems, did not agree with Richards's vision. They would expand home economics in their own way, to sometimes devastating result.

CHAPTER 3

Food Will Win the War

At the end of 1910, Ellen Richards declined reelection as American Home Economics Association president. It was "high time for the younger folk to take over," she said.[1] What she didn't say was that she was ill with heart disease. Not even her husband knew; he had been away the night of her first angina attack. There was no need to worry anyone, Richards thought, prudently pinning her doctor's name to her office wall. But walking up the three flights to that office became a struggle. At a January lunch in her honor, where she was awarded about $25,000 in today's dollars for research, friends noticed she looked pale. Richards hid her condition until March 22, when she had an attack during the night and had to call in the doctor. Nevertheless, she continued to work from bed, keeping up her strength until she had completed an essay for MIT's fiftieth anniversary. On March 30, 1911, she died.

MIT lowered its flags to half-mast. The *Boston Globe* shared her aphorisms and devoted several columns to her memorial service at Trinity Church, the sanctuary smothered in flowers and crowded with illustrious guests. As the choir sang hymns—the widower, too upset to sing with them, sat in the congregation—the pallbearers set the coffin before an open door of the church to bathe in the sun and fresh air Richards found so healthful. Scientific to the last, she had requested cremation. Friends and family grieved not just for themselves but for society: "If she could have lived ten years longer how much good she could have done," Robert Richards wrote Annie Dewey. He supported Caroline Hunt to write a biography, which she published in 1912. As part of the editing process, Hunt sent many letters and diaries to Melvil Dewey. No one knows what happened to them.[2]

Richards had done her work. At the start of the 1910s, about nine hundred elementary and high schools taught home economics, as did more than two hundred colleges and teacher-training schools. Now others would carry it on. Only twenty-seven of those colleges offered a full home economics course resulting in a bachelor's degree.[3] Home economists wanted recognition and credentials, and a place where they could run the show. Where women could study experimental science instead of fruitlessly knocking at the locked doors of all-male labs. Where they could create more home economists in their image. A department of their own. They set themselves to building a women's empire.

What a pain. Flora Rose and Martha Van Rensselaer hustled down the hall to the Cornell food laboratory. Once again, a fancy guest was on his way and his minders hadn't planned for dinner. The university president had scoffed, "Cooks on the

Cornell faculty? Never!"—but he was quick to take advantage of the food laboratory now that it was there. Once Van Rensselaer, alone and at the last minute, resorted to serving creamed codfish, baked potatoes, and cornbread, to the Cornell host's horror: "Martha, these people live at the Waldorf!"[4] Impromptu catering was all in a day's (extra) work for the two women fighting to establish home economics at a practically all-male university. If they were ever to get a better budget or the title of "professor" they would have to sell their value, even if it meant swallowing criticism of a dinner dished up under duress. Really, the guests were lucky the dinner was edible: Van Rensselaer was such a lousy cook she had once dumped a cup of coffee grounds into a cake recipe that called for a cup of coffee.

Van Rensselaer had other strengths. Born in the sticks to an insurance agent descended from an old New York Dutch family, she received a better-than-average education—not college level, but at a coed private school set on thirty-five acres, where she went on to teach. But she felt like a river dammed to a trickle until she stumbled upon her true passion after successfully running for school commissioner in 1894. (The local newspaper endorsed her, praising her integrity and skill.) After a day of inspecting schools and supervising teachers, she lodged with farm wives and learned about their hardships. The women who put her up worked so hard and yet their lot was so meager—tragic, even. They worked alone, without even mail delivery. They wanted help with their jobs. Cornell's agricultural college issued instructional leaflets for farmers. Van Rensselaer wondered: Why didn't Cornell help the wives?

Fortunately, a Cornell agriculture administrator had the same thought—and because he knew Melvil Dewey, he had a front-row seat to the developments in home economics. In 1900 he hired Van Rensselaer to create a reading course for farm women. The college didn't think it mattered much. They put Van

Rensselaer in the basement next to the steam pipes. When she asked to take bacteriology—so she could teach women about the microbial activity in dishcloths, she explained—the professor said, "Oh, they do not need to learn about bacteria. Teach them to keep the dishcloth clean because it is *nicer* that way." But Van Rensselaer was someone who blasted her way through obstacles. And she and her boss were onto something. She and the agriculture dean wrote to the five thousand men on the mailing list for the farmers' course, announcing the home economics series and asking their wives to tell them how many steps they walked in a day. More than two thousand women responded with relief and gratitude. "I cannot tell you what it means to me to think that somebody cares," one wrote. "My life is made up of men, men, and mud, mud." Soon the course had six thousand subscribers,[5] and Van Rensselaer not only sent out reading material but piloted an on-campus home economics winter course. Among the experts she roped into lecturing for no pay in snowy Ithaca was nutritionist Flora Rose. Ten years Van Rensselaer's junior, Rose had grown up a Denver society girl as pampered and hothouse as her name, feeling as stymied as Van Rensselaer. After years yawning in ballrooms she ran away to Kansas State and then Columbia University to study domestic science.

When Van Rensselaer's boss okayed a degree-granting home economics course in 1907, she urged him to hire Rose. In turn, Rose refused to outearn or outrank Van Rensselaer. Shrugging, the dean let them run the program jointly and waited to see how things shook out. "Quite frankly, I have not found two people, especially two women, who could for long work together successfully and on an equal footing," he said. Things never shook. The women took to each other like bread and butter. Rose thought that Van Rensselaer was a visionary and a powerhouse. Van Rensselaer strode up to a lecture platform with her hands thrust in her cardigan pockets like she owned the place, giving speeches in her deep voice. Truth be told, she was intimidating—in public. In private, Rose soon learned, Van Rensselaer was the ultimate absentminded professor. She lost everything, even an umbrella labeled with her name and address. She was also hilarious, ready to dress up as a bear to amuse friends and to joke about her shortcomings. When Van Rensselaer tried to become a pig breeder, it went predictably and comically south. She fed the sow so much she couldn't mate; after a diet, the pig turned out to be barren; a replacement pig outgrew its pen; and eventually Van Rensselaer sent "Pigretta Hammeta Van Rensselaer" to pasture, writing, "I shall urge her to remember her early home and family."[6]

Van Rensselaer, in turn, was impressed by Rose's precise scientific mind, attention to detail, ease with people, and refinement. Rose started a problem at A and worked through to Z. Their strengths fit each other's weaknesses. Rose planted their garden, laying down the seeds with infinite care. Van Rensselaer raked the leaves, pulled the weeds, trimmed the paths, and planned out the overall design. For "Miss Van Rose," as the pair was known, shared not only a job but a home. Everyone treated them as a couple, for so they were. Home economics, that Donna Reed of a subject, was partly created by two women essentially married to each other. They may not have been mothers of humans (or pigs), but their department was a "lusty child which needs very careful attention," Van Rensselaer wrote.[7]

Not only the department's activities and students needed attention but also the people who controlled its funding. Van Rensselaer and Rose knew that college administrators supported home economics only if they saw its clear practical value. One or two home economists had overtly put in place a more theoretical vision—and lost their jobs. For instance, idealist Caroline Hunt, the first home economics professor at the

University of Wisconsin, tried to create intellectually demanding classes focused on social justice. She fought with administrators for five years. Home economics should "teach women the social significance of the control which they have over wealth," she wrote the University of Wisconsin president in her reluctant resignation letter. "I see no place for cooking and sewing in such courses except as they give an understanding of materials and processes." At Cornell, Miss Van Rose paired science courses with an extensive network of resources for farm wives—and, of course, those obligatory dinners in the cramped agriculture building. Finally one of their meals paid off big. They fed scalloped cabbage to a brassica-hating state legislator who was deciding whether to appropriate the modern equivalent of $4 million for a home economics building. When it came time to vote, he declared, "I want to vote for the woman who taught me to eat cabbage."[8]

Despite Richards's work at MIT, the expansion of home economics wasn't all science, empowerment, and social change. Even though women professors wrote the curricula and textbooks for grade schools, they were not in charge of the public school system. White men were, and to them, home economics meant *housework*. At the same time that home economists were building power in universities, public school administrators were discovering the power of the home to keep women down. Especially girls who were not native-born whites. Around the country, these administrators began shuttling girls of color into home economics.

In Augusta, Georgia, white school-district leaders decided that older African American girls should spend half their time in home economics—to learn to be servants, the program's supervisor wrote in the *Journal of Home Economics*. That education would also give those young women the knowledge to fix their own homes, which were "utterly lacking in system, cleanliness, and comfort" due to African Americans' "original racial instincts" and their poverty after "the support of the wealthy slave-owners was withdrawn." How pathetic, the supervisor wrote, continuing her racist remarks, that they tried to conceal their squalor "with a few flowers and broken ornaments."[9]

Similarly, US Office of Indian Affairs housekeeping curriculum booklets depicted Native Americans as slow learners who, once educated, would be appalled by their families' habits—particularly by their tiny living quarters overrun by dogs. (A proper household had just *one* dog, the office instructed, and it should not sleep with the family.) In New York City, a night-school English-language textbook presented the ideal American woman as one who stayed home. It taught men the phrases "I wash my hands. I sharpen my pencil. I read a book," while teaching women to say, "I wash my hands. I wash the dishes. I set the table."[10] Home economics seemed an ideal way to impose the American (white, middle-class) way of life on newcomers, administrators decided. Even among people who were the opposite of newcomers, predating English-speaking colonizers. A California superintendent, J. A. Cranston, wanted to create a segregated school for Chicana girls with a heavy emphasis on home economics. Employing stereotypes, he billed it as the ultimate personalized learning. He told his school board that home economics drew on the girls' natural warmth and maternal instinct while correcting their bad habits and preparing them for their predestined futures as maids, teenage mothers, laundry workers, and factory seamstresses. It was "the only solution to the Mexican Problem," he said. The school board gave its approval. The segregation would not be overturned until 1946, and it required a California Supreme Court decision that classified Mexican Americans as white since it was still legal to segregate Black students in separate schools.[11]

On occasion, such attempts to use home economics against immigrants and people of color failed. When reformist New York City mayor John Purroy Mitchel in 1915 tried to institute a curriculum that emphasized manual training in immigrant-dominated schools, families protested for ten days. Thousands of students, some still in elementary school, went on strike. They not only paraded and picketed but stoned school buildings, beat up students who crossed the picket line, burned textbooks in the gutter, and pelted police with bricks and bottles. A girl orating from a soapbox at PS 72 brought Lexington Avenue traffic to a stop. The next mayor, Brooklyn judge John F. Hylan, relied heavily on immigrant support and promised that these "boys and girls shall have an opportunity to become doctors, lawyers, clergymen, musicians, artists, orators, poets."[12]

These moves to limit opportunities of immigrant and non-white students came from men outside the field. But what made such developments even more insidious was that they also drew on xenophobia and racism brewing within home economics. Home economists celebrated the fact that the field was making inroads in education and, at the least, did not care about or were willing to accept the message that public school chiefs implicitly sent that housework was demeaning, third-rate employment for people they considered to be of limited capacity. The *Journal of Home Economics* ran articles describing immigrants as dirty peasants who threatened public health. "Unless we wish to see the immigrant colony develop into a germ breeder for the whole community, we must teach these people simple rules of sanitation," wrote Annie Hansen of the North American Civic League for Immigrants. She considered them shiftless and resistant to the experts' efforts to promote personal and home cleanliness. She did not note that these were poor families with no indoor bathrooms, whose access to water generally consisted of a pump in the street. Hansen and her like pigeonholed these families, saying that the children needed school lunches to Americanize them and the mothers needed cooking and nutritional instruction for cheap foods to keep their husbands from going out and getting drunk (and so that employers could keep paying sweatshop wages). Even a Jewish home economist criticized the New York Jewish diet for going too heavy on the pickles.[13] And while they did not seek to back up their opinions with quantifiable data, others were putting a scientific shine on hate.

If you asked Lenna Frances Cooper to identify the mother of home economics, she would not have said Ellen Richards. No, for Cooper, the mother of home economics was Ella Eaton Kellogg, the wife of health guru/cereal magnate John Harvey Kellogg. Cooper lived with the Kelloggs after leaving her Kansas home in 1898 to study nursing at John Harvey's medical spa, the Battle Creek Sanitarium, affectionately nicknamed "the San." She looked after the Kelloggs' children and ran the food service for the institution. The Kelloggs nurtured her in turn. A few years into the Lake Placid conferences, John Harvey, who never met a health bandwagon he didn't want to jump on and drive, sent Cooper to Drexel Institute in Philadelphia so she could start a home economics school at the San. Even before Cooper finished Drexel's two-year food science program, she had joined the ranks of the Lake Placid chosen. "At Battle Creek we have besides diets for special conditions, diets for special diseases," she said at the 1906 conference. She described the San's empowering practice of serving food in one-hundred-calorie portions, which "enables patients to balance their own menus."[14] (Would she have liked today's one-hundred-calorie snack packs?)

Cooper embraced the San's wellness doctrines. She believed in long walks, no makeup, eight glasses of water a day, a vegetarian diet, and the power of nutrition to transform health. It all integrated exceptionally well with home economics, especially home ec's growing collection of nutritional analyses that made it easy to swap beans for meat. Through the Kelloggs' long-running magazine *Good Health*, Cooper's guidance spread far beyond Battle Creek. Every month, she suggested delicious, vegetable-heavy, seasonal dishes and explained the science behind their health benefits. "After the long period of canned and stored vegetables, one's appetite has a keener edge for the fresh, green things, and just to name the new vegetables makes the mouth water," she wrote in the summer of 1916.[15] She promoted avocado and agave, and published a Thanksgiving menu that featured the Kelloggs' nut-based meat substitute Protose. Some of her claims have been disproved—for instance, that the citric acid in grapefruit cleansed the digestive tract and increased the alkalinity of the blood. But even so, Cooper's advice sounds strikingly modern. *Good Health* is to our eyes a remarkable blend of ahead-of-its-time wellness advice, women's rights advocacy, and Grape-Nuts ads . . . alongside racism. For the Kelloggs—and the Deweys—were getting more and more into eugenics.

English geneticist Francis Galton first used the term "eugenics" in the 1880s. Soon the concept crossed the Atlantic, with proponents such as Yale professor Irving Fisher, who also devised calorie counters. He proposed eating more vegetables and instituting measures to improve public and occupational health such as shorter work shifts in factories. That put him in line with the Kelloggs, who, by 1911, were promoting eugenics in *Good Health*, saying that mating had to be controlled to produce better human stock. Not so coincidentally, eugenicists ascribed scientific, biological deficits to people of color, southern Europeans, the Irish, people with disabilities, even people who had the bad luck to contract tuberculosis. They advocated for forced sterilization.

Though it's not surprising that scientists who thought they could create a better society would be interested in the new theories around heredity, it is deeply dismaying to realize just how widespread eugenics was in the 1910s, and how many people seriously believed it. In 1914, the Kelloggs organized their First National Conference on Race Betterment, and invited Annie Dewey to speak as the representative of home ec. The eugenicists embraced home economics, because they thought that some heritable traits could be cured by right living. Oddly, even Booker T. Washington spoke at the Kelloggs' first Race Betterment conference. In his speech, he first gave Dr. Kellogg his "deep personal gratitude" because Margaret had hired a San-trained African American nurse to restore him to health several years earlier. Washington defended African Americans against the beliefs of eugenicists who wanted to exterminate Black people. "The Negro has lived and is still living and intends to live," he said. "That is not an easy thing for any dark-skinned race to do when it is near you." He then thanked the audience for "what you have done in bringing about race betterment among my people." Apart from that, his speech was one of his standard appeals, asking for the white audience's support to better the Black race—not through such horrors as sterilization but through education, friendship, temperance, and the like. He spoke the first day, and then left for other engagements.[16]

Annie Dewey was much more accommodating. As early as 1907, she had written in a draft magazine article that home economics held "the hope of staying the tendency of race degeneration." She also suggested that home economists build

closer ties with Battle Creek and the Race Betterment conference. Emma Gunther, who ran the American Home Economics
Association hotel-management section with Annie, rejected the
idea of holding a meeting at Battle Creek, writing, "That would
interest some of us very little." Caroline Hunt helped African
American women rally for suffrage. She responded to Annie's
enthusiastic note about the Race Betterment conference simply
by saying she had read about the event in the papers. The other
home economists, as far as I can tell, did not dive into eugenics
as the Deweys did. However, the profession did not shun Battle
Creek's home economics school, which Cooper ran. Flora Rose
gave its 1914 commencement address.[17]

Richards was not ready to condemn eugenics. However, in
nature-versus-nurture, she came down squarely on the nurture side. As early as 1905, Richards coined the term "euthenics" in response to eugenics. This was home economics taken
to its highest philosophical tenets. She defined "euthenics" in
one of her last books as "the betterment of living conditions,
through conscious endeavor, for the purpose of securing efficient human beings." Eugenics "must await careful investigation," she wrote. In contrast, "euthenics precedes eugenics,
developing better men now, and thus inevitably creating a better race of men in the future. Euthenics is the term proposed
for the preliminary science on which Eugenics must be based."
Before anything else, people had to use the knowledge they
already had to modify their environments for better health.
This response to eugenics may sound overly measured by our
standards; however, by comparison, Fisher had written for the
US Senate, "A race that can not hold its fiber strong and true
deserves to suffer extinction through race suicide," and advocated banning marriage for people with transmittable diseases
and sterilizing "imbeciles," criminals, and paupers.[18]

Did Cooper believe that some groups of people were

congenitally defective? I have found no proof one way or the other. *Good Health* became the official organ of the Kelloggs' Race Betterment League, and preventing race degeneration was a tenet of the San's home economics school.[19] Cooper did not mention eugenics in her food column, but she continued to publish menus in a magazine alongside screeds that advocated the segregation and sterilization of "defectives," and detailed supposedly scientific evidence that African Americans were inferior beings. Ella Kellogg was one of her closest friends. Cooper eventually left Battle Creek for a job at a conventional hospital in New York, though she maintained her ties in Michigan and went back for visits. The few biographical materials about Cooper focus on her accomplishments in dietetics. Given her longtime work for Kellogg institutions, her support for Ella, and no words against eugenics or the Kelloggs on this issue, it would seem that Cooper was not troubled by the theory.

Government support for home economics steadily rose in the 1910s, with a focus on the farm. Social scientists quantified Van Rensselaer's observations about rural isolation, poverty, and lack of resources. Farm families, they recognized, needed help. To raise the rural standard of living, Congress created the cooperative agricultural extension service through the Smith-Lever Act of 1914. The act formalized and expanded colleges' existing community efforts—such as the USDA "experiment stations" of the 1890s and George Washington Carver's traveling educational service—and created jobs specifically for women as "home-demonstration agents." From now on, rural women across the country would have their own Van Rensselaers sharing the latest and best ways to manage the home side of the farm. In theory, at least. It wasn't always easy to install these new home-demonstration agents. Some state and

county politicians refused to allocate money for their salaries—
shouldn't women just know how to do that stuff? Most women
agents were funded only part-time and had to provide their
own transportation. If an area could afford only one extension worker, it would be a man. Matters were even worse for
women of color. In New Mexico, where the majority of women
spoke and read solely Spanish, the home-demonstration agent
was almost always an English-speaking Anglo. The Southern
extension service was segregated, with white universities in
control; white leaders forbade education foundations like the
Jeanes Fund to augment Black colleges' extension funds. Florida Black home economics agents were called "assistant agents"
and had to have white agents approve their reports. Georgia
had two Black women serve the entire state.

Nonetheless, these jobs, where they existed, opened possibilities. Home-demonstration agents worked on their own
most of the time, sometimes carrying guns for protection. They
chose their topics and wrote their materials based on what local
women needed. They were uniquely independent, which could
cause problems; some farm women were skeptical of these typically unmarried government upstarts. One town greeted its
agent by having the town band play "Hark from the Tomb a
Doleful Sound." Soon enough they would change their tune.

One leader of Black land-grant education did not live long
enough to see the extension service come fully to fruition.
Though Booker T. Washington refused to slow down, he was
aging. He leaned on "Maggie," who worried about him. Traveling in the North in the fall of 1915, he became seriously ill.
He insisted on coming home to die, which he did just a few
hours after he arrived at the Oaks. He was fifty-nine. Telegrams
poured in from luminaries worldwide, and former president
Theodore Roosevelt commended Washington's service to his
country, though Margaret's hot temper flared at the absence

of a message from President Woodrow Wilson. "I suppose I ought to be *mellow* but I am not. I hope that every paper will brook him thoroughly," she wrote her husband's secretary, Emmett Scott. The blow was followed by a horrifying shock: her longtime clubmate Adella Hunt Logan threw herself to her death on campus the morning of Washington's memorial service.[20] Washington added "Mrs." to her husband's unused stationery and kept going. She did not miss a single meeting of the Tuskegee Woman's Club, whose minutes book crossed out Logan's name. She remained the head of "women's industries," demanding but compassionate when students made mistakes, under new Tuskegee president Robert Moton. She could not stop to mourn. The country was ramping up for a war Wilson had promised not to enter.

CAN YOU BE RELEASED TO HELP US ORGANIZE THE HOME ECONOMIC WORK IN THE FOOD CONSERVATION DIVISION OF THE FOOD ADMINISTRATION WE NEED YOU NOW.[21]

US Food Administration director Herbert Hoover was in a panic. "Food will win the war," he had declared, and after the US entered the fight, almost 1.2 million Americans quickly signed a food-conservation pledge. But would they actually cut back on the staples of meat, wheat, and sugar when restrictions were voluntary? That would require transforming American diets. It would require a home economist. So Hoover telegrammed Rose in July 1917, begging for help. She turned him down, not wanting to leave Van Rensselaer or their work. Instead Van Rensselaer urged Cornell's agriculture dean to get involved, proposing to refocus her department on thrift and asking for the modern equivalent of $200,000 to send home economists around the state that summer. She pointed out that such activities benefited the university's reputation as well as

the public good: the war offered "an unequaled opportunity to
make [our] value felt," she wrote. She succeeded in the request,
and put home-demonstration agents in thirty-three counties
where they had not been.[22]

Everyone in home economics saw that opportunity. Public-
school home economics classes turned their attention to war
work. Forget fancy embroidery or sewing your own underwear.
Now students made garments for the Red Cross—everything
from layettes for orphaned babies to hospital scrubs. To conserve new fabric for military uniforms and surgical supplies,
classes also remade and mended old garments, even unrav-
eling and reknitting sweaters. Governments and universities
poured cash into the new extension service; like an irrigated
seed, it blossomed. Home-demonstration agents turned rail-
way cars into traveling food-conservation classrooms, and the
farm wives who had resisted government intrusion toured
them eagerly. The professionals extended their reach by training armies of volunteers who could signal their commitment
by wearing the US Food Administration's signature wrapped
pinafore, called the "Hoover apron."

Margaret Washington, who had signed up for the Red Cross
in 1914 upon seeing which way the wind was blowing, helped
coordinate food-conservation efforts among African American communities in Alabama. Her colleagues were so successful that Hoover hired Tuskegee professor Ernest T. Attwell to
spearhead such initiatives across the South. Washington also
cooperated with the white-led Council of National Defense
Woman's Committee to recruit volunteers and distribute seed
packets so people could start school and community gardens.
The Tuskegee Woman's Club sent Christmas notes and gifts
to every Tuskegee alumnus in the service; with the Red Cross,
club members helped make five thousand sandwiches for Black
recruits waiting for the train to boot camp. In 1918, Tuskegee

was granted a charter for the country's first African American chapter of the Red Cross.

Lenna Cooper focused on the need to feed wounded soldiers, both American and European, at the front and at home in military hospitals. In 1917, she and Cleveland colleague Lulu Graves created the American Dietetic Association. The one hundred attendees at its first conference wrote to Hoover and the Council of National Defense offering themselves as *the* solution for military medical-nutritional needs. The following year the surgeon general, now part of the War Department, named Cooper supervising dietitian for the army. For the new position, she was to develop a dietetic plan, supervise army hospital kitchens, and hire all dietitians for the service. In seven months Cooper brought on 350 dietitians—the first women besides nurses to serve in a US war. The results, at first, were you-have-to-laugh-in-order-not-to-cry. One dietitian found herself overseeing two hospitals, forty nurses, and 2,700 patients. "Oh! how I do love those plans that are made by people that sit in swivel chairs at mahogany desks," she gibed.[23] Some had no proper kitchen at all and found themselves feeding wounded soldiers out of a pup tent. There were no rules governing how they should work or be treated; army men didn't want to take orders from women cooks there on a lark (as they saw it). Ingredients ran short—except when something arrived by the truckload. But once the soldiers saw the results, they asked for more dietitians. Cooper told the surgeon general that the army should create a permanent dietitian corps, with good salaries and authority, plus a military-dietitian training program at Walter Reed General Hospital.

But still, Americans kept eating their meats, wheats, and sweets. In late 1917, Hoover asked Van Rensselaer to take over the US Food Administration's home economics work. Van Rensselaer decided she had to serve the greater good. She secured a leave, bid a reluctant farewell to Rose, and went to Washington with a young Cornell alumna, Claribel Nye. They arrived at the Food Administration office to a stack of complaints from Americans obsessed with their neighbors' unpatriotic gluttony. One woman asked for the government to crack down on "food slackers." Another proposed giving only limited rations to German American children. A third woman, identifying herself as "A widow a Patriot. and American Citizen," asked, incompletely, "How long will we be compelled to support a great army of retail dealers in lifes necessities at PRUSsian prices, and women and children being drafted to farm and factory work in order that these white aproned clerks, of candy, news papers, cheap jewelry &c &c, attorneys, village lawyers, insurance men, real estate dealers? adinfinitum,?????" At least there was one writer who did not complain: Miss Janet Elizabeth Miller, who wrote, "Dear Mr. Hoover, I am a little girl 5 years old, and I lick the platter clean."[24]

No wonder they had hired a home economist!

Emotion fueled those letters, and that's what the Food Administration needed to latch on to, just as the Red Cross had, Van Rensselaer wrote Hoover in a memo. To get Americans to stint their bellies, the government had to tug at their heartstrings. "It is time to do something besides knit," she wrote. "Women ought to be appealed to romantically, persistently, effectively, to leave knitting to those who cannot do anything else, and to put real honest-to-god brains into the production of food, the self-support of the community in food, and the conservation of food."[25]

For Van Rensselaer, the job was a whirlwind. She immediately dove into writing plans and newsletters explaining "why citizens should conserve wheat when there is still wheat used in the manufacture of beer" and telling conservation workers it was unpatriotic to snack (that one couldn't have been popular).

She had recipe booklets translated into foreign languages even though her staff said immigrants wouldn't read. She commissioned menus for people who managed restaurants, hospitals, state fairs, and logging camps. The voluntary recommendations were daunting: if possible, Van Rensselaer's team wrote in April 1918, people should "*use no wheat* until the next harvest"; if they must buy wheat, they had to buy an equal weight of another grain as well.[26] To help, Rose and her team undertook meticulous research at Cornell on substituting corn for wheat, low-sugar cakes and oatmeal "pudding," and enticing ways to eat cowpeas. Home economists had already highlighted inexpensive legume protein sources; now they advanced vegetarian cooking by leaps and bounds so that meat could be kept for the military. (Butter, fortunately, could not be sent to the front due to spoilage, so Americans could eat as much of that as they wanted.)

True, the bureaucracy drove Van Rensselaer up the wall. Doctors reviewed the recipe booklets as if they knew nutrition better than home economists, and they took so long to approve them that conservation guidelines changed in the interim—to the tune of fifty thousand copies of *Sugar Saving Desserts* printed with outdated sugar limits.[27] Still, when Van Rensselaer's leave expired, she extended it.

Before she could serve out the second leave, the war ended, on November 11, 1918. The government turned off the lights so abruptly at the Food Administration in December that a school lunch booklet sat at the printers, never to be sent. Cooper's position was discontinued the following summer despite the many ill and wounded people. Though Van Rensselaer and Cooper felt grateful to have served their country, they were not entirely satisfied with the experience. Van Rensselaer rued all the material that her team had developed but not distributed due to bureaucratic delays. Cooper was angry that the government treated demobilized dietitians as second-class military citizens. They didn't get the bonuses they were promised and would not be recognized as former military employees, which meant no pensions or health benefits. For the rest of her life, Cooper would fight for the military to recognize her recruits.

Nonetheless, on the whole, home economics' star had soared. Everyone recognized that the American soldiers were the best nourished in the war and that US food conservation had saved displaced Europeans from starvation. More than three-quarters of a million people had volunteered for the US Food Administration. Students had clothed soldiers and refugees—250,000 garments from Chicago alone—earning the Red Cross's gratitude and maybe even instilling a permanent sense of service, teachers hoped. Veterans had been not only healed but educated: "The men are coming home from the army knowing more about home dietetics than the women," Cooper said. "American housewives will have to look out for their dietetic standards from now on."[28]

And the government had embraced home economics for good. For the first time it was funding secondary school vocational education and college vocational teacher-training programs, through the Smith-Hughes Act of 1917. Home economics was the only vocational subject the law recognized for girls. Tuskegee's teacher-training course immediately filled up, and Washington asked Moton for more staff. (She also finally began using the term "home economics," which was in the Smith-Hughes law.) International leaders recognized home ec's value as well: Queen Mary begged British teachers to study home economics, and the king of Belgium hired Rose and Van Rensselaer to study refugees' health.

The Hoover apron, Van Rensselaer reflected back home in Ithaca, was really quite a useful garment. Her department recommended it in its farm wives' reading course.

The American Home Economics Association emerged from the war with more than 1,300 active members plus two new honorary members: Director and Mrs. Hoover. The group "stands face to face with the greatest opportunities and responsibilities which it has ever had," wrote its president, Michigan State home economics dean Mary Sweeney, who had worked for the US Food Administration and the US Army.[29]

Home economics had won its war for recognition. Now its leaders could improve the American way of life, particularly women's lives, through thrift and technology. They were at the start of their golden age.

CHAPTER 4

Perhaps It Wasn't Really a Man's Job After All

With the start of the 1920s, the first phase of home economics drew to a close. Annie Dewey died in 1922 after suffering from heart trouble for years. In a poem she left unfinished in her typewriter, she implored people not to mourn. Her husband Melvil built a marble shrine to her memory at Lake Placid, which displayed her ashes in a stately urn. The American Home Economics Association started a scholarship fund in Annie's name. Even pompous Melvil had to admit that his wife would have liked the latter more than his ostentatious memorial.

World War I inspired Margaret Murray Washington to think globally, as it did for many people. In 1922, she gave up editing the National Association of Colored Women's Clubs newsletter and founded the International Council of Women of the Darker Races of the World, the first Pan-African group aimed at women. She continued to run domestic science at Tuskegee, promoted Black-history education, and joined the Commission on Interracial Cooperation. Washington had never been at the forefront of the women's suffrage movement, because "there are certain things so sure to come our way that time in arguing is not well spent. It is simply the cause of right which in the end always conquers, no matter how fierce the opposition," she wrote. However, after the Nineteenth Amendment was ratified in 1920, she took three Tuskegee women colleagues to register to vote, the first Black women to do so in Macon County, Alabama. On Thursday, June 4, 1925, at age sixty (or maybe sixty-four), Washington died at home after an unspecified illness of about five weeks' duration. News reports as far away as the United Kingdom heralded her legacy: her tireless dedication to Tuskegee, young people, and Black people, particularly women. Five days after her death, six pallbearers bore her coffin into the Tuskegee chapel. It was a warm afternoon and the long service was replete with the music she loved—hymns, spirituals, Chopin—and many messages to read, including from the National Association of Colored Women's Clubs, Delta Sigma Theta, the City Federation of Nashville, and President Calvin Coolidge. "What a marvelous example she has set for the womanhood, not only the black race, but of all races and of all nations," Tuskegee president Robert Moton said. "And we can rejoice in the great victory which she has won, through great struggles and difficulties, for she had them. She suffered much in many ways and from many angles, but she never swerved in her faith in God, and her faith in her fellow men."[1]

The woman born into want in rural Mississippi left an estate valued at the equivalent of $750,000 today. Portia, Booker Jr., and Davidson Washington quickly sold the contents of the Oaks, the home that had hosted so many luminaries. Their action drew rebuke from Virginia's *New Journal and Guide*, whose editors argued that "Dr. Washington's home and its contents should have been preserved as a perpetual memorial," like that of President George Washington. Even the *Journal of Home Economics* acknowledged Washington, though only months later, in November, in a brief news item: her death, the editors wrote, "deprived the Negro race of one of its great figures."[2]

Margaret Washington's grave with its wide, majestic marker stands today at the top of a rise on the Tuskegee campus, far above the small, lichen-encrusted headstones of her two predecessors, Olivia and Fanny. Over to the side, in a bower of trees, their husband lies alone. "Mrs. Washington is asleep—not dead," said Jennie Moton, Washington's successor as Tuskegee president's wife and home economics dean. "Can a woman die whose ideals live?"[3]

Four-and-a-half years after the Great War ended, home economics won its government reward. On July 1, 1923, President Warren Harding created the Bureau of Home Economics under the US Department of Agriculture. Its purpose was research detailing "the scientific basis for the mechanics of living": not what to do in the home, but why; not recipes, but principles. Among the letters suggesting ideas for the bureau was one from University of Missouri home economics chair Louise Stanley, who thought it needed a director who was a woman scientist with leadership skills and the ability to envision how the new department could help women across the land. She recommended Iowa State's home economics dean. Instead, she got the job herself. Stanley, a Tennessee farm girl who had topped off degrees from Peabody College, the University of Chicago, and Columbia University with a PhD in physiological chemistry from Yale, bore wire-rim glasses and a calm countenance. Along with her academic position, she was the American Home Economics Association's legislative chair, with experience advocating on Capitol Hill. Stanley wanted to raise the US standard of living and show the value of household work. Literally. "It is desirable to know on a wage basis the contribution which a woman makes to the home income in doing the various household tasks," she wrote in the *Journal of Home Economics* shortly after her appointment. Knowing how hard it was for a woman to find work in science, Stanley went on a hiring spree to create a professional home for her peers in nutrition, textiles, and economics. Not only was Stanley the highest-ranking woman yet employed by the federal government and the highest-paid woman at the USDA, but her bureau became the largest employer of women scientists of any institution in the country.[4]

In its first few years, even short on funds, Stanley's team cranked out scientific research articles by the score. They studied the vitamin C content of green tea, how rats responded to thiamine deficiency, how the body processed the calcium in spinach, and the best ways to soil fabrics for laboratory stain-removal experiments. They roasted 2,400 cuts of meat to determine the best cooking methods, aided by an extensive taste-testing program. They found that potatoes stored in the cold did not make good potato chips and that honey had "valuable food properties but is low in vitamins,"[5] foreshadowing the disappointment of 1970s hippies. They began working toward standardized clothing measurements and a simple plan of nutrition requirements based on food groups. They advocated for standardized kitchen equipment such as measuring cups, and promoted the metric system. And they studied how women spent their time, which their test subjects recorded themselves on a circular grid. Along with writing professional papers, they turned all this research into women's-magazine articles and direct-to-consumer bulletins on topics such as "reindeer recipes" (Stanley wrote that one), no-stir ice cream, fitting home-sewn clothes to your body, and making rompers that toddlers could put on themselves.

In 1927, the Bureau of Home Economics distributed more than two million copies of its bulletins. By 1929 its budget, though still low, had more than doubled to the modern equivalent of $2.5 million. It soon received fifteen thousand letters per year.[6]

The bureau was far from the only entity hiring home economists. In the 1920s, home economics became the jobs engine of Richards's dreams—and not just because all those new home economics classrooms needed teachers. While women had to fight to enter male-dominated workplaces, if they cloaked their ambitions in suitably feminine garb, they could get challenging jobs. Including in business. "Food manufacturers and producers, makers of household equipment and furnishings, cooperative educational organizations representing entire industries, banks, department stores, and advertising agencies are some of those profiting by the help and judgment of the woman with special home economics training," the appropriately named editor Marie Sellers explained in the *Journal of Home Economics*. The new home-ec businesswomen formed Home Economics Women in Business, an American Home Economics Association chapter, with ninety-one members to start. Close to half worked for food companies or food-promotion trade groups, 20 percent were journalists, and 11 percent worked for utility companies.[7]

Several currents intersected to create the new field of business home economics. One was, well, *current*. The first all-electric range appeared in 1917; in 1920, 35 percent of households had electricity—the ultimate advance in demolishing drudgery—a percentage that had doubled by 1929. However, these new electric devices were far from foolproof, and they required education and training. For instance, with thermostats now built into ovens, all those recipes that called for a dish to be baked in "a quick oven" had to be redone to specify degrees Fahrenheit. Women wrote to college home economics departments asking for help in choosing household appliances. Should they replace their icebox with one of those new "refrigerators"? How cold did food need to be kept? To answer the technical questions, colleges created new curricula. The most famous became Iowa State's pioneering "household equipment" course. It was electrical engineering, camouflaged. The college pitched the knowledge of how machines worked as being essential not just for career women but for housewives. A fictional story in the Iowa State home economics magazine featured an alumna who was preparing for dinner guests when her electric stove broke. "Of course this was a man's job, but could she wait until an electrician came?" the heroine thought. She triumphantly pulled out her pliers and saved dinner. "So simple! Perhaps it wasn't really a man's job after all," she concluded.[8]

With the economy booming, manufacturers of household goods zeroed in on women's spending power as consumers. Companies needed home economists to write instructional and marketing materials, develop recipes, answer customer questions, and back up their new promises of lab-tested consistency: Gold Medal Flour, for instance, promised that its kitchen testers baked with every batch of flour. On the other side, representing the consumer, home economists tested those products in independent labs against advertising claims, and home economics journalists stood for informed coverage against less-educated authors who "unwittingly give the reading public perverted ideas of our work and belittle home activities by space fillers," as *Ladies' Home Journal* editor Anna Merritt East asserted.[9]

These new roles created a tension in the field. Companies saw women consumers as "intelligent buyers" to be informed—and exploited. The business home economists were on the side of capitalism, and their job was to sell. Government and academic home economists advocated for thrift, and some thought their business colleagues had sold out. To be sure, education and money overlapped in both sectors. Business home economists saw themselves as representing consumers, ensuring that they got durable, useful goods that were worth their salt. Many modeled themselves after extension workers, going on the road to meet with housewives. For that matter, the federal Bureau of Home Economics worked hand in hand with industry. Refrigeration companies funded the bureau's public health refrigeration research. When demand for cotton fell, the bureau put together a program to promote the fiber, including developing home sewing patterns for consumers and advising manufacturers on durability and starching technology.

At any rate, the "HEWIBs" were a great success. None other than Martha Van Rensselaer was a founding Home Economics Women in Business member; along with studying war-refugee nutrition in Belgium and co-running the Cornell home economics program, she moonlighted as editor of Butterick Patterns' *Delineator* magazine. American Home Economics Association president Mary Sweeney stood fast against criticism, knowing that her members needed those jobs. No one illustrated that need more than Lillian Moller Gilbreth.

Gilbreth was one of the smartest women ever to hide behind a man. Born into a wealthy Oakland family, she wrote poetry and became the first woman valedictorian of the University of

California, Berkeley. She earned a master's degree, then met a dynamic young industrial engineer, Frank Gilbreth, on the eve of her Grand Tour of Europe. Despite her early accomplishments, Lillian Gilbreth was timid behind her cloud of pale red hair. Though Frank called his wife "Boss," she was the beta dog to his boisterous alpha. He made the remarkable decision that she would join him in his engineering career, no matter how unheard-of that was, *and* that they would have a dozen children: six boys and six girls. During their engagement, she indexed his first book. She should get a doctorate, he decreed, so that factory owners would respect her. And so she did, as the Gilbreths became efficiency experts and developed their pioneering Gilbreth System, finding the "One Best Way" to accomplish a task through an innovative method of filming, studying, and then systematically minimizing workers' motions. Everything Frank willed came to pass, down to the balance of children. They earned the equivalent of $4,400 per day plus expenses as consultants for clients such as Kodak.[10] Only two major things happened outside the plan: their second daughter passed away in childhood due to illness, and in 1924 Frank died suddenly at only fifty-five years old, near home at the Montclair, New Jersey, train station, mid-phone call, while enthusiastically telling Lillian his latest idea.

Everyone expected Lillian to buckle under the grief. Friends and relatives offered to adopt some of the children. Instead, the widow found her steel spine. She was determined to keep the family together and carry on her husband's legacy. In less than a week's time, she left to give the speech he'd been scheduled to make at a conference in Prague. "There was really only one consolation, and that was work!" she thought.[11]

If only men would let her do it. Over the next year, Gilbreth flailed and floundered, receiving rejections at every turn. Though engineers respected her as much as ever—she was one of three women in the seventeen-thousand-member Society of Industrial Engineers, albeit an honorary member, because only men could belong for real—clients, even those who had become friends, dropped their contracts. They couldn't have a woman telling men in their factories what to do. With the family bank account running low, Gilbreth made a decision that saved her bacon: she would become a home economist. "Mother thought one way she might get motion study contracts was to apply timesaving methods to the kitchen. Manufacturers would listen to a woman, she believed, when the subject was home appliances," her children Ernestine Gilbreth Carey and Frank Jr. later wrote. "If the only way to enter a man's field was through the kitchen door, that's the way she'd enter."[12] Gilbreth combed through the couple's archive of household investigations, ran a new series of motion-study experiments on chores, and wrote *The Home maker and Her Job*.

Efficiency had long been a focus of home economics research. It was the opposite of the Fitbit era: Van Rensselaer's very first Cornell bulletin for farmers' wives was called *Saving Steps*. At the moment, the nation's star efficiency expert was Christine Frederick, a best-selling housework expert who promoted the time-saving principles of Frederick Taylor, the Gilbreths' mentor and later rival. Frederick tested equipment at her home, which she dubbed "Applecroft Experiment Station." In her 1919 book *Household Engineering*, Frederick called her readers "a great band of women investigators." She told them how to arrange their kitchen, buy sturdy labor-saving devices, and set a schedule so that their work would be easier, faster, and less exhausting. Use your brains, she wrote: "Today the woman in the home is called upon to be an executive as well as a manual laborer."[13] Though Frederick was known popularly as a home economist, she had no training in the field. After she wrote a book called *Selling Mrs. Consumer* in 1929, telling advertisers how to dupe women, professionally trained home economists decried her as a betrayer of the cause and a sellout of the sisterhood.

But even Frederick couldn't out-business Gilbreth. "Housekeeping is an industrial process," Gilbreth once wrote, and the home was a factory, complete with brute labor—that would be the children. *The Home-maker and Her Job* addressed the housewife as Gilbreth would a foreman, and you practically needed an MBA to put her system into effect. Children should do as much as possible so as to free up the highly skilled mother for complex tasks. "Handling the machinery and repairs can be done by much younger members than we usually think possible," she wrote. "Inspection is a part of the training and only the overinspection need be done by adults." (By "machinery," she meant mops and brooms.) It also made sense to send some work out—"I consider that doing washing at home is almost as mediaeval as setting up a spinning-wheel," she told one interviewer—and to buy cheap stockings that could be discarded when they wore through instead of darning expensive ones. *The Home-maker and Her Job* called for time sheets and preprinted task-reminder slips for each member of the household; to save motions in handwriting, homemakers should label slips for their children by number instead of by name. The book had an enormous amount of jargon: Gilbreth told housewives to analyze task order by "Calendar When" versus "Sequence When." She had them create Simultaneous Motion Cycle Charts and assess whether family members were carrying their fair share of the work: some, she wrote, were "one hundred percent parasites." Women could undertake their own motion-study experiments by recruiting a child to follow them around trailing a spool of string. All to a joyous, albeit clinically stated, end: maximizing "happiness minutes."[14]

The book made a splash, and the home economists who

rejected Frederick embraced Gilbreth—even though the latter had no home-ec training either. More important for Gilbreth, readers and businesses embraced her. Soon she had all the work she wanted. She coordinated a high-profile home economics seminar for housewives at Columbia University, set up the *New York Herald-Tribune* Homemaking Institute, and became friends with Miss Van Rose. She told a household equipment company to design its iceboxes—the predecessor of the refrigerator continued to coexist alongside the newer appliance—so that women didn't have to stoop to get eggs, milk, and butter, and to add a drainage hose and pump to the new electric washing machines so users didn't have to drain soapy water into a bucket. She promoted herself as a parenting expert and evidently enjoyed it, judging by the cover letters to magazines preserved in her archives. Her most lasting impact was in designing the contemporary kitchen. General Electric and the Brooklyn Borough Gas Company, one of the few utility companies run by a woman, hired Gilbreth to entirely reenvision the food workspace. She went about designing the kitchen as she would a factory station, with everything close to hand, in three sizes, including two for small apartments. New technology opened up new layout options, she recognized: an icebox had to be near the back door for ice delivery, but a fridge could be placed where convenient so that the homemaker could do everything practically standing in place. Gilbreth also put shelves at a height to cut fatigue and added a wheeled service table and a kitchen desk, later marketed as the Gilbreth Management Desk. The resulting compact, L-shaped "Kitchen Practical" layout cut the distance walked in making a lemon meringue pie from 224 to 92 feet.[15]

So keen was Gilbreth's reputation for engineering efficient home products for women that Johnson & Johnson hired her to consult on the ideal maxipad. Gilbreth dove into consumer research, tabulating surveys and conducting focus groups. What she found made her furious. Periods could keep you out of a job: MetLife, she learned, wouldn't hire women with "menstrual trouble." Gilbreth wrote the maxipad report over Christmas on her Frank B. Gilbreth Incorporated letterhead, exhausting her supply of exclamation points describing busy women wasting their time trimming enormous pads to size and clipping them to their clothes with pins that rusted and stained. Every manufacturer copied Kotex's distinctive box, so everyone knew what you were carrying home. "This napkin is entirely too large, too long, too wide, too thick, and too stiff," she wrote of the best-selling Kotex. Of Gimbro Nap: "There is no sense to this title, and one would probably have to repeat it a number of times to the clerk and finally ask in exasperation for a sanitary napkin." In short, she concluded, "all existing equipment is probably wrong"—because no one had studied the One Best Way to manage menstruation due to a silly, unscientific taboo that hampered women's lives.[16]

Gilbreth had hitched her wagon to the right star. Her scheme worked perfectly. True, her 1928 follow-up *Living with Our Children* drew a couple of sneers, including a review subtitled "Mrs. Gilbreth's Precepts for the Management of Children Are Admirably Adapted to the General Run of Youngsters but They Somehow Seem Not Quite to Fit One's Own." But mostly people went gaga over Gilbreth. To be sure, having "Eleven Children—*and* a Career," as one magazine enthused, was quite a feat. ("Charmingly wholesome" children, at that.)[17] But journalists credited her parenting expertise to her fertility, not her academic and professional qualifications as an organizational psychologist and industrial engineer.

They couldn't have been more wrong. Though Gilbreth loved her children (and knitted in meetings), she had no interest in housework. Her children called her creamed chipped beef DVOT, which stood for "Dog's Vomit on Toast." She always had professional help. "We considered our time too valuable to be devoted to actual labor in the home. We were executives," she told the National Federation of Business and Professional Women's Clubs. Ironically, it was Frank, not Lillian, who found household efficiency fascinating. Frank who presented at the American Home Economics Association conference way back in 1912, and who blurbed Frederick's *Household Engineering*. Frank who set up the millisecond-saving home and personal-care routines, detailed in *Cheaper by the Dozen*, that kept the family running smoothly; Gilbreth thought they were too regimented, and let them lapse after he died. Her home kitchen was huge, old-fashioned, inconvenient, and equipped with an icebox. No matter: she didn't use it—the cook, Tom, did. (According to her children, Tom liked it that way.) Keeping a spotless house, she used to say, was like putting pearls on a string with no knot at the end. And she thought that the ultimate solution to inefficiency went beyond turning children into drones. "The answer to home problems is to teach men how to combine a career and a home," she said.[18] Gilbreth's primary interest remained the business world. She continued to run a small motion-study course for corporate executives. She was using home economics to stay afloat, for as long as it served her.

If the media treated Gilbreth as a character, it simultaneously featured a whole lot of characters who were treated as real women. Companies had begun creating fictional spokeswomen, also called "live trademarks." The spokeswomen, portrayed by actors, attended events and appeared in written material. Aunt Jemima was the first, launched at the 1893 Chicago World's Fair alongside Richards's Rumford Kitchen. The primary African American spokeswoman, she was followed, starting in 1920, by Armour's "Marie Gifford," Carnation's "Mary Blake," and Spic and Span's "Ann Bradley," among other characters, all white.[19] In 1921, the most enduring trademark of them all made her debut. Flour company Washburn-Crosby, manufacturer of Gold Medal Flour, created the "Betty Crocker" character after a 1921 mail-in puzzle game generated sacks and sacks of unsolicited cooking questions from housewives. Three years later, the company hired Marjorie Child Husted to run cooking workshops around the country. Husted was a native of Minneapolis, where Washburn-Crosby was based, and had worked for the Infant Welfare Society, the Red Cross, the Women's Cooperative Alliance, and Creamette. She traveled around the country to give promotional cooking classes, and she had a method for addressing customers' needs: in every city, she recruited high school girls to observe homemakers and report how they cooked. She was so effective that Washburn-Crosby promoted her after one year to director of its Home Service Department.

That's when she started working on the new technology that provided an even better way to reach customers than live classes: radio. Everyone started to produce homemaking radio shows—cooking schools, universities, radio stations, and corporations. And anyone could join in. (Everyone and anyone white, that is: as of 1930, only 8 percent of African American families owned a radio, compared to 44 percent of white families, with rural Black radio ownership virtually nonexistent; the only radio shows by and for African Americans were a few music programs in cities.) Small Shenandoah, Iowa, had two stations, KFNF and KMA, launched by competing plant-nursery owners to promote their businesses. For universities, radio was a virtual way to do home-demonstration extension work. Kansas State started a show in 1924; within two years, two dozen colleges joined the parade.[20] Journalist, trained dietitian, and cooking-school owner Ida Bailey Allen hosted *The National Radio Home-Makers Club* on CBS Radio. Women devoured these shows, particularly their recipes. That makes the programs' power clear, because radio is inarguably the worst possible medium in which to share a recipe. Announcers repeated instructions and ingredients, and reminded listeners that they could write in for a print copy.

Businesses that catered to women took note. Taking advantage of the fact that there was no line dividing advertising from editorial content in those days, companies such as Butterick jumped in to produce shows, often featuring their new fictional spokeswomen. Of those, nobody did it like Betty Crocker. Having honed her chops teaching women in person, Husted took on the bigger challenge of scripting a radio personality to teach from afar. *Betty Crocker's Cooking Show of the Air* debuted October 2, 1924, on Washburn-Crosby's own station, WCCO, whose signal reached as far as California. To participate, all women had to do was cook Betty's recipes and mail in reports on how the dishes came out, with a grocer's signature testifying that they had used only Gold Medal Flour. At the end of the year, 238 women who had completed the course came to a "graduation" ceremony at the radio station. The next year the show expanded to thirteen stations, and forty-seven thousand more people "enrolled." It was, Betty announced proudly, the largest cooking class ever.[21] In 1927 NBC picked up the show to air across the country. Betty Crocker's voice sounded nasal in New Jersey and drawling in Texas, for each station or station group had its own local announcer read the role.

Various members of the company's home economics team developed recipes, mailed them out upon request, and answered letters. Husted wrote the scripts, informed by her knowledge of how ordinary women cooked and what they wanted, knowledge she kept current through continued field research that included watching women in their kitchens. She learned, for instance, that whereas test-kitchen staff scooped flour into a measuring cup and gently leveled it off with a knife, women at home tapped the flour down in the cup— which packed in more flour and led to leaden results. After Washburn-Crosby became General Mills, the company standardized Betty's approach. According to company policy, Betty was always dignified, always a lady. "She must stick to home economics and never discuss her private life, which would be rather dull anyway," the policy said. Betty admitted she had a team, but no one ever, ever revealed that Betty did not exist. In turn, listeners took Betty to their hearts. One elderly woman wrote saying the only reason she didn't want to die was that she would no longer get Betty's recipes. Maybe that problem could be solved, she said: "I shall send in a call to St. Peter." Even women who weren't housewives loved the show, such as one who wrote, "I have listened to every one of your cooking school programs and have decided that I'm not a very good housekeeper. I'm really glad I'm still single."[22]

Seeing the popularity of these radio shows, the Bureau of Home Economics created its own Betty Crocker in 1926. "Aunt Sammy" was Uncle Sam's sister, though many listeners thought she was his wife. Like the bureau itself, Sammy had a wider purview than the kitchen, sharing information about sewing, money, cleaning, and home décor as well as menus. Bureau communications lead Ruth Van Deman wrote most of the scripts, sometimes repurposing bureau pamphlets. As befit a fictional character employed by the federal Agriculture Department, Aunt Sammy could be tough. "Matilda" had better set the breakfast table neatly, because, Sammy warned, "I heard of a man once who left home because the tablecloth was always askew." She dispensed diet advice with verve to poor "extra-stout". Katy, whose tears ran from her "plump cheeks, and bounced from her double chin, onto her ample bosom." When Katy squeezed into a dress, "well—I'll leave it to your imagination. Curves and detours—you know what I mean," Aunt Sammy said, rather cattily.[23] Katy would have to give up her mayonnaise dressing!

Sammy's advice to Katy showed the extent to which the bureau listened to women. Stanley and her team actually tried to shy away from advising on weight loss. They thought that proper nourishment was what mattered; weight would take care of itself. But the twenties popularized a skinny silhouette, and so many women wrote for advice on "reducing" that the bureau developed a form letter urging them to avoid fad diets and make sure they got all their nutrients before cutting back on food. An agency with no power to enforce its recommendations and limited funding to get its message out depended on responding to its public. So weight-loss advice it was. Sammy's connection to her listeners became as strong as Betty's: her 1927 "radio recipes" cookbook sold fifty thousand copies in a month and became the first cookbook to be printed in braille.[24]

The homiest radio hosts of all, however, were real, breathing women, though they, too, were not exactly what they seemed. the radio homemakers, just-folks who "visited on the air" sharing household tips, tidbits of family news, home economics developments from extension services, and cookie recipes. The Driftmier clan was nothing special, Leanna Field Driftmier's daughter wrote later on: "We're just small-town, Midwestern Americans who have been fortunate enough to claim you as our friends."[25] That ordinariness was what Driftmier and the other "radio homemakers" traded on. But was it ordinary to convert a bedroom into a soundproof recording studio, then ad-lib a radio show? To have a busload of fans troop through the kitchen while you ate breakfast, expecting a tour and a snack? To manufacture imitation vanilla with your face on the bottle? To set a microphone on your kitchen counter as you mixed a cake, and when the eggs turned out to be rotten, to continue mixing with an empty bowl while your daughter quietly dumped the stinky stuff out back?[26] That's what life was like in the Driftmier house after Leanna, mother of seven, turned homemaking into a media career as thoroughly as any modern shelter blogger.

Born in 1886, Leanna Field grew up on farms in Iowa and Southern California, then taught school. She took a "manual training" course at the Los Angeles teachers college, walking through orange groves to catch the streetcar in the dark, and ended up a skilled builder who helped construct her parents' stone chimney. She was twenty-six years old when she returned to Shenandoah, Iowa, to help her sister Jessie run a camp that was the start of 4-H. That's when she met Martin Driftmier, a widower with two toddlers. They married the following year, and Leanna permanently charmed her new stepdaughter by making her a dress festooned with embroidered scallops and a blue ribbon sash. Leanna Driftmier's radio career began about a dozen years later, in 1925, a financially and emotionally draining year in which the family moved cross-country twice and her husband took a job in New York, leaving her home in Shenandoah with seven children aged three to sixteen. Her brother Henry Field, a seed-company entrepreneur, had recently started radio station KFNF. There was no such thing as radio job training in those days: station owners pulled in whomever they could to fill air time, including their siblings. Terrified of speaking on the air, Driftmier pretended to be in church and sang on her sister's *Mother's Hour* show. But soon she started talking, and didn't stop for decades. Her sister switched to chatting about horticulture, and Driftmier renamed the mother's show *Kitchen-Klatter*.

The schedule was punishing. The Driftmier kids remembered cleaning the kitchen after their big, home-cooked weekday lunch, with much klatter, while Driftmier shut herself into her home office. Just after 1 p.m. she left for the studio. Saturdays were toughest of all. The family broadcast morning worship at 7 a.m. Then Driftmier hosted *Kitchen-Klatter* at 1:30 p.m. and a 3:30 p.m. children's show that featured her daughter Margery singing songs that listeners requested. All the children had jobs around the house. Lucile, the oldest daughter, helped with the correspondence, which was heavy, because Driftmier rapidly became incredibly popular. In December 1926, a guest host asked listeners to surprise Driftmier with Christmas gifts. In came four hundred dishtowels, two hundred bath towels, sixty aprons, thirty-five pairs of embroidered pillowcases, and uncountable numbers of cookie boxes, cakes, candy boxes, washcloths, potholders, hankies, doilies, and other linens.[37] The children were still using the linens when they grew up.

With all the radio homemakers, it's remarkable the extent to which their identity as "just a homemaker" was a fiction. It was professionalized parenthood. Even when the hosts recorded from their kitchens, and no matter how much they spoke from their own experience, radio homemaking was a career. Many radio homemakers were divorced or widowed, and held multiple roles at the stations. For instance, Doris Murphy, a widowed mother, hosted a homemaking show on KFNF rival KMA, served as the station's women's director and news reporter, edited the station's monthly magazine, organized monthly events at KMA's one-thousand-seat auditorium, and solicited her own on-air sponsors. Murphy eventually cofounded American Women in Radio and Television. The jobs paid, albeit badly, and the hosts weren't compensated for the snacks they fed to those busloads of fans coming to their houses or the time they spent entertaining them, though

KMA owner Earl May did once replace a homemaker's carpet, worn through by all the visitors. That was although the products they recommended flew off the shelves. Radio homemaker Jessie Young could squeeze a dozen commercials into a one-hour program. One radio homemaker got on the mic to host her show the day after her husband died, and told her listeners about it. No wonder listeners felt a connection.

While these women were making their family lives into radio programs, home economists in academia wanted students to experience what it meant to raise a child. In the 1920s, the maiden home economics college administrators got baby fever. The strangest offshoot of the professionalization of parenthood came in the form of a new resident in university home-management living-lab practice cottages, the practice baby. Not a sack of flour or a doll but a real, live human child, to be raised in the most scientifically approved manner.

Surprising as it sounds, when the Lake Placid group codified home economics, they largely omitted parenting advice. President Taft founded the Children's Bureau in 1912 in the Department of Labor, but the American Home Economics Association's 1913 syllabus omitted childcare altogether. Perhaps it was because the women in charge, as noted in chapter 2, rarely had children of their own. For a woman, pursuing a career usually meant remaining unmarried or at least childless. A look at the personal titles in the 1926 *Bulletin of the American Home Economics Association* shows that the field's leaders were overwhelmingly single. However, the study of childhood was on the rise academically—as was the market for parenting expertise, as Gilbreth's experience showed. By 1921, the Children's Bureau infant-care booklet ran to more than a hundred pages. And as home economics college programs became more popular, their students included not just women willing to trade family for career but future homemakers—more than 80 percent of home-ec majors married, Iowa State home economics dean (Miss) Anna Richardson told the American Home Economics Association in the mid-twenties, around the time the association created a homemakers' section.[28] Among its goals was to study household pursuits so society would recognize homemaking as a profession. In 1924, philanthropy put the final finger on the scale: the Laura Spelman Rockefeller Memorial Fund began granting money to study child development. The American Home Economics Association voted to develop childcare curricula, and home economists began trying to persuade college agriculture deans and the US Department of Agriculture that children merited scientific research as much as wheat did.

Flora Rose approved of the new focus on parenting. Even at academically prestigious Cornell, 42 percent of home economics graduates became full-time wives and mothers, and an additional 12 percent held jobs outside the house while being married. Rose and Van Rensselaer established a nursery school and a statewide network of child-study clubs that cooperated with New York State's new parent-education bureau, also funded by Laura Rockefeller, while Van Rensselaer taught a course on the history and economics of marriage that included the open consideration of birth control and cohabitation.[29] The practice baby, however, was the real attention-grabber. The first, "Dicky Domecon," was just three weeks old when he arrived from a Syracuse social services agency. (All the Cornell practice babies would get the last name "Domecon," short for "domestic economy.") "We have had much pleasure this spring and summer in feeding our practice house baby," Rose wrote a colleague in February 1921. The six-month-old boy weighed eighteen pounds, she reported. "His flesh is firm and pink, and his eyes a brilliant blue. For a common, or garden baby, we all think him quite remarkable."[30]

Like Dicky Domecon, home economics practice babies typically came from adoption agencies or orphanages, though occasionally they were loaned directly by families whose mother was unwell or father working far away. Oregon Agricultural College's first practice baby, Patsy, was the toddler of a widowed home economics major who herself participated in the management-house care. Upper-class students lived in the practice home for some portion of a semester and rotated in as "baby manager" for a couple of weeks each, planning and carrying out the baby's meals, naps, baths, playtime, and discipline; caring for the baby's clothes; and setting up substitute care during class time, all under faculty supervision. (Faculty also stepped in during term breaks.) Practice babies lived on campus for anywhere from a semester to a year, at which point they were made available for adoption. From there, the colleges could not keep track of the babies, because adoptions of that era were closed. Students often made scrapbooks to remember the babies by. They had plenty of newspaper clippings to include, because press coverage was extensive—and sickeningly coy. Journalists cooed that the babies would be spoiled rotten by so many mothers. They dwelled on the inevitably "bouncing" charges' newly chubby cheeks and sparkling, big eyes, and made tiresome jokes: "If Baby Kathryn Marie gets from under the cover some cold night and takes cold, a co-ed will receive a demerit mark," the *Boston Globe* warned. Babies ready to be adopted were said to be "graduating." The articles emphasized that the babies came from good families. Amid so much literary drool, it's really quite a relief to read a note in a Cornell student paper that mourned Dicky Domecon's departure "with a few tears from our editorial fountain pen," as "the source of much freak news for this neighborly journal."[31]

Still, underlying the fluff was respect for the universities' methods. "There will be no kissing of little baby feet; there will be nothing of that kind. Baby Kathryn Marie is to be raised in the most approved scientific manner," the *Boston Globe* continued. Home economist lab-tested consistency wasn't just for flour. Perhaps the surest sign of social approval came from prospective parents. Couples clamored to adopt practice babies. The *Boston Globe* reported that thirty-five families had applied to adopt "tiny Rebecca Murphy" of the University of Maine; after the article ran, six more families added themselves to the list. That same year of 1929, the nation's top government homemaking expert followed suit. "Dr. Stanley Is Now Mother by Adoption," the *Washington Post* proclaimed.[32] Louise Stanley, who lived with women housemates, chose Nancy, a sixteen month-old who had been cared for at the University of Iowa. The newspaper speculated that Stanley wanted to keep a child in the house now that her roommate Mabel Willebrandt was moving out with her own adopted daughter. Apparently the adoption fell through. The 1930 census lists Louise as living with Nancy Stanley, but the latter was her adult sister. Stanley's obituaries and a dissertation on her do not mention a daughter.

With practice babies, as with the press coverage of Lillian Gilbreth, the press and the public imposed (and home economists sometimes sold) a narrative of women's traditional roles on a situation that did not much resemble it. In reality, practice homes looked less like the married, heterosexual, nuclear household for which they ostensibly prepared students than the feminist communes of a later era.[33] There were no husbands, and women shared tasks equally. Nor was the work anywhere near as unrelenting as actual parenthood: the

University of Minnesota baby manager had hands-on responsibilities for only four and a half hours per day, because education came first.

Thanks to that education, home economists had now established domains of their own, in government, business, and households. That authority would serve everyone in good stead after October 1929.

CHAPTER 5

It's Up to the Women

"Housewives are not the only people interested these days in inexpensive meals. Girl scouts are also interested. So is the President of the United States," Aunt Sammy enthused in April 1931.[1] President Hoover wasn't doing much to stanch the Depression's panic and unemployment, but he could at least eat, with public fanfare, a dinner whose educational value was topped only by its carbohydrate count—a kludgy bill of meat loaf, pea soup, potatoes, cabbage and carrot salad, wheat muffins, and lemon bread pudding, prepared by Scouts for just $1.89. Dining with the president were Louise Stanley and Lillian Gilbreth, who was now the chair of the women's division of the President's Emergency Committee for Employment.

Home economics was at its best in hard times, and when the Great Depression began in 1929 after a brief decade of plenty, its professionals leapt to help families in the crisis.

Unfortunately, the man who had spearheaded rapid, top-down hunger-response efforts as the Great War's food czar did nothing of the same as president when the Depression hit. The crisis would soon be over, Hoover assured the public. Home economics professionals tried to take up the slack, but their efforts remained scattered and localized as the unemployment rolls grew. Nothing seemed to get traction. Not Gilbreth and Stanley's weekly newspaper service with shopping lists designed to fend off malnutrition, which home economics classes then turned into menus. Not Gilbreth's presidential committee's "wise spending" campaign, centered on articles and booklets encouraging women to hire people to fix up their houses and gardens, thereby helping alleviate unemployment. In fact, the reverse happened: as companies laid off married women to retain jobs for men, women began to do things themselves that they had previously hired out. Looking for guidance on tasks such as reupholstering, the number of rural women in extension homemaking clubs rose from about 640,000 to 760,000 from 1930 to 1931. Even big efforts didn't make much difference. The Red Cross received 500,000 bales of cotton from Congress, traded it for cloth, and gave the fabric to thousands of home economics students to sew garments for the needy, including 2.8 million cotton sweaters. It wasn't nearly enough. Moreover, what aid existed wasn't always circulated wisely. "The distribution of food, clothing, and other relief supplies was in many places in the hands of well-meaning but inexperienced persons who were unable to use the resources to the best advantage," the *Journal of Home Economics* editorialized in 1933. And the financial crisis threatened home economics itself. Though the class seemed obviously useful in tough times, the school-funding crisis made it nonessential at a time when teachers in some places were already waiting for an endlessly delayed payday. With dues in short supply, the main body of the entire profession, the American Home Economics Association, almost went under. Membership fell by one-quarter; conference attendance went from about 1,650 in 1931 to barely 900 in 1932. The association cut its budget, its staff, two annual issues of its journal, and its journal subscription price. Then, in March 1933, the bank that held its money failed. "Zero hour—or below. Icebound in the red sea with everything frozen but our spirits," business manager Keturah Baldwin reported.[2]

Fortunately for everyone, the home ec turnaround was about to begin, thanks in part to a First Lady with a tin palate.

Eleanor Roosevelt became a mover and shaker in New York politics in the early 1920s as her husband Franklin D. Roosevelt recuperated from polio. At a meeting of the new League of Women Voters, she met a fascinating woman named Flora Rose who told her about her inspiring work—and converted Roosevelt into a powerful ally for Cornell and the home economics cause. Roosevelt helped convince the New York legislature to upgrade the department's status to the New York State *College* of Home Economics, and attended Cornell's annual Farm and Home Week so many times she lost count. When her husband became governor of New York in 1929, she persuaded him to allocate funds for a new, larger home economics building at Cornell.

In late spring 1932, as its cornerstone was about to be laid, Martha Van Rensselaer died in a New York City hospital. She had hidden the seriousness of her illness from almost everyone. She worked until the day before her death, holding conferences in her hospital room, dressed and evincing her usual dry humor. Encomiums poured in to Rose full of loving comfort. Gilbreth referred to Rose and Van Rensselaer's "perfect friendship" in her letter, writing as a fellow widow: "For her, of course, the going was beautiful. Her last waking words with you—then to sleep into the other world. But for you, my dear, only those of us who have lived thru a sudden parting know what it is." Eleanor Roosevelt sent two pages of scrawl, starting, "Couldn't you drop 'Mrs. Roosevelt' with me? I would like it if you could." She continued, "Though the loneliness is great, the world is so much richer for those of us who knew and loved Martha that it makes it the more imperative to try to carry on the things she stood for in her life." Governor Roosevelt, who was about to be named the Democratic presidential nominee, sent a brief, typed letter with a handwritten postscript: "I am really deeply distressed—and I shall miss my old friend greatly."[3]

In June, Rose dedicated the new home economics building at Cornell to her late partner: Martha Van Rensselaer Hall. She carried on doing the work of two as she had during the Great War, only now without an end point. "Wherever I go as you say I am reminded constantly of Martha," she wrote a friend. "That is perhaps the greatest joy which I now have. I feel her magnificence and courage now as I have ever felt them and I want always to be in those surroundings which we together have made. For that reason I am going to try to keep the home which we both have loved so much and I want my friends to come to it and share with me the very beautiful thing which constantly I feel in going in and out of the rooms we so enjoyed." And to the stern University of Wisconsin home economics dean Abby Marlatt, "I have a fine philosophy about the whole situation but alas I am human, and life necessarily will be a [sic] difficult from now on."[4]

The Roosevelts invited Rose to the presidential inauguration—not just to the swearing-in, with a seat in the president's stand, but to the Washington Cathedral service, a governors' dinner, a private reception with the president and his wife, and a private buffet lunch. Rose treasured the invitation for the rest of her life. But the greatest honor the Roosevelts gave to Flora Rose was to elevate her and Van Rensselaer's life's work. Eleanor Roosevelt discussed it in her very first interview as First Lady. She planned to focus first on housekeeping, the Associated Press reported. Along with cutting White House expenses 25 percent in accordance with a new presidential policy, "I want to try out here some of these new foods that Flora Rose and others are developing at Cornell University," Roosevelt said.[5] By that she meant the nutritionally supercharged "Milkorno," made of cornmeal mixed with dried-milk powder and salt, which she had sampled at the university's Farm and Home Week. It was, essentially, famine food. Cornell followed up with the similarly fortified "Milkwheato" and "Milkoato."

Then Roosevelt published a book, *It's Up to the Women*. Where Hoover had once said "food will win the war," she said women would win the Depression. It was a home-ec book through and through, advocating household budgeting, smart spending, training children to follow routines and keep house, and treating maids (if you had one!) with the same regularity and dignity as a worker in a factory. Given the complexities of nutrition, "the mother of a family should look upon her housekeeping and the planning of meals as a scientific occupation," she wrote.[6] Over and over again Roosevelt told readers to get help from a home economics school to learn how to manage money, care for a baby (recommended for both men and women), arrange their kitchens for optimal efficiency and least fatigue, choose durable furniture that could be easily kept clean, and remake old things. She specifically credited Rose several times, especially for her school's budget-conscious menus.

Alas for the refined president and his hungry guests, Roosevelt practiced what she preached, enthusiastically promoting

Milkwheato and Cornell's emergency-relief menus. Perhaps they ate the Tuesday bill of fare from *It's Up to the Women*, which included a lunch of hot stuffed eggs in tomato sauce with mashed potatoes and prune pudding, and a night meal of peanut butter sandwiches with apple-cabbage salad on the side. Over the years, she would mention home economics well over a hundred times in her "My Day" newspaper column, describing numerous visits with Gilbreth, Rose, and Stanley. In teaching home economics, Flora Rose "is really giving an education in democracy," the First Lady wrote.[7]

Despite the similarity between the prune pudding menu and Hoover's Girl Scout meal, everything had changed. Franklin Roosevelt's New Deal funded a myriad of home economics emergency-relief projects to put Americans back to work and strengthen the country. The Civil Works Administration paid for nursery schools. Housing experts designed lodging for Tennessee Valley Authority dam workers, placing fireplaces next to electric heaters to combine modern convenience with local custom. The Federal Surplus Products Corporation bought twenty-five million pounds of Milkwheato to distribute to the unemployed. (This era brought a less-nutritious, longer-heralded home economics food development as well: Toll House cookies, created by home economics teacher–turned–restaurateur Ruth Wakefield.) The Works Progress Administration was especially productive. Its National Youth Administration paid African American girls to get job training in home economics. Bureau of Home Economics textiles chief Ruth O'Brien got the go-ahead on her long-planned project to create standardized clothing sizes for children and women, an enormous research endeavor eventually requiring more than five million distinct measurements of almost 150,000 children and 15,000 women. (All were white.) The bureau hired unemployed people to take the measurements, more than eight hundred for the children's project and five hundred for the women's.[8]

And then there was school lunch.

For generations, schools did not serve lunch. Many city schools were built without kitchens: students went home or bought snacks from pushcarts. Kids in the countryside brought food to eat. School lunch had long been a plank in the home economics social-change platform, because it solved multiple social problems at once. It energized children to learn; gave an opportunity to teach nutrition and cooking; reduced truancy; tempered poverty; and saved children from the "poisonous" snacks of the streets—"pretzels, candy, or pickles," the *Journal of Home Economics* noted in 1913. The ethnic element of that description points to another goal: school lunch could be used to "Americanize" immigrant children, and through them their families, by introducing them to what was considered middle-class fare. As early as the 1890s, the New England Kitchen took charge of Boston school lunches despite obstruction attempts by janitors who had supplemented their salaries with snack tables. By the end of 1914, New York City offered lunch to more than twenty-four thousand children, plus a three-cent morning snack of crackers and hot milk "for anaemic, ungraded and crippled classes." The city did make an effort to appeal to immigrant tastes, with a long list of soups including tripe, Scotch broth, obergritz with potatoes, and minestrone.[9] Some other districts followed suit. Still, school lunch remained a local affair. It never came close to paying for itself, and relied heavily on volunteers and charity. In 1932, the *Journal of Home Economics* begged fruitlessly for government support for school lunch, which could quickly feed six million malnourished children.

When Roosevelt came into office, he found, of all ironies, a disastrous surplus looming in the hog market. Midwestern farmers had bred too many pigs, glutting the market, and they didn't have enough corn for feed due to the ongoing drought. To prevent the farm depression from growing even worse, the new administration announced that it would buy and slaughter five million surplus pigs, including one million heavily pregnant sows, then preserve some of the meat in salt and give it to people on the relief rolls. It sounded like a good idea, but the results were gruesome. Farmers, sensibly, off-loaded their smaller stock. However, commercial processing equipment designed for full-grown hogs couldn't manage piglets, some of which escaped from their holding pens and ran down the streets of Chicago and Omaha, squealing. Some of the meat had to be ground into fertilizer or animal feed, which people claimed was simply dumped into rivers. The pork that made it to the public was so salty as to be almost inedible: "This pork takes a lot of rinsing," one man told the *Boston Globe*. The waste, with so many people hungry, infuriated the public. In response, the administration scrambled together a more systematic plan to deal with agricultural surplus: send it to schools. The government combined food donations with monetary support, and thus started school lunch as we know it. The program was a major success. It nourished children, supported farmers, and even created jobs. By the time the Depression ended, federally funded school lunch programs operated in every state, served more than two million lunches per day, and employed more than sixty-four thousand people.[10]

Even as the Depression threw many people out of work, it provided opportunities for home economists to launch careers. Three women in particular would take the opportunity to change their lives, and the lives of countless others.

Three decades after the Lake Placid conference excluded African Americans, Black home economists were still separate and highly unequal in the profession. African Americans made up 24 percent of the South's population but only 12 percent of southern extension staff, even as Black families bore the brunt of economic hardship. The American Home Economics Association rarely mentioned Black universities in its journal and practiced segregation: one could not join without belonging to a state affiliate, and the southern state groups refused to include African Americans. To extend some nominal support to southern African American professionals while not rocking the boat, the national association formed a "cooperation" committee that was evidently wholly ineffective. It encouraged Black home economics leaders to form their own groups; many already had, under the auspices of the National Association of Teachers in Colored Schools. Then the committee recommended that the AHEA invite a delegate from those groups to the AHEA's annual meeting, and make a reciprocal visit. The suggestion went nowhere.[11]

Undergraduate programs at historically Black colleges had improved in quality and quantity. Tuskegee, for instance, converted its home economics program to full collegiate status and began granting bachelor of science degrees in the subject in 1929. Still, Black colleges had little money for research, and none offered the home economics graduate degrees that were becoming necessary for advancement. African Americans simply had to leave the South for that. Supporting those degrees became a priority for several foundations that had financed public and undergraduate education for African Americans and now opened up to graduate students. The Rosenwald Fund, for example, gave grants to twenty-five women of color between 1929 and 1931 for postgraduate home economics study. Still, home economics at predominantly white northern universities could be segregated as well. Ohio State undergraduate Doris Weaver, a Black Cleveland socialite, sued unsuccessfully to live in the whites-only practice house, a case that made headlines across the Black press for months. Home economics chair Ruth Lindquist declared "that as long as she stayed at Ohio State University there would never be a colored girl live [sic] in the Home Management House." Weaver earned a bachelor's degree through alternative coursework and became a professor at nearby Wilberforce University, a Black college. Despite prejudice, Black women did find universities that would admit them for advanced home ec degrees. Between 1925 and 1933, at least forty-one women earned master's degrees, including the memorably named Pinkie Thrift, who would go on to lead home economics at Southern University in Baton Rouge. Of them, twenty-seven attended Columbia University, six Iowa State, three Cornell, and one each the University of Chicago, Ohio State (graduating in 1927), the University of Kansas, Kansas State, and the University of Southern California. Among the Cornell graduates was Flemmie Pansy Kittrell.[12]

Kittrell was born in 1904 to rural North Carolina sharecroppers. The eighth of nine children, she was petite and, she admitted later, perhaps a little spoiled; she dragged her feet doing farmwork but was always on time for school. "I had the benefit of many of the privileges that my older brothers and sisters had had, without having to work for them," she said.[13] Still, life wasn't easy. By the time she left for Hampton Institute, three of her siblings and her father had died. She spent a decade at Hampton working her way through high school and college. Fortuitously, she arrived just early enough to attend its soon-to-be-discontinued high school, and late enough to earn a bachelor's degree at its newly elevated college. Kittrell was interested in political science, not home economics—the home was so ordinary, she thought, you already knew all about it— until one of her high school teachers gave her Caroline Hunt's 1912 biography of Ellen Richards.

Though Kittrell became a home economics professor at Bennett College after graduation, her mentors encouraged her to gain more education while working. Cornell accepted her to its master's degree program. She was anxious about going: it was six hundred miles away, and she didn't think she would know anyone, though it turned out that there was a small group of Hampton alumnae earning their master's degrees at the same time. Kittrell stood out among the graduate students for her focus and insight. She "had a real contribution to make to the field of home economics," Rose wrote. Recognizing her promise, Cornell and a few foundations funded her part-time studies. After earning her master's degree, Kittrell made the highly unusual decision to keep going. As of 1930, only fifty-one African Americans had earned PhDs in any discipline, and Cornell had awarded its first home economics doctorate degree only that same year.[14] Rose herself did not have a doctorate, and Kittrell's adviser had earned hers only a few years earlier.

At the university in small-town Ithaca, Kittrell found a global perspective. Cornell, including the home economics school, prided itself on its internationalism. Rose and Van Rensselaer had earned medals from Belgium for studying malnutrition among survivors after the Great War, and their renown drew students from around the world. Cornell home economists believed that rural communities, globally, had more in common than they had differences, and that banding together brought strength. Solving hunger, they believed, would help calm countries with political instability. More broadly, discussions of social impact infused the coursework. In Kittrell's adviser's Family Studies course, they weren't sweeping and sewing; they were using the family to change society. Along with pursuing her research and studies, Kittrell joined the Women's International League for Peace and Freedom, one of the few Black women to do so, and the YWCA, which also promoted international work. She was delighted to find political science in her chosen career of home ec.

Prejudice still existed. During Kittrell's years at Cornell, the dean of women forbade Black undergraduates to live in the women's dorm, reversing the policy of many years, though at least at first, Kittrell apparently was still allowed a room there. Kittrell kept her head down and worked. She ignored the university's racism. "I did not have problems in general because I wouldn't allow myself to have problems. . . . [I] didn't want to have any special favors. I worked hard and I just got results," she said later. That attitude went over well with her white professors, who praised her for being "less race conscious than other negro students," and, a racially coded comment, said that she was "forceful without being insistent." Kittrell spoke later about only one instance of racism, when a male instructor deliberately gave her a failing grade on her French translation exam. She retook the exam and, after he failed her again, insisted on seeing the professor's dictionary, which he could not provide.[15] Two home economics professors came to her rescue, writing letters on her behalf and challenging the scoring. She passed.

However, Kittrell was vocal about the desire she shared with her foremother Margaret Murray Washington to lift up her race. She studied African American communities in rural North Carolina, finding staggeringly high infant mortality rates. Like the Hampton booklet from 1911, her goal as a professor was to train leaders, not maids. "We do not train specialists in home economics programs to work in other people's homes!" she said.[16] Her professors admired her drive and commitment to the African American community, as well as her focus: she had a plan and she followed it.

In 1936, Kittrell became the first Black woman to earn a

doctorate in nutrition. She continued working at Bennett, now as dean of women. Greater things were in store.

A New Mexican family sat around the table with their visitor, the home-demonstration extension agent. They tucked into beans with fragrant chile sauce and toasted, whole-wheat tortillas. Their guest, however, got a special meal: fried potatoes, corned beef from a can, and white bread. White and pink, salt on bland. When the agent, Fabiola Cabeza de Baca Gilbert, asked them why, they said, "We thought you wouldn't like the kind of food we poor people eat."[17]

No wonder they thought that. Home economics had shown little regard for Latinos. The New Mexico extension service hired just one bilingual home demonstrator during its first fifteen years, and that woman only temporarily, though half the population spoke only Spanish. In the 1929 book *Americanization through Homemaking*, a Southern California home economics teacher portrayed the Mexican American diet as leading to crime. "The noon lunch of the Mexican child quite often consists of a folded tortilla with no filling," she wrote. "Such a lunch is not conducive to learning. The child becomes lazy. His hunger unappeased, he watches for an opportunity to take food from the lunch boxes of more fortunate children. Thus the initial step in a life of thieving is taken."[18]

But de Baca, the first Latina hired full-time by the New Mexico extension service, wrote her own rules. Born in 1894, she grew up on an affluent, 100,000-acre ranch in La Liendre in the US territory of New Mexico. De Baca loved the silence, colors, and grandeur of el Llano Estacado, the Staked Plains, a place she described as having "loneliness without despair." She was five feet tall, with blue eyes, tiny feet, a soprano singing voice, and dark hair she disliked. Her community called themselves *Hispanos* and were proud of being descendants of the Spanish conquistadors—de Baca's father sent her twice to study in Spain—in their pride separating themselves out from Latin American indigenous peoples. The family ranch was largely self-sufficient, including in herbal medicines. Even de Baca, the owner's granddaughter, had to work, though she shirked kitchen duties as much as possible to go horseback riding. Once she rode back to find that someone had set the dirty plates in a line to the well. "The poor dishes were thirsty and started out for relief," her brother explained.[19]

De Baca was ambitious, and she was taught to give back to the community, even as her family's fortunes declined. In 1918, her father lost his ranch to drought. For fifteen years she was a teacher, at first in a one-room stone schoolhouse with a dirt floor and not even an outhouse; children were told to go behind a juniper tree. She boarded with a family and wrote her own bilingual materials. At the same time she became the first woman in her family to attend college, earning two bachelor's degrees—one in teaching and the other in home economics. The Hispano community was thrilled when she graduated with the second, at the age of thirty-five. They thought home economics could do much to elevate their community. De Baca agreed. "Psychologically, these people needed encouragement and orientation," she wrote. There was "a large field for the extension worker who understood their language, their social customs, and their food habits."[20] The Hispano family's shame over their cooking, which predated Anglo food in the region—and during the Great Depression, when anyone who had enough to eat was fortunate—showed how badly she was needed.

Like all extension agents, de Baca brought women the latest science from universities. That included canning, which was controversial in rural New Mexico. Most farm women had no running water, and almost no one could afford a pressure cooker, essential for safely canning most ingredients. Besides, they had a long tradition of drying food to preserve it. However, de Baca saw extension as an *exchange* of knowledge, "to extend the work by way of passing it to friends, neighbors, and relatives," she wrote.[21] In many ways she considered the country women, not herself, to be the experts. She didn't want to eliminate food preservation by dehydration. Not only did the extension service endorse the practice, but de Baca loved the strings of dried chiles festooning houses and knew they could be used for store credit locally. She just wanted to persuade farm women that the modern way was better in some cases. In this effort, she addressed the Spanish-speaking reader as a respected and knowledgeable steward of her own family's resources. Each homemaker knew how much her family would consume, she wrote in her Spanish-language canning guide. In contrast to the white "Americanizers," she advised that extension workers should start with traditional foods when teaching people to plan menus and cook.

De Baca thought this way not only because she was Latina, too, but because she had a larger vision for her work. Along with relieving poverty and hunger, she wanted to make her compatriots proud of their heritage. Her adult life revolved around that mission. In her mid-thirties she married Carlos Gilbert, a charming and successful insurance broker who, to her family's intense disapproval, was a divorced father of two. Alongside him, de Baca became a trustee of the League of United Latin American Citizens. "LULACs" honored their dual heritage and advocated gradual political reform. The league's code told them to "honor your country . . . respect your glorious past and help to defend the rights of your own people." De Baca cofounded Santa Fe's Sociedad Folklorica, adorning her home with weavings and organizing parties and dances to which she brought the traditional New Mexican cookies she loved to bake. (She was so generous that her nieces and nephews called her "Aunty Santa Claus.") The marriage ended after about a decade, but her commitment to her heritage never waned. Despite her Eurocentric upbringing, de Baca also treated Native American women respectfully. She was the first extension agent assigned to the northern New Mexico Pueblos, where drying food was even more omnipresent than among Hispanos, and learned to speak the Pueblo languages Tewa and Towa.[22]

Over the years, de Baca became legendary in greater Santa Fe. Even a horrific car accident that scarred her face, took her leg, and required two years' convalescence didn't stop her: she got a wooden prosthetic leg and hired a driver. She reached an estimated 80 percent of Santa Fe County farm families. She bought clothing patterns for women to share and designed embroidery patterns for them to sew and sell to tourists. Within five years from when she joined the extension service, half the farm families owned pressure cookers, and within ten, almost all owned or could borrow one. In one year alone she helped families can 407,500 quarts of food, valued at the modern equivalent of over $1 million. With drought and depression, 1935 "would have been one of the worst calamities ever experienced had it not been for timely financial aid from the Agricultural Drought Service and the food preservation program," the extension service reported. The farm women appreciated not only the resources but the rare social outlet de Baca's extension clubs provided. "It has been a change in their lives to get together once a month regularly," she wrote in 1930, after her first year on the job. "They have gained much spiritually. It has started them to think along the social side of life."[23]

Through all this time, de Baca recorded her clients' stories, folklore, religious rituals, recipes, and wisdom in notebooks.

In 1939 she shared their recipes in *Historic Cookery*, one of the first cookbooks devoted to Mexican American recipes, including such classics as chile sauce, masa, atole, panocha sprouted-wheat pudding, and menudo. "Recent research has proved that many of our basic foods—chile, beans, purslane, lambs' quarters, goat's cheese, and whole grain cereals, for example—are highly nutritious," she wrote in the 1946 edition. Who needed Milkwheato? *Historic Cookery* was a hit. Over the next decades it was requested by a hundred thousand people, from almost every state in the country.[24]

In October 1938, Louisan Mamer, a Rural Electrification Administration home-demonstration specialist, steered her blue Ford convertible and trailer off the road and onto a field in Anamosa, Iowa. She and her male colleague were loaded down with appliances—refrigerators, stoves, agricultural trimmers, a chicken brooder, irons—along with stacks of pamphlets and two circus tents. Less than two years before, the local farmers had formed the Maquoketa Valley Electric Cooperative, transforming their lives. Now Mamer would show others why and how to do the same. She was debuting the Electric Circus, her idea to educate and entertain rural families.

As late as 1935, more than eight of ten US farms were still in the dark. Mamer knew that life all too well. All her childhood she had mowed, raked, and hauled timber from the Illinois River bottomlands like a man, using heavy Belgian horses. She'd had to. Her father needed her labor. But so did her mother. And thus Mamer also minded her siblings, tended the two-acre vegetable garden, canned for winter, churned butter, baked bread, and butchered, on top of studying. In her spare minutes she cracked pecans to sell so she could afford college. All "sans electricity, sans running water," she said later.

She arrived at the University of Illinois at Urbana-Champaign in 1927 with the modern equivalent of $14,000 from pecans, a fashionable suntan, unfashionable broad shoulders, a walk that cut through the quad like a harrow through a field, and a plan to be a writer.[25]

Which became a bit of a problem. Mamer, a realist, faced the facts in her elegant Georgian dorm in her sophomore year. Although she was an honor student, she didn't stand much chance of getting a job in journalism. Editors thought women's nerves were too fragile for deadline pressure. Her *Women in Journalism* book warned her to specialize in an area that "demands the distinctly feminine background and experience," such as beauty, shopping, tearjerker stories, or advice for moms.[26] The career disparities were clear in what happened to the university's journalism grads. The men went to the *Chicago Tribune* and the Associated Press. The women went to the church altar. Maybe Mamer could have been the exception, but she wouldn't risk it. Her family hadn't recovered from the postwar agriculture price drop, and her uncles were bunking with her parents on the farm. Plus, she had to admit, she didn't really have anything to say. She decided to change her major to home economics. That way she would learn something to write about, and have a career where she didn't have to compete with men.

Mamer was a smart cookie, and she made a smart call. In the height of the Depression she got a job straight out of college teaching secondary school. In the late spring of 1935, she saw a newspaper squib not three inches long announcing a new New Deal project: the Rural Electrification Administration, which was dedicated to bringing power to the farm. The newspaper said the agency wanted to reach five hundred thousand farms, almost twice as many as had electric power now. The ad sought employees with a "pioneering spirit."[27] Power on the farm! The thought grabbed Mamer as nothing in her classroom had. In the Roosevelt electricity program, Mamer saw more than a job and a paycheck. She saw a longer, healthier, fuller life for women. No more headaches caused by squinting at books or mending under a sooty kerosene lamp. She saw laundry day freed of its shoulder-busting agony—lugging tubs of water from the pump up onto the coal stove, boiling dirt-encrusted clothes and linens, rubbing them by hand, wringing them through a hand-turned wringer, hanging them to dry, and ironing them with a seven-pound hunk of metal left to heat on the stove. The laundress froze in winter and steamed in summer. The average farm woman worked sixty-four to seventy-seven hours a week, not counting the farm jobs. Doing everything by hand the hard way and bearing a lot of children was killing women at an early age, Mamer thought. Look in the cemeteries, and you'd see maybe two wives for each farm man. She wrote in so fast, the Rural Electrification Administration wasn't even hiring yet.

Over the next three years, Mamer wrote booklets and traveled around talking to women's clubs trying to get them to see the benefits of electricity. Yet they hesitated. Farm men and women knew, in theory, that electricity would make their lives better. However, with the Depression grinding on, fields blowing away in dust, and unsettling news from Europe, it just seemed too risky and expensive. They knew all about the negatives, but they couldn't see the advantages. Farmers and their wives quailed at the thought of soliciting neighbors to form the necessary electric collectives, taking on debt, hiring an engineer, erecting power poles, running lines along roads, wiring their own buildings, collecting fees, and changing almost every way they'd run their farms for generations. Some feared they'd get electrocuted or burn down the house—electricity was the same as lightning, right? That's when Mamer had a brainwave. If they got manufacturers to donate equipment, they could take it from place to place and create a mini–World's Fair at the electric cooperatives that were already up and running. It would be an educational expo to show off the world of electricity and inspire attendees to set up their own collectives and power up. An electric circus. So there they were on a field in October, setting up the tent.

The next morning, people started to arrive. A few dozen, then a hundred, then five hundred, from miles and miles away. They read the displays and inspected the electric chicken brooder that could prevent those horrible mornings when they realized that the kerosene heater had malfunctioned overnight and wiped out an entire brood. Mamer, the star of the show, seemed to have eight arms. She made salads and ice cream, demonstrated bright lights, cooked what the REA newsletter described as "beguiling hams" in the oven, and ran an ironing race, which, surprise surprise, the electric iron won.[28] Then came the grand finale. Two of the community's most important men stepped up to the stoves, tied on aprons, and set off on a cooking duel, accompanied by Mamer's patter and the audience's glee. At the end, the audience chose the winner by acclamation. The funniest way possible to show the simplicity of electric ranges, she realized, was to show that even a man could use them.

That Anamosa event was the first of many thrilling nights of the Electric Circus. Over four years, one million people in twenty-six states ran their fingers through electrically husked corn kernels as an extension agent, easily audible through a microphone, described the process. They touched a (shut-off) electric fence and walked down a midway filled with equipment dealers whose trucks caravanned behind Mamer's vehicles. Their children thrilled at the electric cow that chewed its cud, gave milk, and mooed. When they got hungry they stopped at the all-electric food tent where dishes stayed warm on hot plates. Mamer slept for only four hours per night, sometimes in her trailer, resulting in a series of expensive fender-benders that spurred a memo from the REA's top administrator: "Get more rest and cut back on the 10- to 12-hour work days."[29] But how could she? After the circus left town, the local women took the initiative and signed people up for the rural electric cooperatives. They bought ceiling lights so they could see to do their work, irons to ease their shoulders, and radios that connected them to the world. As Mamer had dreamed, she was literally empowering women.

As 1939 opened, home economists exhaled. They had come through the tight-money years. The national association was now solidly afloat, with dues, journal subscriptions, and advertising coming in above budget. Membership had almost doubled from the low-water mark of 8,726 in 1933 to 16,300. Conference attendance reached record highs. At least 1,326 additional African American home economists worked in southern states and could not be American Home Economics Association members.[30]

Rose decided to retire while Ruth O'Brien began putting her finishing touches on her women's clothing sizes project. The president of Hampton reached out to Kittrell: Would she return to become the college's first Black dean of women? Gilbreth, having saved her career through home economics, turned her focus back to business. Despite her honorary AHEA lifetime membership, she largely dropped her home economics work after Purdue hired her as its first female business professor. Her exception was a 1950s project examining adaptive housework for women with heart trouble—work that also drew on her past projects with Frank. Gilbreth's 1946 passport listed her occupation as "engineer."[31] Mamer kept on espousing electrification, with a revised assignment. She had to turn the Electric Circus into the Electro-Economy tour. Another fight was beginning.

CHAPTER 6

Clothes Moths Work for Hitler

"We are suddenly in the front line of defense," the *Bulletin of the American Home Economics Association* wrote.[1] After the field's stellar performance in the Great War, there was no question that home economists would help fight World War II—and early: President Roosevelt ramped up US defense activities more than a year before Congress declared war on Japan, Germany, and Italy. Major home-ec players included Mary Barber, food consultant to the secretary of war; Florence Kerr of the Works Projects Administration; Helen Mitchell, nutrition director in the Office of the Coordinator of Health, Welfare, and Related Defense Activities; and of course the lead women of the Bureau of Home Economics: Louise Stanley, Ruth O'Brien, clothing designer Clarice Scott, nutrition director Hazel Stiebeling, and communications director Ruth Van Deman.

Well ahead of Pearl Harbor, the Bureau of Home Economics

put aside its usual research and responded, essentially, only to war requests. When the government imposed mandatory rationing of cane sugar in May 1942, the bureau was ready with sugar-substitute dessert recipes. (Stanley and her crew had been developing recipes using honey, corn syrup, sorghum, and cane syrup all along, starting where the US Food Administration left off in 1918.) For soldiers, bureau scientists figured out how to sterilize wool, treat cotton against mildew, and improve the flavor and nutrient retention of dehydrated food. For civilians, they devised ways to preserve fruit with less sugar in jars that used less rubber, and tested ten different cotton-stocking designs at once, replacing silk and nylon, on a massive knitting machine that entertained schoolchildren on field trips. The bureau issued radio talks and brochures with the immortal titles "99 Ways to Share the Meat" (peanut butter omelets, anyone?) and "Clothes Moths Work for Hitler." It swiftly set standards for equipment to feed twenty-five thousand refugees in southern France, and helped the Red Cross buy that equipment. War agencies used the bureau's extensive research on American consumption habits to make a range of supply and price-control decisions. The war would last long enough that the bureau had to recalculate its recipes to give cooking times for glass and ceramic saucepans, as metal had gone to the war effort. The public, shall we say, ate it all up: in 1943, the bureau distributed an all-time high of twenty-eight million bulletins.[2]

As women joined the war workforce, the Bureau of Home Economics addressed a question that might sound frivolous but had possible life-and-death significance: What should they wear? The National Youth Administration asked Clarice Scott to design outfits for women in a range of defense training jobs. Scott knew firsthand how limited and awkward women's work clothes were. Growing up on a five-hundred-acre farm in Illinois, she typically wore a washed-out dress or an old men's jacket; when company stopped by, she raced to change before they could see her. "The woman who does hard, active work has been the forgotten woman of the fashion page," Scott said to listeners of the bureau's radio program. "No one ever designed an outfit for doing such things as milking or working in a factory." Leaving aside ugliness, a loose jacket or dress could get caught in farm or production-line machinery. Neither men's clothes nor old dresses suited the purpose, because they weren't designed for it. For the NYA project, Scott conducted task analyses of various farm, factory, medical, and laboratory jobs. Then she designed more than a dozen patterns that *did* suit the tasks. These outfits were thrifty with material, easy to clean, simple to make, safe around machinery, comfortable to move in, and attractive. "Every seam serves a purpose," Scott promised. Most of the patterns had box seamed crotches to allow for squatting and stooping. The two-piece farm suit had snap-on, snap-off sleeves, and ankles that could be cinched to keep out dirt and grasshoppers. The nurse's uniform remained crisp without starch, which provided the "dignity that nurses want." The belt of the mechanic's suit immediately unsnapped if it caught on anything, to avoid pulling the worker into machinery or damaging the suit. A dress for scientists had pockets high on the chest, out of the way of counters and vials; it was wraparound, with the back cut surplice-style and on the bias "so the arms have plenty of freedom for the reaching and stretching that laboratory work often requires." To publicize the designs, Eleanor Roosevelt hosted a fashion show. The press went nuts over the "practical but snappy togs for the well-dressed milkmaid, farmerette and defense factory-ette," as the Associated Press described it. "Working Girl Can Keep Good Looks," the *Washington Post* proclaimed.[3] The bureau provided patterns to manufacturers rather than selling directly, so there's no way to know how many of these outfits were made, but photos from the period show uncountable comfortable Riveting Rosies.

All these activities changed American lives for as long as the war lasted. The bureau also undertook a project that changed American lives to this day. After Congress authorized a military draft in the fall of 1940, experts' worst fears about the American diet proved true: one-third of the men called up for service failed their physicals due to nutrition-related factors. Clearly, it was not enough simply to keep people from starving. They had to eat the right amounts and combinations of food. Nutrition gained a new purpose: military defense. Home economists revived the slogan "Food Will Win the War" and argued that the US needed a national food policy. President Roosevelt agreed. It was clear that "food and nutrition would be at least as important as metals and munitions," he said.[4] With that in mind, the quasi-governmental National Research Council created two boards in late 1940 to develop and promote such a policy, the Food and Nutrition Board and the Committee on Food Habits. Hazel Stiebeling of the Bureau of Home Economics, Helen Mitchell of the Children's Bureau, and University of Chicago home economics dean Lydia Roberts joined the FNB to determine what Americans should eat.

This wasn't new work for Stiebeling and Roberts, who had worked on nutrition standards internationally for several years as part of an international League of Nations committee. That group published its abstruse results in 1936, and they barely made a ripple. Stiebeling was the first to argue for a consumer-friendly, easy-to-understand set of nutrition guidelines that included "recommended daily allowances" for various nutrients. As 1941 opened, the Food and Nutrition Board put its collective heads together to hammer out a list. It was a tough task given that, then as now, health studies often contradicted each other and interest groups hovered to make sure their products didn't get short shrift. Stiebeling was familiar with political pressure. When a 1935 Bureau of Home Economics bulletin suggested that some people might reduce their wheat intake, wheat-belt senators moved to fire any USDA employee who advised eating less of any agricultural product. Stiebeling and Stanley won only by bringing in experts who showed that the bulletin's menus would actually increase wheat intake overall.

Roosevelt gave them a deadline: the May 1941 White House National Nutrition Conference for Defense. The night before the conference, the Food and Nutrition Board still had not finalized its recommendations. Its male members were nowhere to be found—probably "out seeing the town," Roberts figured, tartly. So she, Stiebeling, and Mitchell met in her hotel room and, like the little red hen in the children's book, they did it themselves. The next day, they unveiled the new American standards for overall calorie intake, protein, calcium, iron, and vitamins A, B_1, B_2, B_3, C, and D. They gave guidelines for healthy civilians, including children at several ages, at three levels of activity, plus pregnant and nursing women. The totals assumed that men weighed 154 pounds and women 123, with no height specifications. Unlike the League of Nations report, it was all as simple as could be, fitting in a five-page booklet whose cover bore a cheery ruler with the motto "A Yardstick for Good Nutrition." They called the guidelines, interchangeably, the Recommended Daily Allowances or the Recommended Dietary Allowances, "RDAs" for short. The board also laid out a set of "basic seven" food groups: potatoes; grains and bread; dairy; protein (eggs, beans, fish, meat, fowl); butter and margarine; green and yellow vegetables; and tomatoes and citrus. Both the RDAs and the food groups immediately became gospel.

At the same time, home economists drew on military

necessity to preserve school lunch—that is, the large-scale version with federal government support. The triumph of the Depression seemed to be on the butcher block, because the agricultural surpluses on which it had depended had a new destination: soldiers. But home economists pointed out that school lunch mattered more than ever, because it grew future soldiers. Besides, mothers had less time to prepare midday meals now that they were replacing drafted men in the workforce. With the RDAs and food groups, lunch could be not only properly nourishing but part of a national health-education program. Despite close to half a century of home economics nutrition promotion, most respondents to a 1941 poll did not know the difference between a vitamin and a calorie.[6]

Together, the farmers and the military agreed to save school lunch. Farmers remembered the agricultural price collapse that followed World War I. To prevent a recurrence, they lobbied Congress to promise to continue buying surplus commodities after the current war. What would the government do with all that food without the school lunch program? No one wanted a repeat of the squealing piglet rampage of 1933. Congress voted to buy surplus crops for at least two years after the war and to subsidize school food purchases while the fighting lasted. The RDAs immediately proved useful in determining which meals would qualify for a subsidy. Under new regulations, the so-called Type A lunch, with the highest subsidy, provided one-half to one-third of the RDAs. It had to include a half pint of whole milk, two ounces of protein, six ounces of fruit or vegetables, a serving of bread, and two teaspoons of butter or enriched margarine.

The new nutrition guidance did not ensure that the lunches would be delicious. Though Stiebeling assured the public that the RDAs could be met by any ethnic, regional, or cultural group's diet, the bureau's suggested menus continued to feature the same old Yankee standards. It didn't help that the president's other food advisory panel, the Committee on Food Habits, which included famous anthropologist Margaret Mead, said that schools could best unify the young American populace by serving emotionally neutral, inoffensive lunches, with no seasonings other than salt.

Home economists mobilized across the country. The American Home Economics Association sent its members wartime-service registration cards. The Rural Electrification Administration loaned Louisan Mamer to the War Production Board. The Iowa State home economics department magazine made wartime career women seem glamorous, reporting that alumnae took jobs with the Martin Bomber Plant, General Motors, General Electric, Johnson & Johnson, Rock Island Arsenal, Boeing, and the WAVES. The university's household-equipment graduates proved especially enticing for defense contractors and laboratories that had to replace men sent to the front. While the federal government and some companies ran engineering boot camps to increase the number of women who qualified for these jobs, Iowa State majors already knew the material and were "especially prepared for key positions in [the] defense industry," the magazine reported.[7]

The federal government backed home economists by putting them center stage in the short film *Women in Defense*. Eleanor Roosevelt wrote the narration, drawing thematically from her Depression book celebrating women's work; Katharine Hepburn read the script, braying, "Yesterday the pioneer woman helped to win a continent. Today with the same spirit of determination, American women are working to save this way of life."[8] The film showed women scientists testing the durability of silk substitutes and dripping experimental nutritional

formula down a guinea pig's maw; extension workers presenting community lectures on how to buy and cook economical,
nourishing meals; and a Bureau of Home Economics designer,
presumably Clarice Scott or Margaret Smith, sketching the
woman's work jumper. Even the factory scenes featured women
sewing and machinists wearing bureau work suits.

Flemmie Kittrell turned her department at Hampton into a
wartime research machine. The US Office of War Information
featured her department's radio programs on soybean research
and nutrition in its public relations short film *Negro Colleges in
Wartime*. She worked with a government nutritional planning
group, changed the focus of her *New Journal and Guide* home
economics newspaper column to "The Family and National
Defense," and promoted 4-H, which was experiencing enormous growth. By 1942 it had almost doubled in size to 1.5
million members, a figure that included more than 275,000
African American children.[9]

Kittrell's feelings about the war effort appear to have been
complex. She worried about her students' reputations. Due
to Hampton's strategic location near waterways and navy
schools, it was one of the country's main training sites for African American soldiers, and Hampton's women students were
called upon to socialize with cadets as a public service; oddly,
they even earned academic credit for dancing with soldiers at
USO events. Kittrell felt deeply uneasy about the freedom with
which servicemen moved about Hampton. "It is so easy to lose
even what little ground we have gained in poise and essential requirements for decent living," she wrote to the college's
male leadership. "Negro women . . . get the least respect and
protection of all women."[10] Moreover, at heart, Kittrell was a
pacifist. She continued volunteering for the Women's International League for Peace and Freedom, and in 1940 attended the
founding meeting of the American Peace Movement in Chicago.

The APM had a platform of stopping war mobilization and profiteering. It also had ties to the Communist Party. Kittrell eschewed Communism, nonetheless, someone at Hampton sent a tip to the FBI in 1941, saying that she had received mail from the APM. From then on, for over twenty years, the FBI monitored Kittrell and interviewed her colleagues and friends, who staunchly defended her patriotism and hard work.

Some home economists got directly involved in feeding soldiers. American Dietetic Association president Mary Barber took a leave from the Kellogg Company to put together nutrition plans, with the Bureau of Home Economics' Hazel Stiebeling, for soldiers, prisoners of war abroad, and Japanese Americans incarcerated in US internment camps. The first male member of the ADA, Captain Claud Samuel Pritchett, joined them in the quartermaster general's expanding Food Service Branch. Both the army and navy hired home economists to rewrite their official cookbooks—the navy's writer was Ina Lindman, by day the head home economist at United Fruit.

Rank-and-file dietitians, keenly aware of the insult and financial injury that followed World War I, did initially hesitate to sign up for military service. The US Army had a handful of dietitians employed as civilians in its hospitals, but as of October 1940, only a few of the four thousand members of the American Dietetic Association had registered with the Red Cross for potential reserve service. Lenna Cooper, now head of nutrition at Montefiore Hospital in the Bronx and the American Dietetic Association's defense secretary, was lobbying for Congress to raise dietitians to military status, which Canada had already done. Such status would provide the authority that was absolutely crucial for dietitians to do their job, she said. The 1940 bill failed, but Cooper gained an important ally: the quartermaster general's subsistence chief, whose daughter was an army dietitian. In 1943 Congress finally agreed to grant temporary second-lieutenant status to dietitians, and Cooper donned her old World War I uniform and recruited whole-heartedly. Eventually the army commissioned close to two thousand military dietitians, and between fifty and sixty dietitians joined the US Naval Reserve Supply Corps.[11] Most found military work an adventure. Some got more than they signed on for. The latter group included Ruby Motley, who was already working in military hospitals when the war began.

After earning a home economics degree from the University of Missouri, Motley worked at the army's Walter Reed General Hospital in Bethesda for five years before transferring to Sternberg General Hospital in Manila on Valentine's Day 1940, as the only US Army dietitian assigned to the Philippines. Manila was considered a tour in paradise: sparkling beaches, lush flowers, the work not too heavy. But the day after Pearl Harbor, the Japanese military bombed US installations in the Philippines, and paradise turned into hell. The army evacuated Sternberg and sent Motley to the hospital on tiny Corregidor Island in Manila Bay. For protection from ongoing Japanese air attacks, the entire hospital moved underground into the Malinta Tunnel network. Even so, Motley had to set up stoves outside, because she was trying to feed 1,500 patients and the permanent kitchen could handle just 300.[12] With no idea when food reinforcements might arrive, Motley served only two meals per day.

Then things got worse. After two months, Motley was transferred to the emergency hospital on the peninsula of Bataan. Four thousand patients lay on beds there under the open sky, surviving on half rations as the enemy advanced. The kitchen equipment was "the poorest in the world," Motley said.[13] There was no refrigeration. She cooked over fire pits as malarial mosquitoes bit, flies contaminated the water, and rats and monkeys ran off with the food. Sometimes they ate water buffalo and horse; sometimes a can of salmon had to feed ten patients. On

April 8, the US military ordered all women medical officers back to Corregidor. It was agony to leave the patients, who knew they were being abandoned to the enemy Slowed by explosions and fire, Motley and the nurses arrived at the dock so late that they missed the rescue ship. They crossed to Corregidor in batches all night long in small boats. Just as the last group left, the Japanese bombed the departure dock and the US general surrendered. The Japanese would make the healthy male soldiers on Bataan march to a prison camp under torturous circumstances, causing the death of many.

Motley knew that Corregidor, the last outpost of American control in the Philippines, could not hold out long. Twelve thousand military personnel were packed into two square miles. The Malinta Tunnel smelled of blood. You couldn't tell night from day. The patients, stacked on triple-decker bunk beds, gasped for breath as the constant bombing filled the tunnel with dust. Rations grew shorter and shorter; water had to be rationed. When the military decided to evacuate a few dozen people to Australia, Motley asked to leave. The colonel refused. "Ruby, you are the only dietitian we have, and we can't do without you," he said. Motley "felt like two cents," she said afterward.[14] Ashamed, she never said another word about leaving. It was too late anyway. As the Japanese landed on the island, the medical personnel signed their names on a bedsheet to serve as a record.

The good news was that the Japanese decided to put the military women in the Santo Tomas Internment Camp in Manila, with the city's residents who were from the Allied countries, instead of sending them to military prison in Japan. They would be neglected, not tortured. The camp's four thousand residents counted three dietitians in total: Motley; Vivian Weissblatt, the wife of UPI war correspondent Franz Weissblatt, who was also imprisoned; and Anna Bonner Pardew, who had a daughter less

than two years old.[15] The camp was a former Dominican college
with ornate buildings, incongruous under the circumstances.
Motley slept in a classroom crawling with bedbugs and shared a
single toilet and a cold-water shower with one hundred women.[16]
The internees set up a management group to assign jobs to their
fellow prisoners. Motley was glad to do it. Not only did she feel
driven to pursue her mission as a dietitian, but she knew that
work was the only way to stay sane through the fear. "The people who went down the fastest were those who didn't have anything to do," she said. "Time to think—that's what ruins you."[17]

Their diet, however, became equally ruinous. At first the
food was palatable, albeit scanty. The internees supplemented
their Japanese rice rations with Red Cross contributions and
the black-market skills of a local woman who bought supplies
for them outside the camp; they called her the "Angel of Santo
Tomas." Motley took over the kitchen and coordinated a large
garden of eggplant, okra, and corn—it took a lot of vegetables
to feed four thousand people. She also discovered a local green
called talinum or waterleaf, which grew quickly, was packed
with nutrients, and tasted like spinach, only with a rather slimy
texture. "We fared much better if we had this green vegetable
along with the rice. Many didn't like it, but they ate it and were
glad to get it," she said.[18] However, after two years, the Japanese cut rations and stopped allowing outside supplies. They
restricted prisoners to a small portion of campus, locked them
in their rooms overnight, and abolished the internees' management committee. The bill of fare for Thanksgiving Day 1944
consisted of plain cornmeal mush for breakfast, thin rice mush
for lunch, and sweet-potato leaves on rice for dinner. Motley
wrote a report to the Japanese government begging for more
food; they ignored it. Rations went down to seven hundred
calories per day. Internees' bodies swelled with pellagra; they
fainted in line as they waited for their bits of food. Three to four

people died every day of starvation and malnutrition. Motley did not know how they would keep going.

Then, on February 3, 1945, Motley and the other prisoners smelled gasoline. This was it, they thought, flooded with dread. The Japanese were going to burn the camp to the ground. Tanks burst through the gates, sending their hearts into their throats. Then they saw that the tanks were American. Nine days later, Motley put a fresh khaki blouse on her wasted frame and walked out of the camp for the last time. She had lost thirty pounds, and she was lucky. Seven people were so physically depleted they died of starvation after the US arrived. The public hailed the military women as the "Angels of Bataan," and the American Dietetic Association made Motley the first recipient of its highest honor, the Marjorie Hulsizer Copher Award, named for a dietitian who served in France in World War I. "I have seen many horrible things, but I have also seen many acts of bravery, courage, and sacrifice that make me proud to think I am an American," Motley told the ADA members.[19]

Even safe (and proud) at home, business home economists' lives and jobs continued to be dominated by the need to address war's privations. We can see the progression of World War II through a new home economics magazine from an unexpected source: J. C. Penney's. Founded in 1902 in Wyoming, Penney's started the Depression with about 1,400 stores and continued to grow over the decade. It was not yet a full-service department store but essentially a dry-goods shop with its own line of fashionable sewing patterns named Advance. The company hired its first home economist, Mary Omen, at the end of 1937. Not long afterward, Omen started a twice-yearly publication for home economics teachers focusing on the stores' strengths. *Fashions and Fabrics* was like a magazine and catalog combined.

It looked like a fashion magazine, with sketches of women posing in dresses. Omen probably based it on the *Delineator*, Butterick's thick magazine that promoted its sewing patterns. The *Delineator* also had fiction and standard women's-service magazine fare, but would soon cease publication.

J. C. Penney's put real money into *Fashions and Fabrics*—it had attached fabric swatches and perforated pages for educational reuse. With patterns costing less than $3 in today's dollars, it seems impossible that Penney's recouped the expense. Making money, however, wasn't entirely the point. Omen's goal was not just to sell fabric and get foot traffic into stores but to establish Penney's as a community resource. Though the magazine was free to home economics teachers, Penney's mailed it only to select state leaders: the rest had to go to a Penney's to get it. (Teachers not near a store could order a copy from Penney's headquarters.) Yet despite the ostensible audience, the "you" the magazine addressed was the student. "Every dress you make will be wearable," it promised optimistically. "You will be mending broken seams, putting in new sleeves, sewing on loose fasteners, rejuvenating with pique and ruching trims, doing everything to prolong the life of the dress because it's your very own dress. You will save money—and, what is much more important, you'll be happy in your clothes and better and more becomingly dressed than ever before."[20]

In the magazine's imagination, those students had well-rounded lives and a range of options for adulthood. They needed dresses for graduation and work, plus the occasional seersucker romper for leisure. "Heigh Ho! Heigh Ho! It's Off to Work You Go," read the copy for the Tailored Frock pattern. "Housewife or Career Girl, day in and day out, you will need a suit. It is the right thing almost any time and sometimes it is the only thing." A pantsuit pattern proclaimed itself the height of "Feminine Masculinity!" The magazine also promoted the new 4-H club uniform for girls, with Omen writing, "We wish to pay sincere tribute to the girls clubs and organizations throughout the country together with their leaders, many of whom are voluntarily offering their services to teach, train, and guide American girls in better living."[21]

That was the first sign in *Fashions and Fabrics* that the US was thinking about war. Very soon, its pages reflected the war's trajectory. First Omen tried optimism. How would the war affect spring fashions? Designers were looking to the military for stylistic inspiration, but taking only the "gay 'dress parade' things," Omen wrote, and in italics, *"We do not propose to let unneeded grimness overtake us."* Six months later, grimness had taken over: Hitler had conquered most of Europe. American patternmakers, who had mostly copied French designers, turned back to their own resources. "The new fashions literally breathe the spirit of America," Omen wrote. Six months after *that*, the magazine's fashion-color palette turned overtly patriotic, with shades such as "Old Glory Red," "California Sun," "Warpath Red," "Navaho Green," and "Rocky Mountain Blue." *Fashions and Fabrics* announced the entry of the US into the war with a cover that bore a war bonds stamp and depicted women saluting. One wore the Red Cross volunteer uniform, one the Bureau of Home Economics coveralls, and one the 4-H uniform. "Sew! For Service and Defense!" the magazine urged. It featured Red Cross patterns for garments like operating gowns, convalescent robes, and rompers for refugee children. Also the recently designed Bureau of Home Economics work clothes. After all, the magazine said, "You're in the Army Too!"[22] An illustration showed women working in a USO office.

Sewing for service and defense wasn't as simple as choosing fabric and a pattern, however. Government rationing not only limited the availability of materials but put strict rules on clothing design so as to avoid waste. *Fashions and Fabrics* gave the long list of prohibitions—no voluminous sleeves or skirts and no more than one patch pocket on a blouse, just to start—and warned readers to expect shortages at Penney's stores. What on earth was a fabric and patterns magazine supposed to do during rationing? "Make Restyling a Success Story!"—that's what. The Bureau of Home Economics put out brochures on how to mend clothing and cut down men's suits for women's and children's garments. *Fashions and Fabrics* gave guidance on cotton stockings and advertised patterns for dickies and accessories using scraps, as well as mix-and-match patterns that let women create seven different outfits. Home sewing benefited women stylistically: someone somehow convinced the rationing board to let home sewers use more material than dress companies could. Fabric belts on store-bought dresses could not be more than two inches wide, but if you sewed your own dress, you could have a veritable cummerbund. Omen made sure to point that out. Even so, as the war wore on and shortages deepened, Omen's challenge grew more and more stark. The cheeriness got hard to maintain as the issues of mend-and-make-over continued and the fabric swatches disappeared, a victim of rationing. The magazine's exhaustion mirrored that of the country. Perhaps people wanted to think about a better future.

The American Home Economics Association was thinking about its future workforce, in the form of clubs for teenage girls. The Depression had generally been a bumper time for youth groups, including Scouts, Camp Fire Girls, the Future Farmers of America, and 4-H, whose home economics division filled state fair displays with canning, baking, and fiber-arts projects. As of 1935, the American Home Economics Association was trying to strengthen its 750 high school chapters because, as director Alice Edwards wrote to a colleague in a letter marked "confidential," they believed the American Vocational Association wanted to co-opt them. Though the 1910s alliance with vocational education had opened up immense financial resources and federal support for home ec, Edwards thought the relationship should go only so far. "It makes me cringe to think of some of the ways in which I believe home economics work might be cheapened and used in support of legislation for vocational education," she wrote.[23] Perhaps more to the point, whoever controlled high school home economics clubs had power over the profession.

But by 1944, the American Home Economics Association had a different director and a different opinion. The school clubs bled money—more than $75,000 per year in today's dollars—and college deans and public school district administrators said they weren't preparing teenagers for careers in home economics. Nor could they compete with other youth groups, which offered insignia, awards, and prizes; to use today's terminology, the AHEA home-ec clubs were not gamified. Some states had gone rogue and founded their own home economics teen groups outside the professional association. So AHEA decided to spin off the high school clubs into a new, separate, national organization. The association would partially sponsor it, but the federal Office of Education would take an equal role, and the American Vocational Association and National Education Association would have seats on its board. AHEA loaned the new group startup money and chose its first employee, Oklahoma home economics supervisor Hazel Frost.

Frost insisted that teenage girls draft the group's materials, unlike Future Farmers and Girl Scouts, whose mottoes and the like had been written by adults. She, AHEA field organizer Gladys Wyckoff, and Edna Amidon, the home economics chief at the federal education office, organized a score of national planning meetings and regional focus groups. They drew crowds of participants who eagerly wrote chants, creeds, and entire oath-of-office ceremonies. That excitement boded well for membership, which Frost knew would be a big lift: with dues at ten cents per member, the new, yet-to-be-named organization would need at least 250,000 participants to break even.

The girls planning the new high school home economics club decided that they would wear red and white, with a red rose as their official flower. They adopted the motto "Toward New Horizons." They pledged to "face the future with warm courage, and high hope." And what would they be in that future? Housewives. As the war soldiered on, American girls, seeing their older sisters work in factories and fearing for their brothers and beaux, evidently had homemaking on the brain. Judging by the records, the adult coordinators do not seem to have pushed it on them. "I believe in preparing now for my future career as a homemaker," one focus group wrote. That line didn't make it, but the creed did include a promise to build "homes for America's future, homes where living will be the expression of everything that is good and fair." Teenagers also chose the organization's name, "Future Homemakers of America." One adult adviser wrote AHEA president Dora Lewis about her disgust over the name. "The [Future Homemakers] name implies rural schools to many persons because of the association of the name with Future Farmers," the letter said. "I regret this but no one comes forth with a better name and you can hardly expect high school students to go beyond us in this thinking."[24] It seems that the adviser's annoyance centered more on the ongoing urban-versus-rural image struggle in home economics than any fear that the name might not be associated with paid careers. Nonetheless, "Future Homemakers" would help identify home economics with patriarchy and what would later be termed the feminine mystique.

To be exact, *some* teenagers would wear red and white: those in states with integrated public schools, and white teens in the seventeen states that had legal school segregation. Southern white organizers would run Future Homemakers. Knowing that those organizers would not accept African American girls, Frost and Amidon reluctantly planned a sister organization. Amidon did not like creating a segregated club but thought it was "the only feasible thing to do at the present time," she wrote Wyckoff. They held separate planning meetings with African American girls, who created their own name, creed, crest, magazine name, and so on. The name they chose, the New Homemakers of America, echoed that of its African American agriculture counterpart, the New Farmers of America. New Homemakers would wear blue and white, read *Chatter Box*, and pledge to promote "justice in the Nation" and "peace in the world." The two clubs would be united at the core, however, by sharing a central office, an adviser (Frost), and board members from the major home economics and education groups.

That was the plan, at least. But when Amidon met with the Black teacher trainers who would be on the New Homemakers board—Marie Clapp Moffitt of North Carolina, Zxlema Price of Mississippi, and Lenouliah Gandy of Oklahoma—she got an earful she hadn't anticipated. African American home economists were furious at the American Home Economics Association. Not until 1944 had the association accepted southern African American members, and then not by ending segregation in its southern state chapters but by doing a runaround: letting members join at-large, without belonging to a state chapter. For that matter, every southern state already *had* Black teen home economics clubs under various names. The American Home Economics Association had never noticed, helped, or funded these clubs, or invited their members to national conferences or leadership positions. AHEA didn't want African

American home economists, Moffitt, Price, and Gandy said, and they didn't need AHEA. They certainly didn't want anyone from AHEA on the New Homemakers board.

This resistance angered the leaders of the American Home Economics Association, who wanted representation on that board in order to play out a complicated power game. They did want to control the teen homemaking groups: they just didn't want to shoulder the whole cost, as they had for the teen clubs of the thirties, and they wanted to placate the American Vocational Association by giving it a role. Amidon backed the African American teachers' decision. Insisting on a board seat "would irritate a 'sore' that would hinder progress now in the new organization," she wrote Dora Lewis. The AHEA would just have to reap what it had sown, take the time to mend the relationship with African American home economists, and hope to join the board later. Amidon assured Lewis that the US Education Office "will try to function in a way to minimize the differences between the two organizations."[25] The AHEA backed down.

The teen clubs were immediately popular. Right off the bat in 1945, the summer that the war came to a close, New Homemakers had close to 20,000 members and Future Homemakers more than 90,000. In just four years, the combined groups met the organizers' goal of 250,000 members.[26]

After the war, most home economists went back to their old jobs: Mamer to the Rural Electrification Administration, military dietetics advisers to their companies. Motley married and disappeared from the dietitian records. Kittrell left for Washington, DC, to lead home economics at Howard University, whose president promised to build her a new home economics building. She continued her relationship with Hampton as its first Black female trustee.

War successes spun directly into the accomplishment of long-held goals. The heroism of the army dietitians and nurses finally won Lenna Cooper's long battle for recognition. President Harry S. Truman created the Women's Medical Specialist Corps and permanently commissioned military nurses and dietitians. In 1946, Congress passed the National School Lunch Act, making the Depression and wartime programs permanent. It was the fulfillment of Richards's dream, and it fed a lot of kids: over the 1950s, participation would double to fourteen million children. That said, the federalization of school lunch had its downsides. The program explicitly set out to encourage the consumption of farm commodities as well as supporting child health, which would affect what kids ate. "No nation is any healthier than its children or more prosperous than its farmers," President Truman said upon signing the law.[27] Though schools had to serve free or discounted lunch to needy children, the new requirements paradoxically made it hard for poorer schools to participate: they were no longer allowed to rely on their traditional free labor force of volunteers to make and serve lunches, and there were no funds to build cafeterias, which many older, urban schools still did not have. The record-keeping and nutritional requirements turned into epic spools of red tape. Also, in reality the program served few of the poorest students due to yet another Jim Crow compromise. Southern states feared that the USDA would wield the money as a cudgel to make them desegregate schools. To assuage that fear, Congress let states distribute the money, and did not set standards for that distribution—so states or districts decided who qualified for discounted lunch. Virginia, for instance, gave barely any funds to Black schools.

That said, whereas home economists' World War I success lasted for a decade, society changed very quickly after World War II, erasing some gains for women. The Future

Homemakers' eagerness for housewifery wasn't the only sign of a pull away from careers and back toward home and marriage. *Fashions and Fabrics* changed overnight. After all those issues promoting strong women working for defense, the spring/summer 1946 issue featured skincare, fashions for the "young homemaker," "a bon-bon of a blouse," and an "hour glass party dress to win a beau's approval"—no work clothes, no 4-H. (It also continued to lack the fun fabric swatches, as fabric scraps remained in short supply.)

The Bureau of Home Economics had been renamed during the war as the Bureau of Human Nutrition and Home Economics. Professionals were uneasy about the implied reduction of the focus on textiles, urban affairs, child development, finances, and sociology. Midway through the war, the USDA moved Stanley over to its new Agricultural Research Administration to do international food research, and it did not move her back. Stanley evinced excitement over the change, but the decision thrust one of the most powerful women in home economics into the shadows, replacing her with a man. Though Hazel Stiebeling soon took over the top job, home economists were right to be concerned. In 1947, Congress cut one-quarter of the bureau's budget.[28] The upcoming slide might be symbolized best by bureau designer Clarice Scott's new sewing pattern for the working woman of 1950. It incorporated a tissue dispenser; pockets for a pencil on a chain, a house key, and bus tokens; and a reusable bag with plastic rain cover. Scott named it "the Shopper's Coat," and it was for homemakers to wear while running errands.

CHAPTER 7

From Coveralls to Housecoats

After World War II, like those bureau patterns, women's lives in the US changed quickly from coveralls and lab coats to housecoats. Wartime jobs ended, and women had to leave the workforce to make room for veterans. The consequences were rapid and obvious. By 1960, more than one-third of women married before the age of twenty, and two-thirds married by the time they were twenty-four. Birth rates bounced up after more than a decade of deprivation and war. The share of female college students fell to one-third, down from half the total number of students in 1920. Almost every man aged twenty-five to thirty-four worked in the 1950s, but only one-third of women. Despite technological advances that made laundry and its like faster and easier, women spent as much time on housework in the 1950s as they had thirty years before: about fifty-two hours per week. For African American families, the rise in housewifery could be seen as a sign of progress, because it meant that men were finally earning enough to support a family. In a 1947 editorial titled "Goodbye Mammy, Hello Mom!" the new magazine *Ebony* celebrated that fact. "Today in thousands of Negro homes, the Negro mother has come home— come home perhaps for the first time since 1619 when the first Negro families landed at Jamestown, Virginia," the editorial team wrote. "The cooking over which the 'white folks' used to go into ecstasies is now reserved for her own family."[1]

Political and economic stressors affected women as well. The US was simultaneously taking a newly dominant place on the world stage and quaking over the Communist threat with its possibility of mutual destruction. Men had trauma from their "good" war, which, unlike in previous and future wars, was not recognized with a term such as "shell-shock" or "PTSD." People moved to the suburbs, and banks and government ensured through racist loan and zoning policies that their settlement patterns would be segregated. Wartime technological developments fed an economic boom that both offered and demanded consumption. Thrift was not only less necessary but, economically speaking, practically un-American. Besides, after fifteen years of rationing and depression, who could blame anyone for consuming?

Though the feminine mystique was real, other currents tugged away from the powerful vision of domesticity, marital stability, and the single-paycheck ideal. Divorce spiked. By 1960, already one in ten of US families were headed by a single mother, and two in ten of nonwhite families. The percentage of mothers who worked full-time outside the home went up as well: every year during the 1950s, half a million wives entered the paid workforce. Women of color were still more likely than white women to be working—44 percent in 1955, compared to one-third of white women—but the latter were catching up.[2]

All these trends added a nervous element to emotional and family life, and often triggered panic. Why were so many families breaking up? Would the USSR, or the US, drop the Bomb? All these new products and ways to spend leisure time—were they making Americans soft? And what was wrong with these kids today, listening to loud music and fawning over James Dean? Home economists responded in ways that would swiftly and radically reshape the field into how most people think of it today: repressive, boring, and trying to keep women barefoot and pregnant. Home economics didn't create these changes. It addressed them; it took advantage of them; in ways its practitioners tragically did not see, it reinforced them; and it suffered from them.

School administrators in the 1910s had embraced home economics as the perfect training for future wives and mothers, and so it became again. The emphasis on a woman as wife, mother, and homemaker was catnip for home economics. In any given year, almost half the girls in public high school—2.4 million—took home ec. The Future and New Homemakers of America boasted 462,000 members in more than ten thousand chapters. Extension agents reached five million homemakers and two million 4-H participants. In 1970, four out of every ten women undergraduates at Kansas State studied home economics. The Vocational Education Act of 1963, later known as the Perkins Act, permanently authorized funding for home economics and home-ec teacher training; less than ten years later, half the girls in public school vocational training programs were taking home economics. The field's PR women made hay, for home economics should be "the most saleable of all professions for women," the American Home Economics Association's 1953 public relations guide said.[3]

It all created jobs. The US Labor Department estimated that there were seventy thousand home economists, including forty-two thousand teachers and professors, twenty thousand dietitians, and five thousand extension agents. They developed cake-mix recipes, wrote textbooks, and gave radio chats, for pay. They did not seem to see the contradiction, the irony, arguably the hypocrisy in building careers telling other women to stay home, often while someone else cooked and cleaned for *them*. No, home economists thought they were training girls for "dual roles"—home and career. Flora Rose, having driven across the country from California at age eighty to be honored by Cornell alumnae, told the women that home economics was "a three-edged tool." It gave women "a means of earning a living before she marries [and] the knowledge and skills to make a good home for her husband and her family. And it opens vistas for productive service and occupation when her children are grown." Unlike in the earlier days of the profession, more and more home economists had dual roles themselves, judging by the names in reports and journals. In an age of Mrs. His Full Name, they listed themselves using their first name and birth last name followed by married last name. African American home economists in particular were almost always married. The *Journal of Home Economics* regularly reported on working mothers. In fact, a group of Maryland homemakers with home economics training complained in the *Journal of Home Economics* that news coverage lionized working women and made it sound like homemaking was so easy it could be done part-time. In reality, homemakers picked up the slack for their employed peers, watching those working women's kids play in the yard and running Scouts and the PTA, they wrote. Working mothers might be psychologically damaging their children, they added, urging home economists to "emphasize the value of homemaking and to build up its prestige."[4]

It hardly seemed necessary. To the contrary, leading home economists gave seemingly heartfelt lip service to the idea that homemaking and motherhood trumped all, no matter how little they followed their own advice. Flemmie Kittrell jet-setted around the world seeding home economics education, as we'll see in the next chapter. And yet she said, "A woman should go no further in other fields than is possible while still doing a good job in the home. If women in any field don't do a good job as homemakers, they don't really make a lasting contribution to the world." Mollie Stevens Smart and Russell Smart, authors and academics, had an egalitarian marriage where they went halves in cleaning and childcare. Yet they wrote a high school textbook warning women against pursuing careers. Marjorie Child Husted, the mastermind of Betty Crocker and the highest-ranking woman at General Mills, brought work home every night and called for equal pay. Yet in 1951, she told the American Association of University Women, "Let's help every woman recognize that true homemaking is still the most important career of all for women." Students adopted that philosophy as well. At the 1957 national conference of the New Homemakers of America, the Oklahoma delegation presented a solemn skit in which a white-garbed narrator intoned, over the strains of "Clair de Lune," that she planned to choose homemaking over a career "because wars may come and jobs may go."[5]

What were all these proto–Donna Reeds to learn? A new era called for new curricula. Especially now that technology had rendered much of home economists' previous material—canning, wash day before the washing machine—obsolete. Fortunately, the burgeoning field of child psychology roared in to fill the gap. Home economists refocused on managing not the physical structure of the household but the people and relationships within it, which they called "family-life education." Nothing could have done a better job of suiting the conservative postwar attitude that sought to keep women occupied within four walls. New textbooks promoted the idea that tending to her family was a woman's primary job—no matter whether she also worked for pay, and no matter what home economists thought they were teaching.

Family-life education had its roots in the 1920s promotion of child development, and began blossoming during World War II. In 1943, Abraham Maslow proposed his now-famous "hierarchy of needs," which posited that humans needed first the physical essentials of survival, then love, esteem, and self-actualization. Three years later, Congress passed the National Mental Health Act, which created the National Institute of Mental Health and made psychology a major public health issue for the first time. That same month, Dr. Benjamin Spock published his paradigm-changing parenting guide *The Common Sense Book of Baby and Child Care*. He spoke at the fifth White House Conference on Children and Youth, in 1950, the first of those conferences to focus on children's emotional needs, not food and shelter. Simultaneously, theorist Charles Prosser, the force behind the two vocational education laws of the 1910s, called for high schools to teach students what they would need to succeed as adults, beyond college and career.

Perhaps most influential of all for home economics was the National Conference (later Council) on Family Relations, founded in 1938 by a law professor, a sociologist, and a rabbi, all white men. There was crossover between the NCFR and home economics from the start: the Bureau of Home Economics' Hazel Kyrk and University of Chicago nutritionist Lydia Roberts attended the first organizational meeting. However, child development, perhaps because it grew out of the medical specialties of psychology and pediatrics, became (ironically) a hotbed of men. And people who affiliated with NCFR held, generally, a traditional view of the family. Though the organization was progressive in advocating marriage counseling, contraception, and honest discussions about sex, the second issue of its journal included articles by eugenicists Frederick Osborn and Paul Popenoe discussing ways to encourage the "right" individuals to procreate, with Popenoe criticizing America's "biologically unsound" tradition of equality. (Popenoe was also writing arch-traditional marriage advice books that ridiculed educated women and effeminate men.) NCFR cofounder Paul Sayre devoted nine close-packed pages in the third issue to dissecting Romeo and Juliet's relationship, concluding that self-sacrificing Juliet was the perfect wife, albeit to a rather immature hero. "The world is divided into two very distinct classes of people: men and women," Sayre said in his first NCFR presidential speech.[6] The American Home Economics Association was thoroughly aware of the differences between men's and women's experiences, but had never seen the need to underline that.

At any rate, the American Home Economics Association concluded after the war that managing personal relationships, not separating light from dark laundry, was the set of skills a homemaker really needed. Perhaps they thought they had fulfilled Ellen Richards's dream of science freeing women from drudgery, and that this was the next step. (Though the 1959 New York City curriculum told girls they should go back to doing their own laundry instead of sending it out—the early home economists would have been apoplectic at that.) Studying and managing human development seemed much more meaningful, with more power to change the world. "Much of the misery and frustration in the adult world is due to the unresolved conflicts, the inability to accept one's self, the lack of understanding of one's own basic motives," Esther McGinnis wrote in 1951.[7] She was about to take a grant-funded sabbatical from leading the Merrill-Palmer child-development institute in Detroit, to train home economists for the AHEA. The "sabbatical" job would run her half off her feet: she met with educators in Mississippi, Indiana, Wisconsin, Illinois, and Iowa in March 1952 alone.

By the end of the 1950s, the American Home Economics Association had adopted a new definition of home economics: "the field of knowledge and service primarily concerned with strengthening family life."[8] Not only was family life a topic on its own, but it organized and infused the entire domain of home economics knowledge. Though high school classes still spent most of their time cooking and sewing, now they learned to cook in order to please their family, cultivate strong relationships, gain confidence, and develop social competence. The point of sewing was not primarily to save money, become a savvy shopper, develop a marketable skill, learn math and geometry in a tactile fashion, or even do something useful with your hands, but to be a delightful woman with a strong and happy family.

The goal of family-life education was lofty: to improve happiness and citizenship by honing self-awareness and helping families function better. However, the reality in high schools did not look like learning to resolve conflicts, accept oneself, or understand basic motives, as McGinnis had hoped. Though the field ostensibly focused on relationships in the home, a reading of two dozen textbooks and curriculum guides shows a whole lot of focus on self-improvement and how a girl could make herself more appealing, especially to the opposite sex. The lessons were infantilizing, dumb, condescending, and only one step away from a teen magazine. In fact, Ohio recommended that junior high home economics teachers stock their classrooms with *Charm*, *Glamour*, and *Seventeen*. (*Seventeen* at this time was carrying articles on the versatility of soup and what to do "if your folks disapprove of the boy you like best." Its sister publication for home economics teachers, *Seventeen-at-School*, suggested ways to use the articles in class.) The textbook writers borrowed a newly chummy tone from these magazines, which contributed to their intimacy. Every teenage girl could and should become more likable, the textbooks said. South Dakota students could assess "How do I rate as a date?"[9] Girls should not waste time worrying—that would put lines in their pretty faces. Nor should they wear black, which would make them look wan, the New York City curriculum guide said (and, presumably, lead to the dangerous playing of bongos). An Alabama teacher observed her students and recorded the flaws each girl had to correct in a notebook à la *Harriet the Spy*, with a whiff of judgment. One girl, for instance, had adoring brothers, understanding parents, and overindulgent grandparents. The teacher concluded that she was inflexible, shy, dependent, and passive.

And what to think about Illinois homemaking students, teenage girls, modeling their fathers' clothes on "Daddy Date Night"? That was, if nothing else, a sign of the weirdness with which high school home economics textbooks addressed sex and gender. Textbooks were prudish, depicting people toasting marriages with ginger ale. Some were euphemistic, describing the physical changes of adolescence not as periods or breasts or erections or body odor but as "changes in pulse rate, blood pressure, and basal metabolism." For all the valorization of wifedom and motherhood, school leaders hated it when girls jumped on the bandwagon *too* young. Data showed high divorce rates for teen marriages: one in five as of 1958.[10] One of the goals of family-life education was to convince students to delay commitment until they were mature. It was backed up by school policies that punished married teenagers, especially girls, especially those who became pregnant. Though many wanted to continue their education, administrators almost always expelled them or pressured them to drop out, and almost none came back. (A pregnant senior close to graduation might be allowed to finish if she wasn't showing.)

What would your life be like once you were married? These textbooks and curriculum guides claimed to represent modern families, which included a smidgen of gender equality. Husbands and wives shared the housework, because America was a democracy, Bernice Milburn Moore and Dorothy M. Leahy wrote in *You and Your Family*. Sometimes they had chapters for boys, as if boys took home economics, which they essentially did not: they made up just three in one hundred home economics students in high school; Cornell did not have a single male home economics undergraduate major, outside of hotel management, in the 1950s. The boys' units were named things like "A Stitch in Time Is Not Sissy." The truth peeped out in vignettes, captions, and photographs (always showing white families), which invariably depicted traditional gender roles. Mother stood at the stove while Father carried a briefcase. She cleaned the house, he raked the leaves. *Living Together in the Family* quoted a boy as saying, "Home is a place my father is proud to support, my mother is glad to keep, and my friends are happy to visit." Splitting the housework meant that Mom could ask Dad for help, and he would cook the occasional meal following a menu his wife had posted, with groceries she had stocked. Who could be surprised by that? When Dr. Spock told men in his 1946 bestseller, "You can be a warm father and a real man at the same time," he immediately followed with: "Of course, I don't mean that the father has to give just as many bottles or change just as many diapers as the mother. But it's fine for him to do these things occasionally. He might make the formula on Sunday."[11]

Ellen Swallow Richards was the first woman to attend MIT. Traditionally considered the founder of home economics, the tireless Richards had both a social conscience and a brilliant scientific mind.
MIT Museum.

Richards used her own money to expand opportunities for women at the institute, including building a women's lounge and laboratory.
MIT Museum.

The first Lake Placid conference brought together white women to create home economics jobs with "adequate compensation" and college classes. From left: Annie Dewey, Maria Daniell, Ellen Richards, Alice Peloubet Norton, Maria Parloa. Division of Rare and Manuscript Collections, Cornell University Library.

Born in Mississippi during the Civil War, Margaret Murray Washington became one of the most influential Black leaders of her day. Her stately, prosperous appearance was part of her message about the power of a middle-class home life to lift up communities. Library of Congress, Prints & Photographs Division, LC-B2-3673-8.

Colleges for Black students pioneered academic home economics.
This photo shows Hampton Institute's weaving class in 1899 or 1900.
Library of Congress, Prints & Photographs Division, LC-USZ62-78715.

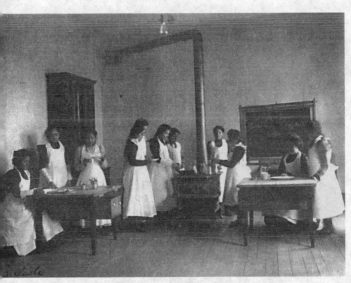

Pennsylvania's Carlisle Boarding School was the country's first federal off-reservation boarding school. This 1901 "breakfast lesson" is an early example of authorities using home economics to train indigenous children in white, middle-class ideals.
Library of Congress, Prints & Photographs Division, LC-USZ62-55456.

A New York City "practice apartment" in the 1910s. Schools and settlement houses taught immigrants to cook a standard, albeit bland, American diet.
Library of Congress, Prints & Photographs Division, LC-DIG-npcc-19631.

Agricultural extension workers used railroad cars, such as Cornell University's car here, as portable community classrooms. The practice took off during World War I to highlight conservation.
Division of Rare and Manuscript Collections, Cornell University Library.

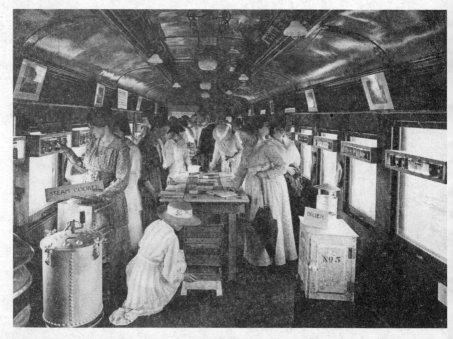

Martha Van Rensselaer, right, and Flora Rose founded and ran the Cornell home economics school for several decades while living together as romantic partners. Here they attend a League of Women Voters meeting at the home of Franklin and Eleanor Roosevelt in the 1920s.
Division of Rare and Manuscript Collections, Cornell University Library.

Eleanor Roosevelt with Rose at Cornell's 1938 Farm and Home Week. The First Lady became a friend and advocate of Rose and Van Rensselaer's work.
Division of Rare and Manuscript Collections, Cornell University Library.

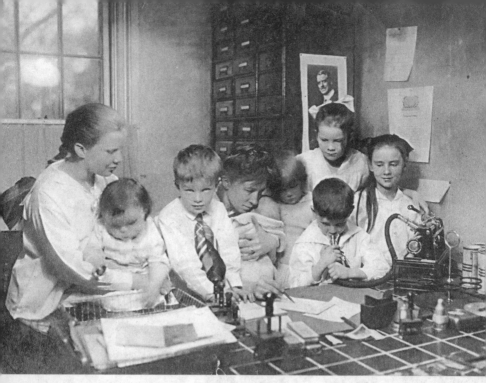

After her husband died, Lillian Moller Gilbreth, the industrial-psychologist mom
in *Cheaper by the Dozen*, supported her large family through home economics.
Purdue University Libraries, Karnes Archives and Special Collections.

Fabiola Cabeza de Baca Gilbert, an early Latina home economist, began teaching in this
one-room school in Guadalupe County, New Mexico, that lacked a bathroom or an outhouse.
Center for Southwest Research (UNM Libraries), no. 000-603-0002.

Chosen to lead the new Bureau of Home Economics in 1923, chemist Louise Stanley became the highest-ranking woman in the federal executive branch. She hired the most women scientists in government, but her job also included stints as a pie-baking judge.

Roosevelt's New Deal included a big push to electrify farms. Louisan Mamer traveled the country emceeing her brainchild the "Electric Circus," which showed off the world of electric power.

The Bureau of Home Economics hired unemployed people during the Depression to measure almost 150,000 children and 15,000 women to create standardized clothing sizes.
Library of Congress, Prints & Photographs Division, LC-H22-D-2003.

With men at war, the Bureau of Home Economics designed work clothes for women in defense jobs. This is the mechanic's suit, with a boxed crotch for easy squatting and a belt that unsnapped if it caught on machinery.
Smithsonian Institution Archives, no. SIA2015-003212.

Iowa State textiles lab, circa 1950. Home economics promoted better living through science, which included examining the chemical properties of fabrics and developing new products.
Special Collections and University Archives / Iowa State University Library.

Dietitian Vivian Weisblatt, far left, was among the women (mostly nurses) captured in the Philippines in May 1942. The women refused to smile for this photo, taken by the Japanese military.
World War II Signal Corps Photograph Collection, United States Army Heritage and Education Center, Carlisle, PA.

The US government taught Japanese Americans in World War II internment camps, such as this home economics class at the Rohwer center in Arkansas.
National Archives, no. 210-G-E360.

Renowned photographer Gordon Parks took this picture of a Bethune-Cookman home economics class for the US Office of War Information, which promoted Black colleges and universities' war efforts. Library of Congress, Prints & Photographs Division, LC-USW3-016032-C.

"Radio homemakers" such as KMA's Florence Falk, shown with a feathered costar, dominated the airwaves for decades with their recipes, household tips, and folksy tales of life on the farm. Iowa Women's Archives, University of Iowa Libraries, Iowa City.

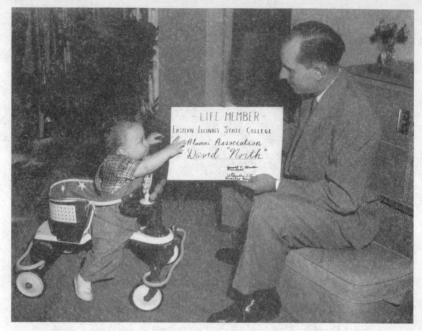

Even as "practice babies" became controversial in the 1950s, the Eastern Illinois University alumni association made the university's foster baby David "North" an honorary lifetime member. University Archives & Special Collections, Booth Library, Eastern Illinois University.

The American home was a political symbol in the Cold War, as Vice President Richard Nixon and Soviet Premier Nikita Khrushchev highlighted in their "Kitchen Debate" at the 1959 American National Exhibition in Moscow. National Archives, no. A10-024.43.12.1.

Military dietitian Bea Finkelstein looks on as astronauts Gus Grissom, center, and Gordo Cooper, right, test her space food in the lab they called "Bea's Diner." U.S. Air Force Life Cycle Management Center History Office.

Glamorous Satenig St. Marie, far right, modernized J. C. Penney's home economics program. Teachers, like these in Detroit in 1961, flocked to the company's educational demonstrations. Bettmann/Getty Images.

Mollie Smart, shown with husband Russell, in India in the late 1960s, wrote child development textbooks that didn't always reflect her own egalitarian marriage and career choices.
Photograph by Ellen Smart.

The first African American woman to earn a doctorate in nutrition, Flemmie Kittrell became a world traveler and one of home economics' most influential leaders.
Division of Rare and Manuscript Collections, Cornell University Library.

HOME ECONOMISTS TO AND FROM COR

1967-

THE WORLD

In 1971, feminist Robin Morgan, shown protesting the men-only policy of the New York City bar McSorley's, called home economists the instruments of the patriarchy.
Bev Grant/Getty Images.

Joshua Eddinger-Lucero competes in a quilting race at the 2018 American Association of Family and Consumer Sciences conference. Title IX barred schools from restricting home ec to girls, and Eddinger-Lucero found a place to thrive in the field.

Danielle Dreilinger photo. Courtesy of author.

Among the new textbooks promoting understanding of human development was *Living in Families*, written by the previously introduced married couple that lived a very different reality from the one they promoted to students. Mollie Stevens and Russell Smart met in 1937 at the Merrill-Palmer Institute in Detroit, one of the best-known child-development programs in the world. She had earned her bachelor's degree in psychology with honors from the University of Toronto, and he was almost done with his doctorate. After a year as colleagues and friends, they began dating and found they'd had perfectly compatible childhoods that were quietly nontraditional. Both had families that had emigrated from the British Isles long before the American Revolution. Mollie was athletic, coaching swimming and softball; her father championed her successes. Russell's mother and sister taught him to knit and embroider. Mollie agreed to marry him only on the condition that they go halves in everything: both would be scholars and both would be parents. (Neither knew how to cook.) Russell's mentor Florence Goodenough, an excellent name for a parenting expert if there ever was one, applauded the decision and urged them to write child-development books together as parents. Which they did.

In 1941, as she finished her master's degree, Mollie was invited to write her first parenting book, which won a prize from *Parents* magazine. She had a gift for conveying science and theory clearly, in plain language and with a warm, sympathetic, often gently humorous tone. *Babe in a House*, published in 1950 and directed at new mothers, promoted breastfeeding but reassured that bottle-feeding was perfectly OK if, for instance, a woman could not make enough milk. If a woman wanted to breast-feed, "the best attitude is, 'I intend to nurse this baby and shall do my best to get ready for it. If I turn out to be one of those women who can't, I'll do a good job with the bottle and it will work out fine,'" she wrote. No one should guilt-trip mothers into any particular behavior, including breastfeeding: "Respect your feelings and let yourself be the kind of person you are."[12]

Mollie followed her own advice on that. Together, the Smarts built a remarkably egalitarian home. They had three daughters, in 1942, 1945, and 1948, and began writing books together when the oldest was napping. Because "Rus" was the morning person, he made breakfast for the family and Mollie handled lunch and dinner. He sewed all their curtains, with matching bedspreads. Professionally, they often worked as a team as well. Though it was Russell who was offered a full-time, tenure-track professorship at Cornell in 1945, Mollie subbed for professors who were out of town and wrote for the extension service; she had office space at the university, plus on-site day care, and felt she was treated as an equal. They even loaned nine-month-old Laura to spend her days as a practice baby in the Cornell home-management house for two weeks when they moved house in town, though they did take her home at night. Laura loved it, her parents remembered (though she looks rather nonplussed in photos from the stay, with plump cheeks and embroidered dress, sitting on students' laps). Colleagues and graduate students came over after the girls went to bed for spirited discussions of family-development theory. In 1953, the University of Rhode Island home economics college dean recruited Rus to chair the child-development department with the promise that Mollie could have a tenure-track job as soon as she wanted.

You wouldn't know any of this from their high school textbook. In *Living in Families*, which the Smarts first published in 1958, gender stereotypes abounded. Though they had written an article in the *Journal of Home Economics* advocating sex education for young people, they described in this book a pair of parents turning their bedroom into a hep combo bed–sitting room by pushing their (ahem) twin beds against the wall. A wife contemplating a career should know that she would always be up against a wall herself, they warned: "A wife who works outside the home has a double job, for she is still a homemaker. Rarely can a woman hire help good enough to replace her services at home. The strain that results is both physical and mental, and it is a strain on the husband as well as on the wife." Fortunately, a homemaker need never be bored, because "she has plenty of opportunity for using her mental ability to the utmost."[13] A photo next to the text showed a woman using her mental ability to the utmost in painting a picture frame.

What would the readers of *Living in Families* say if they knew what living in the Smart family was like? Equality at home was a cornerstone of their marriage. And yet the Smarts wrote this claptrap. Reflecting on the contradiction decades later, their daughter Laura, a family scientist herself, concluded that her parents were researchers and academics, as such, she said, they based their textbooks on the scholarship of the time, and that scholarship was biased. They also suffered from the same shortsightedness as other home economists, not realizing how radical they were or how privileged Mollie was to be respected as a professional equal. On top of all that, they had to write what would sell. States exercised tight control over the content of high school textbooks—particularly Texas, with its huge market and conservative mores.[14] Evidently censorship was the price the Smarts paid to do the work they wanted. The price might also have been paid by their readers, who absorbed all the guilt and pressure to conform that Mollie disregarded.

After high school graduation, the home-ec classroom got even worse.

The repressive messaging of family-life education reached its omega in the new college curriculum trend: the marriage course. This was not the old sociological or anthropological classes that studied marriage as a societal institution but classes that taught students how to be married, with the explicit goal of reducing divorce. They began taking hold in the late 1930s and received a boost during World War II when the army began making them available for soldiers awaiting active duty. By 1961, more than 1,200 US colleges and universities offered a marriage course.[15] Sometimes it was in the home economics department. Other times it was home economics–adjacent, in the sociology or social work department, sometimes required for home-ec majors, sometimes for everyone. Student demand evidently drove supply: the biggest problem, teachers reported, was keeping class size down. In a big departure, men were almost as likely to take the marriage course as women. When the Cornell home economics college discontinued its two marriage courses in 1957, it lost most of the men who took its courses, according to its annual report. There was no explanation of why Cornell cut the classes, though home economics dean Helen Canoyer did say the department had upgraded the undergraduate child- and family-development difficulty level due to the preponderance of family-life education in high school. Maybe those marriage courses were easy As . . . though others reported that students were surprised to find they had to study for the class.

The standard textbooks were written by luminaries of the National Council on Family Relations. Robert O. Blood Jr.'s *Marriage*, Henry Bowman's *Marriage for Moderns*, Evelyn Millis Duvall and Reuben Hill's *When You Marry*, and Meyer Nimkoff's *Marriage and the Family* promoted a model of marriage that was middle-class, companionable, democratic, deeply fulfilling emotionally and sexually, and lifelong. Which sounds nice. Except that they also said that a woman's place was in the home. No wonder someone at the University of Michigan, presumably a student, scribbled on the frontispiece of *Marriage*, "This book is totally and completely SEXIST."

Like Catharine Beecher a century earlier, family-life specialists often disdained parents as needing better training. "Parents represent the last stand of the amateur," Duvall wrote.[16] It was particularly imperative to reach those immature married teenagers before they went too far astray. Despite a social-science veneer, the authors described anything outside the nuclear model as deviant or immoral. Only heterosexual, nuclear, intact families were acceptable. Duvall voiced the consensus when she wrote that divorced or single-parent families, which she called "broken," could not teach healthy attitudes about parenthood. The danger was that these were social and medical scientists, experts, so their pronouncements held real weight.

Everyone, and especially every woman, should marry, they said. The only alternative was "a lifelong celibate career." Women who couldn't find a mate should move to Sacramento or Alaska, where men abounded, or lower their standards. Then, whom to marry? A person like oneself. These authors marshaled reams of data—data that conveniently supported gender and racial stereotypes—showing that "mixed" marriages usually failed. Even ridiculously minor differences hurt. Bowman warned against marriages where the woman was taller, because she would not respect her husband when he tried to wield authority. A Protestant marrying a Catholic was akin to trying to leap a crevasse. Partners should be the same age: if the woman were younger, she would become a widow "when she is too young to stop living and too old to start over," Bowman wrote. If she were older, her husband might find her ugly after menopause. Though even an age-mate might lose his head in middle age over a fresh young thing. Which would probably be at least partly his wife's fault, because she had let herself go. The only difference between partners the authors mostly did not address was the one most obvious to us, race, though Bowman warned that biracial children would be miserable because they would have "white aspirations" but be unable to fulfill them due to their "colored" appearance.[17] (Mildred and Richard Loving, who later brought the lawsuit that ended miscegenation bans, wed in 1958.) None went so far as to say that men and women were too different to marry each other, of course. They followed Freud in stating that same-sex attraction was normal only as a passing, immature phase for teens. Some home economists still lived with women as either romantic partners or long-established roommates who became chosen family, including Flora Rose, now retired in Berkeley with her former student Claribel Nye. No one spoke of any such arrangement as anything other than platonic, because publicly known homosexuality meant career and sometimes actual suicide.

No detail was too picayune for the marriage-course authors to enforce convention as scientific gospel, even when they got the biology wrong. Working-class people had stronger sexual responses than middle-class, and girls led boys on because they did not experience strong arousal and did not realize how excited their date was getting, Duvall and Hill wrote. Eloping was dangerous, as was delaying the honeymoon. Most engaged women got their hymens medically stretched, Blood wrote, because in only 10 percent of cases was the membrane sufficiently elastic on its own for honeymoon sex to be comfortable—a tragedy when many couples would never have so much sex ever again, he claimed. The authors all advocated abstinence until marriage lest partners become permanently alienated from their friends, their families, and their personal values.

Given those attitudes, it's no surprise that these books

warned against married women getting jobs. They worked overtime to tell women that there was fulfilment, control, and variety, not just drudgery, in homemaking. The need for a second salary was an illusion: Madison Avenue had snowed women into keeping up with the Joneses, they wrote. Society's veneration of wage-earning occupations did not mean that they mattered more than housekeeping. No one could replace Mom at home. Though women might think they had time for a job, they really didn't with all the many new, intellectually demanding tasks in housewifery these days. As for using a career as a tool for self-expression, most people, of both sexes, didn't have much of a self to express, the authors scoffed. Besides, it's not like the husband would pick up the slack at home, Blood wrote: working wives still did 75 percent of the housework compared to homemakers' 85 percent. To ensure marital happiness, a woman should get a job only if her husband's paycheck truly was inadequate. He suggested volunteering. Judiciously, Bowman concluded that a young woman should still train to work as "a sort of insurance policy" if her fiancé or husband died or ran off. Of course, she must simultaneously prepare for homemaking. How about majoring in home economics? he concluded. Duvall and Hill unbent just enough to endorse jobs for city women whose children were older. It may have been relevant that Duvall was . . . a working city woman whose children were older. She was the only one of these authors to propose any societal solutions, including community kitchens, nursery school, and shorter workdays. She knew from her own experience that extra money from Mother's work wasn't frivolous. Before earning her doctorate in human development, she had written articles for Christian parenting magazines. "Five dollars meant meat on the table augmenting the macaroni and cheese," she wrote years later. "The long-term rewards were becoming established as a published writer."[18]

So, cross your legs, stretch your hymen, and sacrifice any career ambitions you might have, and you could be happily married. That was the promise. Would it work? Who knew, Bowman said. He freely admitted that there was no research evidence that the marriage course improved students' partnerships. But who cared, he wrote: there was no research evidence that most of the liberal arts curriculum was "effective" in whatever it aimed to do either.[19]

In this atmosphere, would the practice baby fly? Hell no.

Eastern Illinois State College was about twenty-five years behind the times when its new home economics dean, Ruth Schmalhausen, established its home-management houses and a practice-baby program in 1952. She asked the state child-welfare superintendent for help finding a suitable infant. He refused, and assumed that was the end of her efforts. Instead, Schmalhausen borrowed a girl from the Salvation Army. There are no details about that baby, but evidently all went well on the college side, because two years later, the department took on another temporary charge, a boy named David, loaned by his mother, an unmarried woman from Indiana. They gave him the last name "North," because he lived in the north practice house. Schmalhausen, the mother, the college president, and the baby's doctor thought the home-management house was the best prospect for the boy. He was premature and weak, and his mother had to work. She would visit her baby, correspond with the department about his progress, and get him back at the end of the year. Living with students was more stable, warm, and peaceful than the alternatives, such as an orphanage, the experts thought—or even an ordinary family with its tensions and squabbles. However, when the *St. Louis Post-Dispatch* wrote a story about David, the state welfare superintendent blew up and opened an investigation. He thought the baby deserved better than to be an experiment. The college wasn't a licensed placement. The separation from the baby's mother was psychologically harmful. A roster of twelve rotating "mothers" was incredibly confusing. A boy needed a father figure, he argued. Freud said so.

The story went, as we would say today, viral. The *New York Times*, the *Los Angeles Times*, *Look*, *Newsweek*, *Time*, and even the military publication *Stars and Stripes* featured Baby David "North," often with photos. *Life* called him one of the season's "famous babies," alongside Desi Arnaz Jr. The coverage mostly sided against Schmalhausen, presenting the practice-baby tradition as both bizarre and dangerous. "Although he looks like a happy, well-loved child, David North may be developing a first-class case of anxiety neurosis," *Pageant* warned.[20] Eventually, the state concluded that it did not have jurisdiction over the placement. The mother was not from Illinois, had privately arranged for the college to care for her son, and had not given him up for adoption or sought government intervention. In September, the college even brought in a new baby to take David's place, Amy "North." The controversy seemed to quiet. But then, the following February, the federal Children's Bureau and Office of Education convened a meeting to evaluate practice-baby programs. They stopped just short of calling for these programs to cease, but said they were rarely what was best for the baby. To learn infant care, the panel suggested the alternatives of making home visits, volunteering at college-run day care centers, and helping in a doctor's office or nursery. At the very least, when home economics programs cared for infants full-time, it must be regulated as foster care, the panel said.

Though the general consensus was that a baby needed one father and (especially) one mother, Margaret Mead, who was not on the panel, questioned the overall stifling effect of the new insistence on the primacy of the mother. In 1954 she called it "a new and subtle form of antifeminism in which men—under the guise of exalting the importance of maternity—are tying women more tightly to their children than has been thought necessary since the invention of bottle feeding and baby carriages."[21] Not only did that view have no anthropological validity, she wrote, but studies across cultures in fact suggested that children were better adjusted when they had many loving caregivers. As in a university home economics practice house.

But the home economics practice baby was on its way out. The babies were getting harder and harder to find, anyway. With Dr. Spock advocating instinct and flexibility, the idea of a regimented scientific upbringing for a baby no longer appealed as it had in the 1920s. The child-welfare system was arranging adoptions younger. From the two-semester stay of the past, typically practice babies now lived at the college for only a handful of weeks before finding adoptive parents. And colleges had started to drop the requirement that students live in a home-management house, because more undergraduates were married and running households of their own.

In theory, family-life education was a deeper, more meaningful way to talk about why the home matters. You could say it was more sophisticated. Popular novels of the time, such as Richard Yates's *Revolutionary Road*, showed what could happen when the perfect living room set mattered more than love and relationships. And what parent hasn't wished that their teenager could occasionally remember, as these high school textbooks taught, that parents are people too?

In reality, however, family-life education was a way to limit girls' horizons. Up until the fifties, home economics textbooks had talked about cooking, cleaning, and decorating as what women *did*. Parenthood was a series of tasks: washing, feeding, taking the baby out for air. You could feel a sense of accomplishment in your abilities, find autonomy in interdependence. The new textbooks were far more intrusive. They talked about who you *were*, your personality, instead of tasks. A person who messed up sewing a seam was just clumsy. But shyness with a date reflected "emotional frigidity and unwillingness to give of the self for the sake of the partner," while talking *too* much showed a lack of sophistication. Heaven forfend if a girl should be rude enough to talk to her date about other boys: "Boiling in oil, were it legal and less painful, would be just retribution!"[22] Moreover, "family life" made the work of the home never-ending, an inexhaustible time suck. You can clean a floor and see that it is clean, even if your cereal-toting toddler topples, spilling food all over, five minutes later. But there is never an end to emotional labor, to cultivating warmth and togetherness or becoming a better person.

Preparing women for homemaking also took the focus off of preparing them for a job. Emotional skills weren't as obvious a résumé-builder as cooking or institutional management. That had consequences, especially for those home economics majors who needed to work. "Any failure to achieve a balance between family-centeredness and profession centeredness will leave our Negro students grossly unprepared for desirable job opportunities. We must admit that a means of livelihood is indeed essential to wholesome happy living," North Carolina Central professor Sadye Pearl Young wrote, critiquing Russell Smart.[23] Finally, family life erased the structural problems that affected the home. The earlier home economists propounded an ecological view: solutions might require public-policy advocacy and an overhaul of the building code. But from the psychological perspective, problems at home were your own fault and your own responsibility to fix. If you could. It wasn't likely, the marriage books reminded young women, that they would manage to change their socialized husbands' minds about homemaking and career.

In the end, the new emphasis on personal relationships was disempowering. No matter what the classes implied, physical surroundings are easier to change than personalities. There is only so much that one person, especially a teenager, can do to improve family relationships. At least the old textbooks said your life would be better if you put up some convenient shelves. And could home economists even have it all themselves? Yes, Mollie Smart could have a career. But she chose to work less when her daughters were young, and then to remain self-employed while Russell's job brought in the pension and benefits. What if she had wanted to be a full-time professor right off the bat? Many universities still had anti-nepotism policies that barred women from working if their husbands were on faculty. When Mollie told the University of Rhode Island that she was ready to move to full-time status in the early 1960s, the deanship had changed hands. The new dean said no.

The most feminist vision of family life at this time came in a discussion of military preparedness. Federal education employee Druzilla Kent advocated a world designed to support families where women worked in defense. The Cold War meant "a prolonged period of crisis" and unprecedented demand for production to support the defense effort, she wrote in 1952. Women would have to take defense jobs, because the male labor force was tapped out. In turn, society and home economics education would have to change to reflect the reality of employed women. Kent called for day care and paid time off to care for sick family members; easy-to-care-for housing; shopping centers that stayed open late; fast, comfortable public transportation; home economics for boys, because men would have to play a real role in managing the household; parent-teacher conferences at the mother's workplace; self-service laundries; and "conveniently located centers where hot 'main-dishes' can be secured at reasonable cost for the evening meal"—hello, New England Kitchen![24] It was the most feminist statement of the time, and it was done in the name of the Cold War, which was driving a lot of home economists to liberation. For themselves, at least.

CHAPTER 8

The Iron Fist in the Oven Mitt

What did home economists think they were doing in sending women kitchen-ward? Not imposing patriarchy. They believed they were fighting the Cold War.

It made sense. Whereas the fifties have emerged in cultural memory as a decade of abundance, home economists felt foreboding, even dread. (Many baby boomers who lived through air-raid drills would say the same.) Besides, all but the oldest home economists had spent their entire careers in wartime or Depression, engaged in existential fights. The January 1952 *Journal of Home Economics* dubbed the fifties the "Defense Decade," writing, "We are again living in a period of national emergency," with a "sudden, vicious attack" possible at any moment. If everyone did her part, peace and quiet might someday reign again.[1] Reading the *Journal* of 1952, it might still be 1942, with ads for US Army dietitian jobs and a National Canners Association brochure called *Canned Foods for Emergency Feeding*. The Bureau of Home Economics continued to put out food-conservation bulletins such as *Cooking with Dried Whole Eggs*, *Root Vegetables in Everyday Meals*, and *Peanut and Peanut Butter Recipes*, the last recommending that cooks stretch meatloaf, already the ultimate meat-stretcher, with peanut butter. There was one key difference between the decades, however. Home economists focused during World War II on changing Americans' behavior, with wheatless days, fabric rationing, and factory employment. They weren't paying as much attention to domestic conditions in the 1950s, peanut butter bulletins notwithstanding. They had turned outward to change the rest of the world.

Internationalism wasn't new in home economics. Even prior to Catharine Beecher, missionaries' wives had taught homemaking skills to the "heathen," finding that before they could convert, they had to clothe. By the late 1800s, domestic work was part of the British colonial curriculum; after the Spanish-American War, the US government sent domestic science teachers to its new colonies. The American Home Economics Association had begun funding exchange students and international programs in the 1910s. For instance, it raised the equivalent of $80,000 to send Lake Placid attendee Alice Peloubet Norton to Constantinople for three years. Oregon State home economics dean Ava Milam spent two years establishing home economics at China's Yenching University in the early 1920s, and subsequently consulted in Asia for fifteen years. During the Cold War, that work gained government support. Now global political leaders agreed with home economists on the significance of the home as a brass-tacks tactic, a way to create large-scale change—and a political symbol. Then–vice president Richard Nixon and Soviet leader Nikita Khrushchev made the latter clear in their famous "Kitchen Debate," when they argued over technological might and the primacy of their respective political systems in 1959 over a literal kitchen. The skirmish took place in a Moscow exhibit of a model American home. Nixon leaned on the barrier surrounding the exhibit and pointed to the dishwasher, showing it off. "In America, we like to make life easier for women," he said. Khrushchev dismissed his rival's boast. "We have such things," he scoffed—and without the sexist expectations: "Your capitalistic attitude toward women does not occur under Communism."[2]

The new United Nations wanted to feed the hungry, and the US needed to calm military threats, gain allies, and support starving countries being courted by Communists. Home economists would try to take free-market abundance and Western-style democracy across the globe, to transform geopolitics by modernizing the home. Their work combined empowerment with oppression, and changed American home economists as much as it did the women they met.

In late 1946, Flemmie Kittrell boarded a plane for a thirty-hour voyage, one of several Howard University professors who had secured State Department work in the brave new postwar world thanks to the DC university's government connections. She was going to spend six months in Liberia conducting the first-ever nutritional survey of a foreign country and helping schools teach nutrition. Though Liberia was about to mark its first century as Africa's first modern independent republic and had long-standing ties to US Black colleges, it remained a struggling country. The elites, descended from freed US slaves, lived on the coast, leaving the interior isolated. Education had only recently become mandatory for children aged seven to sixteen. The country's location near the equator meant a challenging rainy season and tropical diseases. Most people farmed at a bare subsistence level, by hand, burning fields for rice, Kittrell read in a study she used in her report. The nation's new president, William V. S. Tubman, begged for international investment: ironically, the country's relative lack of exploitation by European powers had resulted in a serious dearth of infrastructure, he said. Reliant on Liberian rubber during the war, the US responded by deepening Monrovia's harbor, creating health centers for Allied troops that also served natives, establishing air bases, and building an international airport.

Over six months, Kittrell traveled with her assistant by "foot, hammock, native dug-out boats, motor boats, canoes, and plane," she wrote, through the rolling hills of the interior, thick with flowers and laced with waterfalls and lakes. She visited the larger settlements and visited public health offices and universities, making side trips to Sierra Leone and Gold Coast (later Ghana). But she spent as much time as possible in remote villages, documenting the diets of more than four thousand families. She watched parents cuddle their children, sing to them as they learned to swim, bind babies to their bare backs with cloth so the mothers could work, and discipline with praise, not slaps. Children learned early to carry heavy loads on their heads while walking for miles and to hull the rice that formed a large part of the daily diet. Kittrell didn't say where she slept, but she spent three to five days in each village and evidently kept up her proper appearance: the residents were shocked by her pressed slacks. (They were shocked by the trousers; we would more likely be shocked at her ability to continue to look neat.) Evidently Kittrell could be comfortable anywhere, with anyone. Authorities warned her that she should not get too "familiar" with the indigenous people in the bush, because they might lose respect for her and she might lose her ability to make them change. Kittrell brushed off the advice, saying, "I know how to treat people."[3]

The visit was a success. Though a tribal chief criticized Kittrell for wearing pants and "bossing the men around," the Liberian government gave her an award for service to the country. "I noted in the hinterland of West Africa much of life that is good and beautiful and at the same time envisioned much to be desired," Kittrell wrote. She informed the government of many problems. People were underfed and malnourished. They had very little access to fish or meat, resulting in protein deficiency and anemia. Despite their hard physical labor, most ate only two meals a day. Men averaged 1,400 calories, women 1,350. Schools were unhappy: teachers frequently whipped their charges, and the courses did not provide practical information that would help at home, such as teaching children in bacteriology class to boil contaminated water to make it safe. Girls rarely went to school because men thought educated women made bad wives—hard to satisfy, with expensive tastes. ("I have heard almost the same reasons advanced in this country," Kittrell wrote, wryly.)[4]

Just three years later she embarked on another study trip, six months in the Indian city of Baroda, now known as Vadodara, to teach at the newly established University of Baroda's College of Home Science as one of the first home economics Fulbright scholars. The timing was fortuitous: Kittrell had to cut her budget at Howard, and rather than sacrifice the home economics building she wanted built or fire one of her few professors, she temporarily took herself off the payroll. The University of Baroda put her up like a princess: screens, sleeping nets, a refrigerator, and even some air-conditioning. Again Kittrell found herself deeply struck by the country, this time by its combination of ancient history and young independence. She admired India's fight for freedom, history of scholarship, and desire for peace. The region's culture "portrays a rare sense of tolerance, long-suffering, and deep understanding of peoples," she wrote. When she visited Nehru's childhood home, she "fell in love all over again" with his philosophy, the educational side of which he had adopted from Booker T. Washington.[5] Kittrell was impressed in particular by two exceptionally accomplished Indian women leaders who brought science to the masses through home economics university education: Amrit Kaur, Nehru's health minister and the first woman to hold a Cabinet-level position in India, and Hansa Mehta, University of Baroda vice chancellor and a member of the UN Human Rights Commission. They embraced Kittrell as she created a structure and degree plan for the department and organized the country's first home economics education conference, which resulted in a new national association. Though Kittrell put in so much work that she even edited and distributed the conference findings, she gave the credit to the Indian women. When she returned to Baroda in 1954 for the university's first home economics graduation, the students welcomed her with garlands of flowers.

The girl from Henderson, North Carolina, became a passionate internationalist, a citizen of the world. When she presented her findings in the US, she liked to wear a sari. The work fed her old political science hunger while helping with physical hunger, too. She traveled professionally in Uganda, Kenya, Japan, South Africa, the Congo, India again, Mozambique, Rhodesia, Thailand, Zaire, Angola, Australia, New Zealand, Burma, and Bangladesh. In the late summer of 1958 alone, she sprinted to Kenya, Uganda, Nigeria, Ghana, and Liberia in an eight-week span. Kittrell promoted some of what the countries had to offer by compiling the American Home Economics Association cookbook *Favorite Recipes from the United Nations*, which featured such dishes as Ethiopian doro wat and Soviet shashlik for eager young gourmets. She was particularly fond of Nigeria, where her predecessor as Howard home economics chair, Madeline Kirkland, established the University of Nigeria's home economics bachelor's degree program. Even as the FBI continued to track her, she worked under the auspices of the United Nations, the Methodist Church, the American Home Economics Association, the Women's International League for Peace and Freedom, the Ford Foundation, and the US government Point Four program, to name a few. She even visited the Moscow exhibition that was the scene of the Kitchen Debate. (There were also home economists working at the exhibition for General Foods and General Mills, showing off their products; American corporations contributed displays.) It all made Kittrell a hero in home economics. Soon she was not only the most prominent African American home economist in the history of the profession, but one of the field's most prominent leaders, period.

Astonishingly, Kittrell continued to run and even expand home economics at Howard during this time. When the new home economics building she had demanded finally opened in 1963, her friend Margaret Mead spoke at the dedication. The building incorporated African, Japanese, and Indian elements, including a large working fireplace designed to evoke an African house. Kittrell hung her own souvenirs and sculptures from her African travels on the walls to make students and visitors proud of their heritage. The 1956 Howard yearbook team called their university "a center of international education," and dedicated the volume to Kittrell, its epitome. Thanks to her influence, in the mid-sixties, fifty-eight recent Howard home economics graduates were working in Africa or Asia teaching and carrying out nutrition studies like hers. Kittrell helped international students enroll at Howard as well, with the idea of equipping them to be of service to their peoples, just as she had intended when she studied at Cornell. At the year-end dinners she hosted for those international students, everyone recited the global-minded creed of the New Homemakers of America, familiar to all African American home economists though less so to white ones: "If there is harmony and love in the home, there will be justice in the nation. If there is justice in the nation, there will be peace in the world."[6]

In a 1960s photo, Kittrell, looking sophisticated in a dark suit with a narrow skirt and cropped jacket, showed off a world map with pins and string connecting her alma mater, Cornell, to the many countries its home economics students had come from and gone to. She might as well have been showing her own itinerary.

Did Kittrell start a trend? Soon tons of home economists were voyaging abroad as money poured in from the US government and foundations. A randomly selected issue of the *Journal of Home Economics*, May 1952, not only mentions American home economists working in Honduras, Agra, Baghdad, New Zealand, and Copenhagen, but includes articles on the Food and Agricultural Organization and the National Conference on International Economic and Social Development, plus not one but two articles on the University of the Ryukyus in Okinawa. When President John F. Kennedy began the Peace Corps, home economists jumped on that ship as well. Sue Sadow—a sexagenarian with a long career in urban welfare, nutrition research in the Middle East, and organizing food for World War II refugees in North Africa and Italy—taught home economics to high school girls in Sierra Leone, then traveled that country demonstrating how to prepare the food that came in aid packages from Western charities. Quoting George Bernard Shaw, Sadow believed, she said, that life "is a sort of splendid torch which I have got hold of for the moment, and I want to make it burn as brightly as possible before handing it to future generations."[7]

The Smarts benefited directly from Kittrell's work. First

Russell spent a Fulbright year at the University of Baroda in 1959 with his wife and daughters. Later he taught at Lady Irwin College in New Delhi, another home economics department Kittrell helped organize, while Mollie studied on another Fulbright at the University of Delhi, at last earning her doctorate. The Smarts would later work in New Zealand on dual Fulbrights as well.

Kittrell also wasn't the only woman of color making big trips. Georgia Poinsette, Allie Holley, Lydia Rogers, Queen Jones, Cecile Hoover Edwards, and the USDA's Patsy Graves, all African American, taught abroad. Fabiola de Baca, the Latina who helped New Mexicans survive the Depression, took a leave from the state extension service in 1951 to train Latin American social workers for UNESCO. She was the international agency's first choice for the job. De Baca took the group to Michoacán, Mexico, where they taught the indigenous Tarascans to improve sanitation and preserve lake fish when they had a good catch.

These new jobs for home economists were thrilling. Why work in Boston when you could, like one former Simmons College department chair, live in Rome and travel in Indonesia and the Philippines for the UN? Helping others internationally also fed personal ambition. It boosted the ego to be recognized globally as experts on women's issues, health, and economic development. In turn, international home economics students came to the US, challenging colleges to make their courses relevant for people who might come from places that varied widely in traditions and resources. The American Home Economics Association published three booklets on "Entertaining Foreign Visitors," with conversation starters, suggestions on what visitors wanted to see, and ideas on what to serve for dinner. The Smarts wrote one of them, *How to Cherish an Indian Guest*.

For all the friendliness, though, it was military might that gave US home economists the opportunity for their most dramatic impact, in occupied Japan. Along with helping its devastated, defeated former enemy recover economically, the US government aimed to permanently change Japan's national character from the authoritarian society that produced kamikaze pilots (as the American occupiers saw it) to a disarmed democracy. They did this not only by disempowering the emperor but through home economics. The Japanese family resembled the Japanese state, with a divine, all-too-powerful, and demanding man at its apex, the American government thought. Mothers who were not subjugated to their husbands would never have let their sons fly suicide missions. The *Journal of Home Economics* endorsed this analysis in 1947, writing, "The Japanese family system doesn't tolerate our concept of democratic family life, but if Japan is really to be democratic it will have to begin in the home."[8] The journal ignored or didn't know about the country's own history of progressive home economics that empowered women. Hani Motoko, the country's first woman journalist and one of its earliest female high school graduates, founded a school and magazine in 1903 that presented marriage as a union of two independent and mutually supportive individuals; the first issue entered the world the day after her first child did. In 1917, Japanese Bryn Mawr alumna Michi Kawai opened a school in Yokohama to teach American scientific housekeeping, fashion standards, and childrearing to "picture brides" so that they would represent Japan well when they joined their fiancés in the US. Kimiyo Onaga taught home economics in Japanese-occupied Korea in the 1930s and had a radio cooking show.

Six months after Japan surrendered, Captain Rachael Johnstone, a nutritional consultant for the occupation army in Tokyo, was already overseeing two home economics schools for Japanese citizens on top of her primary job of supervising sixty headquarters kitchens that fed fifteen thousand people a day. She used the former Siamese embassy as a practice house.[9] The following year, Hunter College home economics chair Dora Lewis moved from New York to Japan to help General Douglas MacArthur revamp the country's high school curriculum. And in 1951, Michigan State professor Eleanor Densmore went to Okinawa, where the US government was building a modern land-grant university. President Truman himself assigned the management of the new University of the Ryūkyūs to Michigan State, whose president, John Hannah, was active in Cold War defense and economic-development groups. Hannah believed that Michigan State's campus was not Lansing but the world.[10]

Densmore, who had been teaching steelworkers' daughters, found herself staggered by the conditions in Okinawa. How to teach modern housekeeping in a place where bombing had driven people to live in caves? The archipelago had lost half its population in the Allied invasion, and the university campus went up on the site of a ruined castle that was one of the deadliest battlegrounds in World War II. Natural resources were limited, machinery expensive, and good farm fields in short supply—the US military had seized large portions of arable land. Even getting the smoky native brick stoves to burn more cleanly was a trial: chimneys blew away in typhoons, oil stoves were expensive, and better-ventilated chimneys ate fuel and made houses hot. The university was severely undersupplied, and students struggled through the English-language classes with dictionaries by their sides. Needing resources, Okinawans raised cash crops such as radishes and onions, while Densmore wanted them to enrich rice and raise goats for milk. (Little did she know that sixty years later scientists would study the Okinawan diet for clues to longevity.) Densmore objected to the residents' Shinto faith, which she thought dwelled on the past, and to what she saw as their selfishness: "Many of them look upon self-government as an opportunity to further their own interests with little regard for the welfare of the people as a whole," she wrote.[11]

Even so, she admired the Okinawans' determination. When her students put on their best kimonos to host dinners for faculty, they looked to her like a bouquet of flowers. "It is amazing that these conquered peoples have been able to pick themselves up and make an effort to return to normal living," she wrote. "Slowly they are groping their way to a better life, and it is our job to try to help them."[12] Densmore and the colleagues who followed her sequentially fought for proper facilities, equal to those of male-dominated departments. The Michigan State home economists designed, organized, administered, and coordinated the Ryūkyūs program, leaving the actual teaching to Japanese professors, particularly Kimiyo Onaga, whom they hired to run the department. They built a home-management house in the Okinawan style, furnished with tatami floors, shoji screens, and low tables, where students cooked local food. Back home, Densmore told homemaker groups about the brave, hardworking women of Okinawa; inspired, Michiganders sent sewing supplies, school dresses, feed sacks for mattress covers, and money for scholarships. Some Okinawan students used the scholarship money to support their education locally; others traveled all the way to Lansing.

Perhaps remarkably, given the deprivation and Densmore's disparagement, American-style home economics caught on. Home economics became a required school subject in 1947— it is still required, more than seventy years later. Okinawan women were excited about transforming their homes and lives through these new methods. Housewives signed up for Onaga's community classes. By 1955, the university had one hundred home economics students. Densmore left only because she needed eye surgery. "This has been the most rewarding experience of my entire life," she wrote.[13]

So was this empowerment or oppression, humanitarian or imperialist? As with all US international activities in the 1950s, it was both. US home economists generally went abroad with earnest intentions. For Kittrell, a devout Methodist, international work was a "moral imperative" for the wealthy US. "If we could ever have enough food and if people are properly fed we can prevent wars," she wrote. The US had destroyed Okinawa, and owed its residents repair. Having embraced Maslow's "hierarchy of needs," home economists thought that people could not do anything meaningful until they had secured basic survival. "Hunger is like a cancer eating away at the very foundations of our civilization," UN Food and Agriculture Organization liaison Florence Reynolds told the American Home Economics Association conference in 1950. The world's poorest people had "no time for improving the mind, or for learning good health practices, or for building roads, or factories, or houses. There is no time for anything but the battle for food."[14]

Home economists were also intensely, professionally curious about home lives in other lands, often nonjudgmentally so. In an era preaching the primacy of the nuclear family, Kittrell didn't blink an eye when praising polygamous Liberian households. Former First Lady Eleanor Roosevelt captivated the fiftieth-anniversary American Home Economics Association conference in 1959 with details of her travels in the Soviet Union. Roosevelt depicted a centrally planned, tightly disciplined society where people had no choice and limited living quarters, almost all women worked, and even little babies learned to do exercises. The people were happy, she said. So many home economists were eager to see homes in the USSR and Europe that four years later they paid the equivalent of $10,000 in today's dollars to attend an American Home Economics Association trip. In twenty-nine days, eighty-five home economists were whisked from an international conference to old-age homes, day care centers, a new planned community going up in the outskirts of Stockholm, and meetings with four ambassadors, pausing to take a sauna in Helsinki. In Moscow they saw brand-new apartment blocks and century-old log shanties, and visited with a homemaker in her apartment, whose kitchen AHEA president Florence Low deemed "meagerly but adequately equipped."[15]

The Americans developed deep affection for the women they worked with abroad. They welcomed exchange students and followed their progress afterward with pride. The feminism disappearing in domestic home economics flowered internationally as the globe-trotting professionals supported the empowerment of women in other countries and sought to raise their status. Hunter College department chair Dora Lewis worried that Japanese women spent too much time learning the domestic arts, an unexpected criticism from a home economics educator. In public, at least, the Americans focused on other countries' strengths. Densmore asked a Michigan State colleague to delete anything in her reports that might "be derogatory to the Okinawan" before circulating them to the rest of the university. De Baca said she never thought of the Tarascan people as poor: "They have plenty of things. Only they don't know how to utilize what they have."[16]

Nor did the American home economists think that they should stamp the world in the US image wholesale. They believed that international projects had to be based on respect and run in tandem with local experts. "Working in harmony with existing cultural patterns is fundamental to successful extension work in any country," a 1957 federal guide said. "Your work is to help the country broaden the opportunity for development of the individual within its own basic cultural pattern." They did not want to overwrite local cultures with American ways. "Unless one is extremely careful there can be great danger from foreign teachers and missionaries trying to impose their way of living from a different civilization," Kittrell wrote.[17] Anyway, they had to rely on the locals. Very few US home economists settled abroad for good. Local women with US graduate degrees led the new international home economics associations sparked by the Americans' activism—in Thailand, Korea, Japan, and the Philippines, for instance. Onaga became a crucial go-between for Michigan State, driving around Okinawa in a station wagon to teach locals how to cook with unfamiliar US food-relief products such as Spam and powdered milk. She encouraged them to adopt US nutrition practices such as eating salad. Michigan State gave Onaga an award at its 1957 commencement, where she shook hands with the graduation speaker: Richard Nixon.

Home economists of color seemed to be especially sensitive to the issues of respect and taking over, perhaps due to the critical eye they brought to bear on their own country. De Baca had, after all, direct experience of American colonialism. When she went to Mexico she had just published her finest work, her memoir *We Fed Them Cactus*, a poetic landmark of Latino literature, at a time Latinas almost never got to publish books. De Baca based *Cactus* not only on her childhood memories but on fifteen years of research and interviews with elders. She described the US government breaking its promise to respect the New Mexican settlers' land claims; the ignorance of Anglo newcomers who thought "the only white people were those who spoke the English language as their mother tongue"; and the warmth, skill, and vanished economic strength of a colonized people. It was a love letter to the land and to a community. From an initial print run of just five hundred copies in 1954, *Cactus* won widespread acclaim when Latino civil rights activists rediscovered and reissued it in 1972.[18]

Of course there was another side, however. The Americans remained the experts, and the locals simply incorporated or adapted their visitors' knowledge. Some Japanese women came to believe that their country was backward. "Our life has become very formal, ornamental, and ostentatious but it is not practical, comfortable, nor healthy," a Japanese home economics teacher wrote. Saying you shouldn't stamp other countries in the US's image could verge on a racist denigration of their capacities. Margaret Harris of Michigan State wrote that one should not apply US standards to "people of Oriental stature and inheritance." Dora Lewis of Hunter College said she would work with "highly trained Japanese educators who are well aware of what their people can assimilate."[19]

And home economists could never get away from the politics of poverty. They believed that poor people were sitting ducks for dictators, because they would follow whoever gave them food. Americans and Communists were competing for influence over "the troubled areas of the world," Michigan State president John Hannah said. Open-minded assessment of the advantages of Communism made home economists all the more aware of the threat it posed. The conclusion Roosevelt drew from her trip to the USSR was that the Soviets' rapid transition from agricultural backwater to industrial powerhouse meant that the US had to prove the value of democracy. "If we don't win the majority of the uncommitted nations of the world, the Soviets will," she said.[20]

Finally, promoting home economics abroad meant at least tacitly accepting US government international policies. All these projects were funded by a Cold War apparatus whose goal was American (and capitalist) influence through the use of soft power. The University of the Ryūkyūs was unquestionably a military project. "Ryūkyūs" was the island kingdom's name before Japanese annexation; choosing it as the university's name was a bid to divert residents' loyalty from Japan, as was making Japanese studies optional. Administrators expelled students who protested US activities or showed Communist sympathies. Densmore, her successors, and Onaga relied on the US military for everything from transportation to demonstrating bread-baking to training dorm mothers (the Women's Army Corps did that). Women students slept on cast-off US Army mattresses; if they restuffed the mattresses themselves, they could use them rent-free. Either the Michigan professors supported the goals of the military occupation or they didn't care as long as they could spread their gospel.

That said, one of the most intrusive international homemaker-education initiatives came from outside home economics proper: the American Red Cross "bride schools" for new Japanese wives of US servicemen. These courses taught the skills to keep a US-style house, assuming that the husband's way would take precedence—everything from how to bake pineapple upside-down cake to how to apply makeup to how to behave with one's mother-in-law. Most of the instructors were volunteers—the American wives and daughters of soldiers stationed in Japan. "The little Madam Butterflys are studying hamburgers, Hollywood, and home on the range, before coming to live in the U.S.A.," a *Saturday Evening Post* photo feature trilled. The article was even worse than the program itself in that it managed to insult absolutely everyone, mocking the wives' permed hair and saying they "have no idea of what to do with a girdle, although they buy them, thus annoying the life out of slightly spreading American women who find the PX never has the right size at the right time because some Japanese bride just bought it, perhaps to hang on the wall of her home as a decoration." One woman featured in the story, Chiyohi Creef, was stunned and insulted to see the published story. "More I read the *Post*, more makes me mad at their writing concerning Japanese Brides," she wrote in her diary, in English, her second language. "Only my husband really knows about me and pride I have in myself."[21]

Once Creef and her classmates relocated to the US, equipped with home economics skills, they would eventually need to buy a new oven or a refrigerator. When they did, they would come into contact with home economists like Betty Newton, who was going to help Creef and lots of other customers make the best of their lives.

CHAPTER 9

Selling Mrs. Housewife

The phone helpline rang at the Columbia Gas Company in Ohio. Another housewife calling frustrated that her stove wouldn't work, or a single man who couldn't figure out a recipe. Home economist Sheila Castellarin picked up the phone. "Betty Newton," Castellarin said.

Everyone across the US loved Betty Crocker. And in the Midwest, everyone also loved Betty Newton of Columbia Gas. Behind Betty Crocker was Marjorie Child Husted, supervising a staff of forty. Behind Betty Newton were several dozen midwestern home economists like Castellarin, working like it was going out of style. If one vein of home economics in the fifties and sixties trained women to be wives, another one targeted them as consumers—and career women were behind it. For an ambitious young woman, business home economics was a good place to be. The sector grew from 3,500 jobs in 1955 to almost

5,000 in 1969. Experts needed to revise recipes to account for more than four hundred new food additives plus innovations such as frozen food, plastic wrap, boil-in-the-bag packages, glass-ceramic (such as Corning Ware), and nonstick coating. Miracle fibers and upgraded appliances required new clothing-care instructions. As supermarkets with their dizzying variety replaced corner stores, household-product marketing became even more important. For every consumer product, especially agricultural, there was a trade association. The *Journal of Home Economics* teemed with mentions of food companies, household-product makers, and lobbying groups: the Florida Citrus Commission, the Aluminum Cooking Utensil Company, Knox Gelatine, Nestle's, United Fruit, Westinghouse, the National Cotton Council. All these companies employed home economists. Say a young home economist felt a fondness for the cow. She could work for the National Dairy Council, the American Dairy Association, the Milk Producers Association of America, the American Dry Milk Institute, the Evaporated Milk Association, Pet Milk, or Borden, to say nothing of all the regional, state, and county dairy promotion groups or the cheese and yogurt companies. It was a newly exciting time for yogurt, or so a Knudsen home economist said in a 1962 recipe booklet: "For 3000 years yogurt just sat there."[1]

Forget being a dowdy teacher stuck in a school: business home economists were glamorous. They knew what was going on in the real world. They earned good money, better than your average working man—Willie Mae Rogers, head of the Good Housekeeping Institute, turned down a Nixon administration post in part because the pay was too low.[2] Their salaries meant they could dress well; when they walked into the American Home Economics Association conferences, heads turned. Satenig St. Marie, home economics director for J. C. Penney's, gave presentations wearing fur hats or maxidresses; she helmed meetings in a midtown Manhattan skyscraper in a jacket that looked like it was made by Chanel. Fashion designer Pauline Trigère created the General Mills test-kitchen uniforms. Business home economists "were the cat's meow," AHEA staffer Gladys Gary Vaughn remembered years later.[3]

And what did they do? A lot. Betty Newton was the public face of Columbia Gas, which had two million customers across five states, and the core of its customer-relations strategy. "We *were* the gas company," Castellarin said.[4] To this day, some women's obituaries say they were Betty Newtons.

Instruction, paired with sales, was the name of the game. Their job was to educate people on the use of gas appliances in the home—and, of course, to promote gas over electric. Not only did the utility company sell power but it sold appliances, both to consumers and to builders. The Betty Newtons were white women. They looked perfect at all times in full-skirted dresses with button-down fronts and regulation round collars and gloves. (At least the company had eliminated the hat rule by the time Castellarin arrived.) No aprons: the idea was to look like professionals, not housewives. They made presentations to homemakers' clubs and schools, trotting out sophisticated dishes for the former and easy, kid-friendly snacks for the latter. (They were permitted to don fancy ruffled pinafores for school and Scout programs.) They were educated, with a bachelor's degree in home economics required. In their labs they took apart new equipment, then put it back together again, so they knew how each device worked inside and out. If an appliance malfunctioned, they called their peers at General Electric or Westinghouse to work it through. Then they visited appliance stores and taught salesmen how to sell the devices, and wrote instructional guides for homemakers and Columbia Gas repairmen. There was a daily half-hour radio program, which Betty Newtons wrote. They produced movies that they loaned to schools. Many people paid their bills in person at branch offices that featured alluring model kitchens, which the Betty Newtons used for cooking demonstrations. Once a year in each town with a Columbia Gas office, the company sized those demonstrations up to a theater, a full-house affair with door prizes and a set created by a company kitchen designer. All free to customers, always. Even corporate customers: When Bob Evans Farms expanded into restaurants, Betty Newtons tested the recipes and designed the menus at no charge, Castellarin said. The customer would use the product, and so Columbia Gas (and Consolidated Edison, and Westinghouse) would eventually make the money back, executives figured.

And the Betty Newtons didn't require housewives to come to them. They made house calls! When a family bought a new stove, fridge, or other appliance from Columbia Gas or a dealer, a Betty Newton automatically visited to help the homemaker optimize her investment. In the early 1960s, utility company home economists handled more than one million service calls a year.[5] Even at those appointments, taking off her white gloves in a woman's kitchen, surrounded by family photos and wedding china, the home economist maintained that her name was Betty Newton. The act was as ironclad as that of a colonial reenactor at Williamsburg. The Betty Newtons enjoyed this element of theater. The anonymity made them feel safe going into strangers' houses. Besides, a woman could get awfully tired of spelling "Castellarin."

The way the Betty Newtons saw themselves, they had the consumer at the front of their mind, always. They didn't encourage waste, even if that might mean more pennies in the gas meter. "We taught efficiency," Castellarin said proudly. Betty Newton told customers they had to preheat the oven for only a few minutes. She redesigned the bill format so customers could understand it. Castellarin found, bought, and had

Ohio State decorate a set of three-foot-tall wooden dollhouses, heavy as heck, so the Betty Newtons could demonstrate ways to save energy in every room. Betty Newton was the commercial heir to Louisan Mamer, who continued to work at the Rural Electrification Administration, less visible but still interacting with the public. In fact, Mamer was Betty Newton's competition. Castellarin devised a timetable of how much faster it was to cook with gas than with electricity, and how much better (she claimed) the results tasted.

Though no longer working in a circus tent, Mamer kept her brio. In 1948, she gave her thoroughly modern manifesto in a rare magazine interview. "My secret ambition is to build a modern house; furnish it modern and Chinese; equip it all-electric and with a husband guaranteed not to wander; [and] operate the whole arrangement at enough profit to provide myself with all the secretarial and other help I would like to have to do my job the way I would like to do it and write besides," she said.[6] One year later, an electrical engineer named Arthur Hagen rejoined the REA after serving in the navy and setting up manufacturing plans for the United Nations in Minsk. They married in 1954, when Mamer was well into her forties. She kept her maiden name. They never built that modern house, but they did live in the beaux-arts Ontario building in Washington, DC. Fittingly, it was a cooperative.

Mamer's trusty stand mixer eventually made it into the Smithsonian. Which highlights one of the key parts of Betty Newton's job: developing recipes. Recipes were big business. Columbia Gas got tons of requests for them. Pamphlets, promotional cookbooks, magazine ads, and packages featured recipes. Columbia Gas bills always included a recipe in the "Betty Newton's Notes" section. There was "Spanish Macaroni" with chili sauce, a no-alcohol "Party Punch" with frozen lemonade, and a gelatin-based potato salad "so delicious you won't have any trouble getting your husband to peel the potatoes." Food companies could easily measure success: Jell-O created a cheesecake recipe that called for a box of instant lemon pudding and saw the flavor's sales climb by almost 50 percent. Home economists created recipes for fussy dishes for company, so the housewife could express her tamped-down creativity or impress her husband's boss with, say, a composed gelatin mold with orange yogurt, grapefruit, mandarin oranges, chopped pistachios, and an avocado. Sometimes it was real food with a sophisticated, decorative accent, albeit one in which appearance was perhaps more important than flavor, such as a waffle with sausage-speared pineapple rings on the side. Sometimes companies worked together, doing cross-promotion. The American Honey Institute's *More Favorite Honey Recipes* (which included a wedding cake with sugar-sweetened "Honey Moon Frosting") featured contributions from "nationally known" home economists representing forty companies and associations, including Sealtest, Sunkist, Ralston Purina, The Frito Company ("Fritos Prune Whip"), the Poultry and Egg National Board, and Heinz—all of course calling for their products as well as honey.' Home economists moonlighted on more frivolous fare: a home economist was credited with vetting the recipes in the 1964 bestseller *The Drinking Man's Diet*. Think martini and steak, hold the potatoes; suave actor and singer Dean Martin was photographed reading the book.

Fancy chefs and food writers like M. F. K. Fisher and James Beard couldn't stand home economics food. Asked to suggest wine pairings for a *House and Garden* brunch cookbook, the latter caustically suggested sweet Mogen David kosher wine. It's true that home economists trying to promote an ingredient could come up with some truly peculiar concoctions. Take, for instance, a General Foods "salad pie" advertised in a 1959 issue of the *Journal of Home Economics*. It encouraged cooks to fill a pie shell with a combination of lemon Jell-O, frozen mixed vegetables, and cottage cheese, top it with a layer of lemon Jell-O mixed with tomato sauce, and decorate it with swirls of the cheese-vegetable paste. A three-year-old's Play-Doh patty-cake would be more appealing. However, contrary to the negative stereotypes of fifties cooking, many home economics dishes were benign and tasty. Researchers found that women *liked* cooking, more than any other household chore. Rather than serving TV dinners as dinner, they preferred to incorporate the new convenience products into their home cooking, such as adding a can of condensed soup to a casserole. Kraft suggested in the September 1962 *Co-Ed* magazine that teens turn a box of mac and cheese into turkey tetrazzini. The popular home economics food textbooks *Meals for the Modern Family* and *Food for Better Living* had ordinary, from-scratch recipes for baked goods, gelatin (not Jell-O) salads, and dessert—hot chocolate, pudding, and the like—with few convenience ingredients. Iowa State students had a food lab assignment where they brought a critical eye to convenience, baking and comparing white cakes made traditionally, from a homemade all-purpose mix, and from a commercial mix. Would these women have had time to make a Julia Child menu without the weeknight canned-soup casseroles? Besides, despite scoffing at commercial shills, Beard was soon writing recipes for corporations, too.

The housewife buying a gas stove or a cake mix wasn't the businesswomen's only audience. Their work filtered into the classroom via teaching aids: films, charts, and posters for schools. With all the new products constantly coming onto the market, textbooks couldn't stay up to date, they argued. Manufacturers and business groups also produced lots of photos that schools and educational publishers could use. General Foods and General Mills had test kitchens dedicated to food photography. The magazine *Practical Home Economics*, itself a teacher tie-in to promote a teen home economics periodical, had pages of coupons for these aids, plus a column that reviewed edu-promotional films. *Two Steaks*, for instance, from the Iowa Beef Producers Association, was "a good example of blended fact and pleasure" that showed proper marbling, texture, and color "with unusual clarity"; the Wheat Flour Institute's *Sandwiches Please* was "a sparkling how-to-do strip, crammed with ideas and facts." In all, commercial teaching aids reached more than two and a half million teenagers in 1962—all potential future customers.[8] On top of that, students cooked and sewed on appliances donated by manufacturers, stores, and utility companies.

Clearly, the introduction of commercial props into schools posed an ethical risk. However, business home economists didn't see that. They saw themselves as educators; J. C. Penney's, for instance, required its home economists to have classroom or extension teaching experience. It was corporations' *other* promotional materials, those not made by home economists, that concerned them. And though the new university-published magazine *Illinois Teacher of Home Economics* urged caution, for the most part the field fell into line. The textbook *Exploring Home and Family Living* used photos from Armour and Company, Household Finance Corporation, American Gas Association, and *Seventeen-at-School* on one page alone. Cleveland's home economics coordinator said that schools' home-grown posters and films simply couldn't compete with the corporations' "scientific research, expert writers, outstanding photography, and plenty of advertising money." She sort-of-praised business home economists for their work: "Most of the time you send us real facts and real information presented in a form that is stimulating. But we also know that sometimes your powers are limited by the advertising people."[9] Anyway, educators didn't shy away from promoting brand names. Pinkie Thrift, the home economics chair at Louisiana's historically

Black Southern University, wrote that a reception included "cheese spread with A-1 Sauce on Ritz crackers, Betty Crocker Devil's Food Cake, and lemonade sweetened with Sucaryl."[10] Thrift herself appeared in an ad for Carnation evaporated milk in the Black press.

Another business sector continued to promote home economists as well: media. Aunt Sammy had hung up her apron, but homemaking radio soldiered on, and it finally included Black women. In the 1940s, some African American colleges, including Fisk, Howard, and Atlanta, obtained radio licenses and started homemaker and home economics programs. WBIG-Greensboro and Flemmie Kittrell's former department at Bennett College in North Carolina created *Gwen's Folks*, beamed to Black and white schools alike. In each installment, Gwen's family despaired over a household problem—say, "Bringing Up Junior," "Investing Money," or "Making Low-Income Diets"—only to be rescued by their daughter's Bennett home-ec education. Broadcasters soon recognized that the many Black women who cared for others' homes as well as their own could spend even more time listening to the radio than the full-time white housewife. Memphis's Willa Monroe became the biggest star in this community in 1949 when she started *Tan Town Homemaker's Show*, sharing recipes and society news backed by soothing music and interspersed with national ads. (The station already aired a show called *Tan Town Jamboree*.) On any given weekday morning, 40 percent of Memphis listeners, of all races, tuned in to Monroe.[11] Following in her footsteps were Alice Wyre in Atlanta; Louise Fletcher in Nashville; Carolyn Shaw in Jackson; Leola Dyson in Norfolk; R. J. Pope in Birmingham; and Delores Estelle, Sister Bessie Griffith, and Laura Lane in New Orleans. Yes, their material focused on the home. But their portrayal of

Black women as knowledgeable, dignified, modern wives and mothers caring for their own families was a huge upgrade from white radio's stereotypes. (Plus Monroe told listeners about her work with the NAACP.) They also provided a meaningful professional foothold. Martha Jean "The Queen" Steinberg, Monroe's successor as *Tan Town* host, became a legendary Detroit broadcaster. The college shows in particular offered Black women a rare opportunity to work as producers and directors as well as hosts.

The white-hosted radio homemaking programs flourished as well. Though centered in the Midwest and explicitly rural, the programs broadcast all over the country. At one point in the 1940s, *fourteen* radio homemakers broadcast live daily from Shenandoah, Iowa, alone, competing at the station over who got the most mail. Usually the winner was *Kitchen-Klatter*, which might receive more than 1,500 letters responding to a single broadcast. Despite losing her ability to walk due to complications from a 1930 car crash, Leanna Driftmier had spun *K-K* into a multigeneration, multiplatform empire with her siblings and children. The Driftmiers produced a monthly magazine, cookbooks, sewing guides, seed packets, and a line of flavoring extracts and cleaning products whose bottles featured the matriarch's face. The magazine included letters from the expanding Driftmier clan, who often appeared on the radio program, with updates on road trips, gardens, babies, and what vegetables they had canned; craft projects; light verse; letters from readers about their hobbies; advertisements for kitchen gadgets, dolls, and *K-K* products; classified ads (many featuring work-from-home opportunities such as GOOD MONEY IN WEAVING); and of course recipes "Tested in the Kitchen-Klatter Kitchen." Its circulation is debated; sources say it peaked at anywhere from 90,000 to 150,000. In the late 1950s, even the lower number meant the equivalent of at least $1.2 million per year from subscriptions alone. In 1954, Driftmier was named Iowa's Mother of the Year.[12] Five years later she retired and sold the company to her oldest daughter but continued to contribute. *Kitchen-Klatter* would become the longest-running homemaker program in the history of radio.

Magazine advertisements and radio were powerful enough, but a new medium promised the chance to reach even more potential consumers: television. That is, if home economists could navigate its requirements. Extension workers and businesswomen were already accustomed to the terror and farce of live demonstrations. Think of Mamer running a cooking contest in the middle of a field, under a tent, with no plumbing. Betty Newtons rehearsed their choreographed motions and tray setups to perfection. They suspended a mirror over the demonstration counter so women sitting at the back of the auditorium could see. If they still couldn't see, well, the Newtons maintained a nonstop patter narrating their actions. However, television posed a new set of challenges. Fortunately the farsighted and innovative Penn State professor Mary Brown Allgood, author of a guide on live demonstration, early on figured out a remarkable array of techniques for TV. In 1953 she published *Television Demonstration Techniques for Home Economists* and laid the groundwork for everyone from Julia Child to Rachael Ray.

"A good platform lecture-demonstrator who is friendly and has an iron constitution can become a good tel-a-structor just by changing a few of her techniques," Allgood wrote encouragingly.[13] Okay, so maybe Allgood wasn't great at coining a term, but she understood that television was a visual and intimate medium. That meant home economists should speak as if to an individual viewer, she wrote. To grab the viewer's attention, every episode should start with an action shot—say, a perking coffee pot. The tel-a-structor should stand aside when she opened the refrigerator so the viewer could see the food. She didn't have to talk all the time; the camera did some of the work. But in return, the camera was a hungry mistress. It demanded constant attention. Every item should face the camera: the bowl you were pouring from ("keep the forearms close to the body and twist the wrist"), the cake you were icing—"one of the most difficult problems to overcome," Allgood wrote sympathetically. "It is a hazard that must be overcome by constant awareness." The tel-a-structor should also use noise consciously to increase interest: the hissing of steam, the snapping of a crisp vegetable. She should beware of unintended noise, and pad the underside of trays and bowls with moleskin so they didn't clatter. Decades later, Castellarin criticized Food Network chefs for banging metal spoons against metal bowls.

Allgood had an amazing eye for the ways that the camera distorted visual reality, and gave tricks to compensate. On black-and-white television, dry ingredients did not show in an aluminum bowl, so the tel-a-structor should not tip the bowl toward the camera until she had added liquid. To make gas flames visible, put pulverized salt near the burner. She gave warnings: wooden spoons with extra-long handles looked awkward, and dish towels and pan holders could "take on queer shapes in the camera's eye." She was also the first home economist to note that, alas, "the television camera makes people look larger than they are." Then there was the clock. A Betty Newton demonstrating dishes for housewives in person might be able to steal an extra five minutes if a dish needed to cook longer, but the TV schedule knew no mercy. If the food didn't cook in time, the tel-a-structor just had to fake it, Allgood wrote. The tel-a-structor could say the camera didn't pick up all the brown. Or plan ahead and "have several batches of the food in different stages," she wrote. In other words, Allgood invented what television now calls the swap-out, when a TV cook slides a raw roast into an oven and slides out the cooked one next to it. Finally, Allgood knew that commerce was king. She recommended three recipes for a half-hour show, which also allowed for "plenty of time to plug the sponsors' products."

Soon homemaking was all over the airwaves, populating the medium just as it had done in radio. In 1958, more than half the television stations responding to a survey offered homemaking programs. And that was before the federal government put more than $160 million in today's dollars behind educational television in the name of national defense. Iowa State, always on the home economics cutting edge, was one of the first colleges to have its own TV station. In the spring of 1951 it created a joint home economics–journalism TV course that produced *Your Home Hour*. Hagerstown, Maryland, public schools experimented with an early version of what we now call flipped learning: a closed-circuit television program presented the lesson while the teacher offered hands-on support in class. Fargo public schools offered "Barbecue Cooking" on TV as part of their adult education program. Cleveland's Western Reserve University even offered a home-management course for credit over WEWS-TV, like online courses now. With television, home economics was using "all the resources of modern science to improve the home life," a federal education official wrote, quoting Ellen Richards.[14] Richards would have approved.

Though Betty Newton was fictional, the connection to the customer—and knowledge of what she wanted—was real. The Betty Newtons learned a lot in those home visits. They saw what equipment customers at different income levels owned and whether appliances worked as advertised. The housewife might complain, might talk about what features she wished her oven had or what would make her life better. The Newtons brought that feedback to their company. Communication went both ways. That's what made home economists so valuable to the company. Betty Newton was "not only a marketer," Sheila Castellarin said. "You were also kind of the touchstone with the customer. You represented the customer viewpoint." Utility home economists were considered among the best-informed experts on what the consumer wanted.

That expertise made them valuable to corporations, and some home economists traded on that expertise to rise in their companies from behind the scenes. Castellarin was one. Ambitious from the start, she worked as a secretary at Ohio State to fund college when her immigrant father wouldn't pay, saying women just got married anyway. After she became a Betty Newton, she signed up for extra opportunities. The company promoted her to home service director, where she oversaw the test kitchens and custom kitchen-planning team, wrote the Betty Newton demonstration scripts, tested all the new machines, and modernized the dress code, dropping the gloves and ordering sleeveless, A-line shifts from her friend Les Wexner, who founded The Limited. Eventually Castellarin became the first female vice president at Columbia Gas. She was just one of the women who used home economics to reach unprecedented power in business. The first women to break the glass ceiling into top management at several major corporations were home economists: Ellen-Ann Dunham at General Foods, Satenig St. Marie at J. C. Penney's, Karen "Lovey" Johnson at Borden, Mercedes Bates at General Mills, Mary B. Horton at Sheffield Farms. It should be noted that most did not have children and many did not marry, giving them more time to devote to their career. Even working in the trenches, the hours were so long that many Betty Newtons quit after marriage or motherhood. Castellarin lived with her parents for her entire adult life. Her mother did the housework. She had boyfriends but remained unmarried and was fine with that. It meant more time for work. "I loved what I did. I had an extremely exciting career," she said. Business home economists had to tread carefully, to manage from below until they got to the top. But these women were able to prove their value in company settings.

The postwar competing narratives of womanhood reached their full complexity in business home economics. From one point of view, business home economists were the ultimate hypocrites: career women who told other women to stay home and were untroubled by ads depicting women joyously vacuuming. Their demonstrations and visits relied on housewives being available during the day. They knew that cake mix didn't taste as good as a from-scratch cake, but they went on churning out recipes for whatever they were selling, be it skim milk, sugar substitutes, or Jell-O in the form of that hideous vegetable pie.

At the same time, the fictional Betty Newtons lived, ironically, in the real world. They sold efficiency and pragmatism, not fantasy like our modern television "shelter shows." The business home economists I've met believed their own hype; gas "*did* perform everything better," Castellarin said half a century later, long since retired. Their recipes let women get dinner on the table quickly so they could fit in everything else they wanted to do, including possibly a paid job. They also developed some useful products and processes. Home economists working for the dry-cleaning association did the work on how to care for synthetic textiles. They created the clothes-tag icons that say whether or not we should tumble-dry a garment. They're why we can now buy turkey in parts all year round. Speaking of turkey, what would Thanksgiving be without the Butterball hotline, which started with six home economists, albeit much later? Or the fried-onion-topped green bean casse-role, which Dorcas Reilly of Campbell's Soup created in 1955? The National Inventors Hall of Fame enshrined Reilly's hand-written recipe alongside Edison's lightbulb.

Home economists needed jobs. And the American Home Economics Association needed companies' money—the ads in its journal, the long rows of three hundred ten-by-ten booths at its conference, the research support: Flemmie Kittrell got some materials for her initial Liberia study from the Firestone Rubber Company, the largest private employer in the country. Some home economists say the field sold out, but they don't have an alternative solution for how home economics and home economists could have thrived as well.

The very existence of business home economists showed the extent of the illusion that veiled the cultural paeans to domesticity. If housewifery were such an unalloyed delight, would experts have had to push women so hard to do it full-time? Which brings up another question. Why didn't the American Home Economics Association resist the 1950s backlash more, or at least try to keep the careers they had established open for the next generation? As we've seen, there are several reasons. The focus on the Cold War and international careers diverted their attention from domes-tic cares. They embraced a subfield that explored interper-sonal relationships—which happened to come from men with repressive ideas about wives. The leaders were used to powering forward against sexism; perhaps they didn't realize how strongly prevailing attitudes had changed since wartime. Business home economists saw themselves as exceptional, as different from Mrs. Housewife, who (they thought) wanted to stay home and make that terrific gelatin salad. Then there was the opposite tendency among some home economists, the failure to see that they were exceptional: Mollie Stevens Smart genuinely did not realize that most married mothers didn't have as supportive a husband as she did. And home economists were human, susceptible to the patriotism that said jobs should go to the wartime heroes, and wanting life to go back to normal, whatever that meant.

At any rate, it did not take long for the leaders in the field to see that the feminine mystique was confining them and other women instead of opening up choices. Did some housewives want a different life? Did some women sense a hollowness behind the image? Because even at the height of its cultural power, home economics was being eaten from within.

CHAPTER 10

New Directions

SOVIET FIRES EARTH SATELLITE INTO SPACE, the *New York Times* shrieked on October 5, 1957. *Sputnik's* out-of-nowhere blaze across the sky shocked and terrified Americans. How did the Soviets get ahead? The answer came quickly: education. Soviet students spent a little more than half their class time on math and hard science. They began algebra in sixth grade and graduated with four years of chemistry and five years of physics under their belts. A seventh grader took zoology, biology, anatomy and physiology, physics, chemistry, geography, agriculture, technical drawing, and math as well as Russian, history, a foreign language, sexual hygiene, physical education, and shop. Pretty extraordinary. Meanwhile, only one-quarter of US graduates had taken any physics at all. Panicked *Times* headlines made the solution clear: "'Drastic' U.S. Gain Urged in Science," "Physicists Begin Campus Appeals," "Eisenhower

Given a Broad Program to Spur Science," and "Eggheads Called Hope of Country." "We need more George Washington Carvers," Vice President Nixon said, using the rocket to promote desegregation in Little Rock. The country could not succeed, he said, if it continued to give Black citizens a separate and unequal education.[1]

The mention of Carver, who had promoted home economics as well as agricultural science at Tuskegee, and who was also an accomplished textile artist and innovator in natural dyeing, might have reminded home economists of their field's history in science. Even now, the field was launching lab careers. For example, Reatha Clark King took a required year of chemistry at Clark Atlanta University for a home economics degree, entered a chemistry PhD program, and went on to do pioneering work for the space race and become a General Mills vice president and the president of Metropolitan State University.

But instead of taking the opportunity to promote the field as a scientific pursuit that the country needed in the Cold War, home economists doubled down on its focus on the family. Which meant that they needed to defend home ec's importance in the curriculum. The month after *Sputnik* launched, American Home Economics Association president Beulah Gillaspie urged the secretary of health, education, and welfare to maintain "a broad, well-balanced educational program which will preserve the human values in education." For its 1958 conference, the association seemed to choose well with the theme "Living with the Changes of the Space Age." But, instead of having a scientist or home economist give a relevant keynote, the association invited the president of the Motion Picture Association of America. The mogul proclaimed that America's most pressing problems, which must be solved before venturing into the universe, were "the sapping weakness of conformity" and the increase in chain stores. "We can explore inner space as well as outer space," he said, sounding like an early wearer of love beads.[2]

The profession's failure to capitalize on its scientific roots was not a shock, because science had been under attack in home economics all decade. Once home economics had been a way for girls to study in women-created labs that were as serious as the men's. Some prewar scientists did continue to update their textbooks, including *Household Equipment* (a core text in the Iowa State curriculum), *Household Physics*, and *Chemistry and Food Preparation*. In the fifties, however, home ec became a way to bar women from science. Advisers pressured women away from majors such as chemistry *into* home economics. Reatha Clark King chose home economics in the first place because it was considered appropriate for a girl. With pressure coming in from all sides—students who felt nervous about taking science, alumnae who said their undergraduate chemistry classes didn't help on the job, and college presidents who sought someplace to put less-serious students—home economics administrators cut hard-science prerequisites from the requirements for a home economics bachelor's degree. Those deans couldn't win either way: North Carolina Central professor Sadye Pearl Young found that students at Black colleges both shied away from the science requirements . . . and were discouraged by cuts to the science requirements.

Most damaging, the government kept cutting the budget and narrowing the scope of the Bureau of Human Nutrition and Home Economics. Politicians argued that a Department of Agriculture bureau had no business dealing with household expenses or textiles or cleaning or parenting. It was pretty obvious where the federal government should put its money instead, they said: military and space research. Fortuitously for the belt-tighteners, the bureau's stalwarts were retiring or dying, including founding director Louise Stanley, economist

Hazel Kyrk, textiles researcher Ruth O'Brien, nutritionist Hazel Stiebeling, and electrical engineer Lenore Sater Thye. The *Washington Post* eulogized Stanley not as the former highest-ranking woman in government or as a director of scientific research but as the "Nation's No. 1 Homemaker."[3] Although the American Home Economics Association temporarily helped the bureau retain some ground through nonstop fighting, the axe fell for good on the Bureau of Home Economics in the early 1960s. The closure decision silenced the biggest mouthpiece for impartial research on home economics. The government demoted it to an institute studying nutrition within the USDA's Agricultural Research Service. The strengthened connection to farming made home economics seem even less relevant as more people continued to leave the countryside.

Some home economics scientific research did still take place at corporations: the trade magazine *Gas Appliance Merchandising* depicted home economists in lab coats. However, by this time most corporate home economists worked in marketing and customer service, not labs. They were marginalized: brought in at the end of the process, not at the start, called on not to formulate the problem but to test others' solutions. Even those gaslit gals in lab coats no longer undertook primary research. The men in charge told them "to envision gas range improvements to delight the heart of any woman, and to make sure that results of research are practical from the consumer standpoint," the trade magazine reported. To adjust chemistry and develop flavors and cake mixes, companies hired "food engineers" and "food technologists"—positions whose names indicated they were jobs for men. A look through General Foods' postwar patents shows no women inventors except for one, Alina Szczesniak, who was not a home economist. Husted, about to retire from General Mills, told a group of advertising executives that they were not using home economists to their full potential.

When she retired, she found that the company paid its top salesman four times what it paid her—even though management admitted her work had produced far more revenue.[4]

University research kept going in a small way. However, while the National Science Foundation and National Institutes of Health funded some nutrition and psychology research, they did not make grants specifically for home economics. At the same time, a new wave of land-grant university presidents sought to upgrade their institutions' reputations from "cow college" to Harvard-of-the-Plains. These presidents began leaning on deans to show their discipline's intellectual heft by hiring more faculty with doctorates. Which meant they hired men. Women were not earning doctorates in home economics. From the fall of 1947 to the spring of 1961, women earned 637 PhDs in chemistry, 925 in biological sciences, more than 1,500 in social sciences—but just 331 in home economics.[5]

There were several reasons for that shortfall. While women scientists still had to brave disapproval, lab doors were no longer completely closed to them in the way that had made home economics such an appealing choice earlier on. Women could now major in the hard sciences—nutrition lab research, for one, was also done in agriculture and medicine—instead of using home economics as a way to pursue these interests. Furthermore, most people who chose home economics as a major had bought the postwar hype: they saw it as preparation for homemaking, not employment; they sought an "MRS" degree, not a bachelor's degree or a timesheet. Study after study gave unmistakable evidence that the likes of Louisan Mamer had left the building. Although the top Michigan State home economics students planned to earn graduate degrees and become married career women, the rest planned to work only until they married or had children. The overwhelming majority "held to the popular belief that 'the woman's place is in the home,'" one researcher wrote. Half the respondents to a survey of Eastern Illinois University home economics majors considered "preparation for homemaking" to be the main purpose of their college education and one-third thought that most women college graduates could best contribute to society through full-time homemaking. College faculty despaired over the seeming disinterest of their students. "One freshman told her family at Christmas, 'I'm not engaged *yet*,'" a professor complained. And if they got that MRS degree quickly, why hang around? Large numbers of home economics college majors married and dropped out before getting a degree. In 1954, US colleges had almost sixty-seven thousand home economics majors but granted only eight thousand home economics bachelor degrees. These women's decisions also meant that jobs went unfilled. The Cornell home economics career coordinator found the shortage of workers alarming. She knew of almost 750 openings for fewer than two hundred graduates, 40 percent of whom were married or about to be.[6] Paradoxically, the cultural priority on being a homemaker was causing the field that once revolutionized housekeeping to crumble from below.

Women in home economics who did continue their education past their undergraduate degree faced further barriers due to sexist attitudes and lack of financial support. The federal government funded hundreds and hundreds of graduate fellowships—but none in home economics. In 1954 there were only thirty-two graduate fellowships in home economics in the US, all funded by invested entities such as the American Home Economics Association.[7] Sometimes the gendered favoritism was explicit: for several years in the fifties, Cornell's only graduate home economics fellowship, funded by the W. T. Grant Foundation, was reserved for men. Some women married academics, intending to combine academic work and career like Mollie Stevens Smart. Yet so many dropped out of

Cornell graduate school to take jobs to "Put Hubby Through" that the graduate dean's wife began awarding them mock "PhT" degrees. Even if a woman persisted, sexist rules—allegedly set to combat nepotism—meant that only her husband would get a faculty job. Leaders in the powerful National Association of State Universities and Land-Grant Colleges cut to the chase and explicitly told home economics deans to hire more men, to whom they paid better salaries than they did women. Ironically, these men usually specialized in the new, hot area of child development.

Worse, male university leaders seized on *Sputnik* to validate their conviction that home economics wasn't intellectually valid—just training for housewives. To them, the very preponderance of women in home economics showed that the field was fluff. This was, after all, still a time when, to rebut the announcement from "a prominent educator" that most women should not go to college, an Iowa newspaper columnist blamed her fellow alumnae because "many women with college degrees do not make the contribution to their family, themselves, and their community that they should."[9] In 1950, Cornell male faculty and staff started a club that explicitly excluded home economics department employees.

It didn't help the battle for power in the academy that a number of longtime home economics collegiate leaders, like their government counterparts, were retiring or dying. Flora Rose died in 1959, followed in the next three years by Claribel Nye, Lenna Cooper, and Eleanor Roosevelt. Shortly after that, Edna Amidon retired from the federal Education Office. Deans Helen Canoyer at Cornell, Grace Henderson at Penn State, and Agnes Fay Morgan at UC Berkeley were among those with retirement looming. It marked the end of a very long era: Morgan, for instance, had worked at Berkeley since before World War I.

Home economics departments did have some successes

against the onslaught. When Hampton president Alonzo Morón tried to cut home economics in 1957, citing its dwindling enrollment and "non-collegiate character," Flemmie Kittrell, a member of the university's board of trustees, mobilized. Two years later Morón quit, claiming difficulties with the board. His successor, a friend of Kittrell's, reinvigorated the program and built a new home economics building. Its name, chosen by alumnae, was Kittrell Hall. However, the University of Chicago closed its home economics department, influential in the field's early years. Columbia University, where so many important home economists had studied and worked, demoted nutrition to subordinate status under science education. One year after Agnes Fay Morgan retired from Berkeley, the campus senate dissolved her department and kicked the subject to the lower-prestige Davis and Santa Barbara campuses. After home economists—and the American Association of University Women—protested, administrators begrudgingly allowed a small nutritional-science graduate program to remain, drawing as much from animal biochemistry as from home ec. They considered only men to run it. Less than a century after Ellen Richards entered MIT, the serious, hard-scientific element of home economics had all but disappeared.

Business home economists saw the shakiness in academia, and it troubled them. They recognized, before the rest of the field, that home economics had an image problem. It lacked prestige. When your problem is image and your professional toolkit is marketing, your solution is public relations. In the late 1940s, Husted, the hard-working woman whose jewelry was 24-karat, had General Mills print a brochure selling home economists on the need to sell themselves. "YES!" a crowd of illustrated, behatted, smiling women hollered. "Let's sell the prestige of Home

Economics! We must glamorize the course and the teachers!"[9] By the end of the fifties, they had succeeded in . . . convincing the rest of the field that they had an image problem. The American Home Economics Association hired PR reps and printed posters for members to display. When analyzing the problem, the business home economists did not dig into systemic issues. They didn't talk about patriarchy or the private disdain for housewifery that underlay its public valorization or the fight for Cold War funding. No, they thought the problem was home economists themselves. They were *dowdy*. (Well, everyone who wasn't a businesswoman. They themselves were *visions*.) Just as the family-life books told girls it was their fault if they couldn't get a date, the new public relations push put the responsibility on home economists to change their look, not their coursework.

That required constant vigilance. They should act perfect in every way. They had to be likable. "If your actions or words make people like you, your Public Relations are GOOD. If your actions or words make people dislike you, your Public Relations are BAD. It is as simple as that," the Washington State home economics association's 1958 PR booklet said. A *Farm Journal* editor told AHEA members that they were too hardened, overly serious, unemotional, sexless. She quoted an unidentified man as asking, "Why do some of them dress like policewomen?!" She asked: Couldn't the *Journal of Home Economics* ever crack a joke? When she read the field's top journal, "it's so hard to find a chuckle," she complained. "A sense of humor makes people more attractive, and people sell professions." She advised the field to get a metaphorical "new hairdo."[10] She did not mention how refreshing it was to read a journal that championed women's professional achievements, nor that when it covered "wrinkle recovery," it meant in blankets, not one's face.

However, one midwestern assistant professor had a

different and better idea about what home economists needed to do. They had to change the substance and focus on what really mattered. Beatrice Paolucci, nicknamed "Beachy" by her family, was the oldest living daughter of an Italian-immigrant coal miner turned mine owner. The Paoluccis had traditional expectations for their children. All would marry and become parents. His son, the future breadwinner, had to graduate from college, Papà Paolucci said; a secretarial course was good enough for his girls, whose husbands would support them. But Beachy contracted polio when she was too young to toddle. She sustained permanent damage to her leg that rendered her, her father thought, unmarriageable. The disability had an unexpected upside: education. "Beachy has to have the best education we can afford because she won't get married and she will need to support herself," her father decreed.[11] She graduated from Illinois Wesleyan in 1942 and became a teacher.

An excellent teacher, by all accounts. Barely five feet tall, Paolucci pushed her students to read, think for themselves, and speak out. She quit a high school teaching job over gender pay disparities—in 1951. Five years after college, she moved out of her parents' house and began living with women friends, which she would do for the rest of her life. She rejected her one serious beau, a Jewish man, in favor of her Catholic faith. Though Paolucci undeniably had physical limitations, she refused to let them constrict her life and rarely accepted help. She kept her nails polished, wore vivid though conservative St. John double-knit dresses, and zipped around in a little red sports car equipped with a hand-controlled clutch. Walking across the Michigan State campus, where she was a professor in the home economics department, she regularly tumbled to the ground, a sight that made Michigan State president John Hannah so uncomfortable that he made a bizarre request of a colleague of hers: "Get Beatrice Paolucci to use crutches.

It pains me so to see her walk." (Apparently it was easier for Hannah to administer a postwar land-grant college across the globe in Okinawa than to have an inappropriate personal conversation with a faculty member.) The colleague, astonished, couldn't think of anything to say to Hannah—and said nothing to Paolucci: "I could never do what he asked. I had come to respect her desire to be independent."[12]

In 1958, Paolucci made a speech at the American Home Economics Association conference that marked her emergence as a home economics philosopher. Borrowing space-race metaphors, she described home economics as a "satellite" orbiting the family, which was "the pivot point without which we have neither purpose nor destiny." Recently there had been "disturbances in the center of our universe," the family. For instance, families had taken on more responsibility for addressing their members' emotional needs; heads of household involved the younger members in making decisions; and they had more choices for leisure and things to buy. Thus the satellite needed to adjust its trajectory, which made for a feeling of insecurity. Paolucci thought big, and her scope was already on display. For instance, she said in the speech that homemaking should be creative—a familiar trope frequently used to try to assuage unwilling housewives' thwarted desires for careers. But she didn't mean artistic self-expression; she meant "the capacity to motivate changes in behavior and to reconstruct one's environment." (She could be a wee bit hard to grasp for anyone lacking a philosophical mindset.) And then she pinpointed an idea about the purpose of home economics that may have never been spelled out before: home economics had to help modern people be happy. That required systematic thought and attention. To attain happiness, Paolucci said, people had to define their goals and values; make intelligent decisions about how to use resources; nurture children; and maintain good relationships in the home. All those skills could and should be taught by home economists. In order to make time for them in the school day, the field should cut down on cooking and sewing, and emphasize instead "the intellectual, interpersonal, and managerial."[13]

Paolucci's words resonated. That year marked the American Home Economics Association's forty-ninth anniversary. The board put Paolucci on a task force to write a new manifesto for 1959 and beyond, for the profession's second fifty years. The good news for home economists is that they found the need for change energizing—it's what had birthed their discipline, after all. Their document *New Directions* declared, "Home economists must be among the first to anticipate and recognize change."

New Directions started by recapitulating Ellen Richards. Home economics, they quoted her as saying, stood for "the freedom of the home from the dominance of things and their due subordination to ideals" and "the simplicity in material surroundings which will most free the spirit for the more important and permanent interests of the home and of society." Never mind that most home economics jobs and classrooms at this time did not espouse simplicity in surroundings and freedom from material things, or that the committee omitted the part of Richards's original quote where she talked about the need to draw on all the resources of modern science. Then the manifesto turned to the present. The US had entered a new and radically different era, and home economics' value depended on its ability to relieve stress and increase satisfaction under modern circumstances, it said. For the 1960s, that meant strengthening families to help people achieve happy, healthy lives. Home economics would do that by addressing eight areas: family relations and child development; economic consumption; nutrition and food preparation; clothing's design, care, and "psychological and social significance"; textiles for clothing and the home; housing and home furnishings; resource management; and "art as an integral part of everyday life." Most importantly, the field would focus on the relationships among those areas "and with the total pattern which they form."[14] That ability to see the larger pattern, the task force said, was what set home economics apart from the fields that specialized in any of the eight domains. It would also become the hallmark of Paolucci's thought.

Would the big new statement convince the Men in Charge that home economics deserved respect, though? Maybe not. Dean Helen Canoyer of Cornell brought *New Directions* to the National Association of State Universities and Land-Grant Colleges' executive committee. She thought they'd be pleased. Instead, a university president—reportedly Eric Walker of Penn State, who thought the point of coeducation was to attract women students who would in turn attract men—scornfully tossed the booklet on the table, rejecting the statement from the field unread. He demanded an investigation into the future of home economics education at land-grant universities. His clear and ominous implication was that it did not have one.

In retrospect, it's hard to see anything that home economists could have done to prove their value and hold on to their positions against men who were simply determined not to respect or include them. Home economists had always worked within the system, bending it to their advantage. They had not risen up in revolt in 1890 to tell women to burn their brooms. Instead they had whittled away at drudgery from all sides, with differing amounts of success. They had brought science into the home to increase efficiency; they had advocated for boys to learn home economics; they had turned domestic tasks into an array of careers. And they had wielded the broom as a weapon to advocate for women. The core problem is that while the founding women home economists could reinvent caring for the home as a way to change the world and their own lives, could flip oppression into empowerment, the men in power didn't have to buy it. The university deans and presidents could just as easily say that girls should learn housekeeping because they were meant to be housewives, emphasizing that the men were still in charge of everything important. Home economists felt anxious. They believed their work was urgent, but also that they weren't making progress. Home ec, they all knew, needed to do more.

CHAPTER 11

New Homemakers
Build the Future

I n the field's early days, home economists joined other social reformers in ameliorating inner-city ills. As consumer activists, they aimed to protect working-class and poor urbanites from unscrupulous merchants selling shoddy fabric and clothes, bacteria-ridden meat from dirty slaughterhouses, and flour whitened with lead. Simultaneously, home economists addressed grindingly poor farm families who drudged away without running water or electricity. That all felt a very long time in the past to home economists of the 1950s, who seemed to live in an eternal middle class. When sociologist Michael Harrington published his exposé *The Other America* in 1962, they were as shocked as anyone to learn of the extent of deprivation in the booming postwar US—especially after they had spent so long working on nutrition. They were chagrined to realize their failure. Through President Lyndon B. Johnson's

War on Poverty program, which he launched in 1964, home economics rediscovered its Progressive Era roots, reemerged in cities, and recharged its social conscience.

Soon home economists were partnering with welfare agencies and studying the low-income consumer. The federal extension service issued new pamphlets and guides, such as a series of nutrition lessons that included instructions on adapting the material for low-income families—for one, home economists should highlight what was nutritious in their clients' existing meal plans, and "point out how easy it is to have a balanced diet by adding to these foods."[1] In 1965 alone, the American Home Economics Association held about thirty regional workshops on working with poor families and funded fellowships for home economics students to study cities. Opportunities opened up: home economists could serve in the new Community Action agencies or staff the women's Job Corps; and Detroit teachers gave night classes in homemaking to low-income mothers, with the goal of building a better relationship with those families.

If home economists' War on Poverty activities evoked the 1910s, one element had changed. Always before, the field had preached that poor families should adopt their middle-class norms. For the first time, they recognized that this approach simply didn't work—and maybe that their ways weren't always superior. For instance, home economists had told low-income homemakers how to shop. But Kansas State professors found in a study that they were already smart shoppers. In fact, homemakers found the items on their grocery lists for 7 percent cheaper than a set of home-ec college students did. Moreover, when asked to improve the homemakers' food choices, the students made wrongheaded suggestions such as replacing hot dogs and hamburgers with liver, and cutting out nutritional nonessentials such as "dried red pepper, candy bars, hot sauce, coffee," and even ketchup—the items that made life worth living or, as the professors professorially put it, that "may have been the ones that added variety and excitement to their menus."[2] Yes, the homemakers could benefit from nutrition information, the researchers concluded. But the students needed to understand the community before they could help.

Also unlike the old days, the lines between helper and helped could blur. The field seemed to be learning. "These people are Mr., Miss, or Mrs. Anybody, U.S.A.; and you and I may very well say: 'There but for the grace of God, go I,'" a New Jersey welfare-department home economist wrote. "Being dependent can be a real, unavoidable, and valid situation brought about by circumstances beyond one's ability to control." New York extension offices trained low-income women to serve as homemaking aides in their own neighborhoods, sharing what they had learned with their communities. Qualifications were basic: they had to want the job, need the money, and make it through the training. The project went well due to the aides' dedication to and understanding for their struggling neighbors and the aides' ability to see the funny side of a situation. One wrote about a mother whose son was wounded in Vietnam, "She doesn't like housework. Well, a lot of people don't like housework, that's nothing against her, but otherwise she is trying." Another aide helped a woman get a new prosthetic leg and clothes for her children, and made a meal plan to turn government surplus ingredients into dishes "that I know that my people love to eat and that their money will be able to reach also, rather than to have them to write out a meal budget . . . of foods that they're not used to eating and would be completely unwanted." Moreover, whereas middle-class professionals might be seen as interfering and judgmental when they gave advice, the aides seemed to be able to give opinions without giving offense. One wrote of a client, "She is a very religious person and she believes solely in leaving things in God's hands . . . and this I have talked to her about and told her not to do."[3]

Home economists even set the terms of poverty itself. The federal poverty line, which determined eligibility for Johnson's Great Society programs, came from Mollie Orshansky, a statistician who spent more than a decade designing diets for low-income families at the Bureau of Home Economics before joining the Social Security Administration. Orshansky combined her meal-planning and mathematical expertise to calculate the standard of poverty. First she figured out how much it cost for a family of two adults and two children to buy food for a "low-cost" diet and a bare-subsistence "economy" diet. It totaled $3.60 and $2.80 per day in the early 1960s, or $30.25 and $23.53 in 2020. An Agricultural Department survey showed that families spent one-third of their income on food, so she tripled the food cost to get the bare-minimum income needed to live in America. When compared against actual income, the results were sobering. One-quarter of US families with children could not afford the low-cost diet and 18 percent could not afford the economy plan.[4]

To this day, many people criticize the federal poverty levels for severely underestimating the cost of living. Orshansky, a Jewish woman from the South Bronx whose Ukrainian parents barely spoke English, knew her index was imperfect. From the start, she said the calculation was "crude," and warned that it worked only if a family had a stay-at-home mother who was an excellent shopper and cook, and allowed for no meals out and no treats whatsoever. "The average family . . . is likely to spend considerably more," she wrote in the paper introducing the calculation. She was not responsible for the Johnson administration's decision to base the poverty guideline not on the "low-cost" diet but on the bare-subsistence "economy" diet, though one could argue that, given the inevitable tendency to seek a cheaper way to do things, perhaps she should not have published the economy figure at all. Nor was she responsible for the fact that poverty administrators held on to the measure for decades through an enormous number of societal and economic changes. Orshansky herself tried to direct the focus to social justice. She emphasized the fact that nonwhite families were disproportionately and persistently poor, that single mothers lacked societal support, and that racism and other structural factors made it hard for poor children to become middle-income adults. She called for interventions to break the race/poverty cycle. As for the poverty line, "the best that can be said of the measure," she later wrote, "is that at a time when it seemed useful, it was there."[5]

And home economists participated in Head Start, President Johnson's new preschool program. Finally, family-life and child-development experts would make a contribution beyond lecturing teenagers on dating mores. Head Start might not have happened without home economists. Flemmie Kittrell conducted some of its pilot studies highlighting nutritional deprivation in cities, and ran a Head Start pilot nursery school for low-income three-year-olds. Mollie and Russell Smart served as consultants, as did Kittrell and Sue Sadow, fresh off her Peace Corps service in Sierra Leone. Johnson's Head Start director knew how important home economists were: he reached out to the American Home Economics Association before the president publicized the program. The association rapidly endorsed Head Start and shot off a memo to its state chapters urging them to get involved. The Smarts wrote a letter to association members as well, giving a more pointed argument. Head Start could solve the field's "rather extensive search for purpose and direction," they wrote. "Here is a chance to act, to reach out, to give and grow, to re-integrate. Let's not lose it. If home economists miss this boat, they may never catch another one like it." That boat, the Smarts noted, held twenty thousand new jobs. To qualify for those jobs, the Smarts suggested that home economists take advantage of a rapid-certification option for preschool teachers. Johnson granted $112 million to more than 9,500 childcare centers in the first summer alone for an eight-week program, funding jobs for an estimated 41,000 experts and 47,000 low-income adults.[6]

Home economists listened. From the start, at least fifty college home economics departments trained Head Start childcare workers. The University of Wisconsin at Stevens Point applied to run a Head Start summer session out of its home-management house, with a college student and his wife living on the premises to provide a familial atmosphere. The University of Wisconsin–Madison created a national poverty research center, with federal funding, that included home economics researchers. Kittrell trained two thousand Head Start workers at Howard, and silenced an unproductive early planning meeting by reminding attendees who they were working for by reciting, from memory, the Langston Hughes poem "Mother to Son": "'Life for me ain't been no crystal stair,'" she said.[7] It certainly hadn't, and the white home economics establishment had blame to bear for that, as they were just beginning to recognize.

Black women were so marginalized in the home economics field that white students who went to inner cities for those AHEA poverty fellowships were surprised to find professionals already there. Throughout the 1950s, as the US Supreme Court officially outlawed racial exclusion in schools, Emmett Till was murdered, and Rev. Martin Luther King Jr. led a bus boycott, home economics continued to segregate. The *Journal of Home Economics* ran just a handful of articles by Black home economists. Several of those called for antiracism to become part of home economics, saying that children learned prejudice at home. In 1951, Howard graduate Alice M. Jefferson became the first African American to be featured on the cover of a major home economics publication, *What's New in Home Economics*, an appearance that *Jet*, a magazine for Black readers, highlighted proudly. Although the national association had established at-large memberships, southern Black professionals still could not join their state affiliates. When a handful of home economists requested membership in the South Carolina group in 1949, its president Elizabeth Watson, perturbed, asked her counterparts around the region for advice. The Alabama and Arkansas directors said they had never faced the issue. The directors in Georgia, Florida, Tennessee, and North Carolina, however, reassured Watson that it was perfectly fine to turn African American women away. She wouldn't even have to say it to their faces: the national American Home Economics Association office "would be very glad to handle the affair without any embarrassment towards the Southern State Association," the Florida president wrote. She herself told African American applicants to send their dues to the national organization, which deposited the national portion and returned the rest "stating that there is no State association for negroes in our State." Not only did Watson follow the Florida president's advice but she kicked out two African American South Carolina members she had discovered during her research.[0] Presumably they had not stated their race in their membership applications.

African American home economists were underemployed. Almost one of five home economics administrators at Black colleges said they had trouble finding jobs for their graduates, and half said the jobs they did find were unsatisfactory. Professor Sadye Pearl Young found lack of jobs was the number-one reason home economics enrollment at Black universities was falling—steeply, in some cases: by 47 percent at Tuskegee; 61 percent at Prairie View; 72 percent at Florida A&M; 79 percent at Pine Bluff.[9]

If *Brown v. Board of Education* had no practical impact on many southern school districts, it had even less on after-school clubs. New Homemakers of America remained a separate, African American organization. 4-H, including its home economics activities, was also segregated in the South. Year in and year out, the Black press persistently criticized 4-H, and just as persistently the federal agriculture department passed the buck, claiming it had no power over states' decisions. "Racial segregation will continue in the 4-H club program for rural youths until the southern states decide to end it," the program's federal supervisor told Baltimore's *Afro-American* newspaper in 1956.[10] Also, the federal department did not use the power it did have. All through the 1950s, 4-H never gave its national scholarship to an African American student, nor did any attend the national 4-H camp.[11]

But even so, home economics flourished in Black communities. Glamorous Freda DeKnight had her popular "Date with a Dish" food column and ran fashion shows for the Black monthly *Ebony*. (Except to note the reprint of her cookbook, which it did not review, the *Journal of Home Economics* never mentioned DeKnight until a decade after her death, when the association established a communications fellowship for Black students in her memory.) New Homemakers achievement degrees—Featherweight, Apprentice, and Advanced Homemaker—required work and garnered recognition. The program fostered a sense of responsibility to one's community. When founding adviser Marie Clapp Moffitt surveyed former New Homemaker student officials years later, everyone who responded said they were successful in their careers. All had graduated from high school, three-quarters from college, and half from graduate school.[12] Gladys Gary Vaughn remembered fondly how she and her fellow New Homemakers went to the Florida state fair on the one day African Americans were allowed to go; they rode on the Ferris wheel, ate candy apples, and held hands with their boyfriends. Vaughn grew up in central Florida in the 1950s as the child of a farmer and a teacher, and chose to study home economics when she went to the historically Black university Florida A&M. Because predominantly white colleges did not hire African American professors, Black colleges had top-notch faculty—experts like Kittrell, who had fought their way summer after summer to earn doctorates from major land-grant universities when the nearer state college wouldn't admit them. Then they returned to teach at Black colleges, which the federal government had starved of research funding. The northern universities were complicit in that racism, accepting reimbursement from southern states for educating African Americans, although rarely hiring Black faculty. Among Vaughn's professors were legends, and they urged her to go to graduate school. First she taught for a few years in her hometown of Ocala. In the evening she visited New Homemakers at their residences, chauffeured by her mother—the young teacher didn't have a driver's license. Vaughn sat with the parents and explained what the girls were working on, then examined the project the student had done to improve her home, taking notes in a spiral-bound notebook. The family always offered food and she always had to eat, no matter how many stops she was making. In 1966, Vaughn took her professors' advice and went to Iowa State to get a master's degree in educational leadership under a Johnson administration program to train future principals. Of twenty scholarship recipients, only two were women, and Vaughn the only African American. She almost left after white fraternity brothers hurled racial epithets at her—she did not come to Iowa State to be disrespected—but the home economics chair and the lone

Black home ec professor together convinced her to stay. She earned her master's, then moved with her husband and began teaching at North Carolina Central. Granted two years' leave to earn a doctorate, she earned a doctorate in two years.

June 1963 was a dramatic month in America. The segregationist governor of Alabama physically blocked three Black students from registering at the state university as a federal court had mandated; President Kennedy sent the National Guard to Alabama to support the Black students, then made his first speech explicitly condemning segregation; and civil rights leader Medgar Evers was assassinated. At the month's end, the American Home Economics Association finally took its own stand against segregation, passing a resolution to desegregate the organization at all levels and "scrutinize" its practices. A profession that promoted cross-cultural understanding and personal development had no business supporting discrimination, the AHEA said. A few days later, association president Florence Low joined the president's National Women's Committee on Civil Rights and promised to "throw open the membership of all women's organizations to all races."[13]

Even then, however, the Future and New Homemakers of America remained as they were. Future Homemakers chapters in thirteen southern states refused to let African American students join. (For that matter, even in Pennsylvania, where Future Homemakers was purportedly integrated, a high school club barred an African American student named Barbara Smith due to her race; she started her own homemaking club and named herself president, and grew up to be the model and restaurateur B. Smith.) The Future and New Homemakers had separate advisory boards and separate conferences. They shared a central office, a small national staff, and a national work program and conference theme—the two boards met together annually

to plan those activities. President Kennedy; Health, Education, and Welfare secretary Anthony Celebrezze; and education commissioner Francis Keppel thought it was high time
to desegregate Future Homemakers, as well as Future Farmers
and 4-H. In July 1963, Keppel called a meeting of the leaders of
the Future Homemakers and Farmers and told them to prohibit
whites-only groups from affiliating with the national organization. That effort did not succeed: the assistant commissioner
for vocational and technical education shot down the proposal,
saying the push for integration had to come from the bottom
up. After Kennedy's death, however, the Civil Rights Act gave
Keppel the cudgel he needed. It let the government withhold
funding from noncompliant entities. (The federal government
was still providing money to Future and New Homemakers.)
Now integration happened without delay. In September 1964,
Keppel wrote federal home economics education director Edna
Amidon, who still oversaw the homemaker organizations she
had helped found, that the groups would have to merge on July
1, 1965. More than seventy-eight thousand New Homemakers
would be folded into FHA.[11]

In the end, the move that some people had resisted for so
long happened quietly. New education commissioner A. W.
Ford told the Associated Press two days before the merger that
there had been no controversy and that he did not expect any.
Maybe that's because the leaders proceeded so quietly that you
might think they were sweeping the past under the rug. The
Journal of Home Economics never announced the merger, nor did
the North Carolina Future Homemakers magazine. The New
Homemakers did not announce their reorganization into the
Future Homemakers either. "Remember, early planning is the
number one rule!" the New Homemakers magazine *Chatter Box*
announced in the spring 1965 issue, which showed no sign

of being its last. The Virginia New Homemakers held one last state conference. It was called "New Homemakers Build the Future."[15]

The most prominent Black home economist of the time was undoubtedly Flemmie Kittrell, and it is difficult to gauge her role in the civil rights movement. The conventional wisdom says she worked behind the scenes. "I never knew her to talk about race relations, but her whole life was a constant flow of *doing* something about them—and not just one variety of people but for all people all over the world," her minister, the Reverend Kathryn Moore, said at her funeral. There have been people who thought Kittrell was too quiet on civil rights, presumably to stay in the government's good graces so it and its favored foundations would continue to fund her work abroad. Some of her political opinions she kept to herself for decades, such as her distaste for the US occupation of Japan. When international audiences asked her about race relations, even when they asked about Little Rock, she expressed optimism. "The inexorable trend is one of progress," she said. Americans didn't need violent uprisings, she said, because "we have a constitution and a way of working things out." Gladys Gary Vaughn believed that Kittrell didn't have to make statements to exemplify Black empowerment: her presence and work were inherently political. She studied southern Black diets and did nutritional analyses of collards and okra, giving dignity to Black communities. If Kittrell mostly put her head down and got her work done, Vaughn said in 2019, when it's a Black woman doing it, "putting your head down and getting your work done scares a heck of a lot of people."[16]

That said, sometimes Kittrell did engage overtly in politics. As a longtime member of the pacifist, predominantly white Women's International League for Peace and Freedom, she insisted in 1958 that their next speakers in Alabama be "a Negro and White woman . . . together"—and then *was* that "Negro," speaking to a thousand students and meeting with Martin Luther King Jr. and Coretta Scott King.[1] During a Methodist conference in 1961, she called ahead to a Maryland diner to make sure it would serve an integrated group. When she arrived with her colleagues, they were refused service anyway. The group sat for the lunch hour as a protest and gave their lunch money to the Congress of Racial Equality. Most sensitively, on a 1967 trip to Zambia, Kittrell boarded a chartered plane to fly into what is now Namibia, ostensibly to conduct a study. In reality, she and her companions, who included the leader of CORE, were conducting a fly-in protest against South Africa's refusal to withdraw from the territory as per United Nations order. As they crossed the Namibian border South African officials' voices boomed over the radio warning that they would be imprisoned if they landed, and possibly killed. They remained in flight until the plane ran so low on fuel that they had to turn back.

Kittrell also visited South Africa that year under the protection of the United States Information Service and the US ambassador to the country. Her introduction to apartheid came before the plane landed in Johannesburg: a white Afrikaner with whom she had been chatting offered to take her bag down but said he would leave it at her feet "for fear that they will identify me with you." Driving around with whites, Kittrell was tailed by the police until they saw the car's American plates. Embassy staff tried to make Kittrell use the building's backdoor; she refused. She visited Bantu miners in a township, who cheered to see a Black woman treated as a dignitary. She promised to tell Americans about their living conditions. At Kittrell's departure, the Afrikaner escorts thanked her for her "discipline," gave her a gift, and said they had enjoyed her visit and hoped she had enjoyed it as well. Kittrell hesitated. She knew she could not cause controversy; nor could she bear to stay silent and let them comfort themselves with the delusion that she accepted their racism. "Well, gentlemen, thank you very much for your courtesy in presenting me this gift, but you know, I have never been so unhappy as I am now, to think that you think I enjoyed my stay in South Africa," she said quietly. "This is the saddest day of my life."[18]

The American Home Economics Association took some steps to put civil rights forward. They had former Urban Renewal commissioner William Slayton address the 1968 conference. "White middle-class America has, in the main, refused to accept minorities into full partnership. This is the basic cause of Negro unrest," he said. "Economic improvement will do much to improve American society, but only with the elimination of discrimination shall we have a truly democratic society."[19] An association task force reviewed the 1968 Kerner Commission report detailing racism in America and concluded that it was required reading for home economists. The task force further recommended that the field overhaul curricula to support urban families; push for community improvement, low-rent housing programs, welfare, and fair lending; support and train home economists for Head Start; and eliminate discrimination in the field.

It wasn't at all clear, however, that the gestures toward inclusion would turn the tide of African American women choosing not to study home economics. Civil rights activism and the new national focus on alleviating poverty, often in communities of color, opened up professional opportunities in social services, politics, and law for young Black women who might otherwise have routed their ambitions through home economics. Spelman, the prestigious Black women's college, dropped home economics in the early 1970s. When a white General Mills test-kitchen supervisor began recruiting people of color in the mid-1970s, she found them resistant: cooking felt like a menial job their grandmothers would have been forced to take. It was starting to look like home economics might need Black and brown women more than they needed it.

The Future Homemakers and Future Farmers mergers did not end inequality in the youth organizations. Black women and girls did not gain the leadership positions in integrated groups that they had held in segregated ones. For years, African American girls received inconsequential, token leadership positions in Future Homemakers, such as secretary or song leader, founding advisory board member Marie Moffitt found. Gladys Gary Vaughn rued the loss of the bond between the school and families that New Homemakers teachers like herself had established: white Future Homemaker advisers in the South, she said, did not visit Black homes. And the history of the African American youth groups has been virtually erased. As part of the merger between the Future and New Farmers, states were told to destroy New Farmers of America records, leaving just one copy in the national office, according to historian Dexter Wakefield. Wakefield wrote his dissertation on New Farmers, using documents from the small NFA archive and interviews with surviving members and teachers, and said that based on his research, he was "pretty confident" that the New Homemakers state organizations were told to destroy their records as well. It seems plausible, because New Homemakers has been all but forgotten. There is no separate New Homemakers archive; the organization formerly known as Future Homemakers has not fully cataloged its papers. Only one library owns a set of *Chatter Box* magazine. Former New Farmer Gary Moore told Wakefield he considered the merger a federal-government-mandated takeover by whites.[20] Furthermore,

Future Homemakers did not incorporate New Homemakers' emblems or justice-flavored creed. The integrated organization uses the original Future Homemakers creed to this day, and as of this writing, its online list of national officers dating back to 1945 did not include New Homemakers.

Black home economists would continue to agitate for justice. In 1970 in Mississippi, African American agriculture and home economics extension workers sued the state for discrimination because—despite the purported integration—white employees retained their former titles as county agents and extension home economists while all the Black agents were demoted to assistant or associate status. Over the five years following integration, the agency appointed eighty-seven people to top-level agent and home economist jobs. All of them were white. The Black plaintiffs won their case.[21]

CHAPTER 12

Beyond Stitching and Stirring

Many of home ec's leaders agreed with Beatrice Paolucci that the field was too focused on skills. Skills that seemed dull, old-fashioned, and simple, at that. The field had to get beyond "stitching and stirring," as they were starting to call the stereotype. "I'm trying to divorce cooking from the concept of home economics," Flemmie Kittrell told the *Christian Science Monitor* in 1964. "Of course we have to cook, but this can be picked up by anyone who can read a recipe." Echoing Ellen Richards and Caroline Hunt, Kittrell said, "With technology freeing women, they have more time to enjoy the arts and make a contribution to the community." Penn State home economics department chair Marjorie East agreed. She thought that classes should stop requiring sewing. Most grown women didn't want to spend time making clothes—many had jobs out in the world—and home economists should support that.

"We do not encourage each family to make its own butter, nor weave its own cloth," she wrote. "Time is the most valuable resource for most families today. Families use money to buy time. They gladly pay for partly processed foods, for automatic washing machines, and for ready-to-wear clothes. We do not want to go backwards and teach our students to spend a lot of their time to save a little bit of money—maybe."[1]

As East's and Kittrell's comments illustrate, in the 1960s, home economists regained their ability to live ahead of the curve. Powered by the field's fiftieth anniversary, the *New Directions* statement, and political events, the field unearthed its roots in social work and took its first steps into the computer era. A businesswoman created a magazine, *Forum*, that promoted a more expansive vision of what home economics could do in the world. An article in the 1966 *Illinois Teacher of Home Economics* suggested "micro-vacations" for the very busy—not only socially productive activities such as gardening, woodworking, playing music, and connecting with one's family and friends, but delightfully useless breaks. To relax, various members of the University of Illinois education department said they liked to slide down the banister, "arrange to be alone in absolute silence for an hour," "daydream about the me that could have been," watch the dishwasher scrub the dishes, call Information in another part of the country to hear the operator's accent, write an angry poem dedicated a two-year-old neighbor, and my favorite, "observe selection of groceries in baskets at the super-market and speculate about the situations in which they might be used."[2]

Home ec even helped launch people into space.

It sounded like an ordinary hearty breakfast: two poached eggs, filet mignon, toast with jelly, OJ, and decaf. Except that

Colonel John Glenn was eating it at 2:23 a.m. on January 27, 1962, before putting on a space suit and crawling feet-first into the *Friendship 7* space capsule, ready to orbit the globe. At about 10:30 a.m., stymied by clouds and probably still full, Glenn climbed back out of the capsule. "Well," he shrugged, "back to Bea's diet."[3] Bea was Bea Finkelstein of the US Air Force, cat-eyed-glasses-wearing dietitian to the stars. Literally. She had engineered Glenn's breakfast to meet the physical demands of spaceflight.

We mock space food today as freeze-dried ice cream and Tang. But as the US raced to catch up with *Sputnik*, space food emerged as a fascinating engineering problem complicated by human nature. Military dietitians had already learned that rations had to taste good or people would just stop eating, putting missions at risk. Through research, Finkelstein quickly found that isolation and seclusion made people eat differently. When men were locked up together, they became everything from fixated on food to territorial to not hungry at all. Eating alone in the dark, as one might in a single-person space capsule, ham on rye tasted, literally, like chicken on white. Then there were physiological unknowns: Would digestion work properly in weightlessness? Would astronauts get space-sick? How much of various nutrients, to the microgram, did humans need? Finally, there were the daunting engineering issues of zero gravity, waste, and the cost of every ounce of weight in the capsule. A crumb could be deadly: floating around, it could easily clog an important apparatus such as the astronaut's breathing system.

Nor was the challenge confined to the time in space. Astronauts would have to be quarantined afterward so they could be observed—there might be space germs; no one knew for sure. Special diets had to start three days before takeoff, prepared to clinically antibacterial standards, for it would be awful if an astronaut got food poisoning in space. That diet also had to be what was delicately called "low-residue," because early space suits left no room for defecation. An astronaut got tea or coffee at that last breakfast only if it did not, shall we say, pop his escape hatch. (Presumably that's why Glenn drank decaf.) The space program knew that danger, alas, from experience. Shortly before starting a delayed 1957 test in a balloon capsule, a frustrated Lieutenant Colonel David Simons grabbed "2 cups of machine-vended reconstituted thin potato soup" and, trapped in his suit, was wracked with nearly intolerable intestinal pains. "Like a man with a gold nugget and a hot penny in his hand, I couldn't let go of one without dropping the other," he wrote.[4]

So Finkelstein concocted high-protein slurries in her rose-pink kitchen lab at the air force research headquarters in Dayton, Ohio, trying the flavors on volunteers. "Surprisingly, by the end of a very few days, most of the men grew to like strange blends of strained meat and concentrated ice cream," a journalist wrote. "Some of the subjects stated that they had never felt better in their lives." Then Finkelstein began testing menus on the astronauts: oregano-seasoned pea purée, tomato blended with rosemary and thyme, baked chicken breast. The astronauts sat in their civvies—colorful printed short-sleeved shirts—at her Formica table at Cape Canaveral, sipping from glasses and eating off trays with silverware as Finkelstein looked on in her white lab coat, beaming. They called the lab "Bea's Diner." One of the astronauts' wives complained that her husband now talked incessantly not about Mom's cooking but about "the way Bea fixes it."[5]

On February 20, Glenn took flight. Twenty minutes in, orbiting far over Nigeria, he snacked on applesauce, squeezing it into his mouth from a toothpaste-style metal tube through a valve in his helmet. He also may have eaten beef with vegetables in seasoned baby food purée form, or munched a malt tablet; reports vary. Glenn wasn't hungry—what adult could be for tube food—but the nutrition team wanted to see what happened mechanically when people ate in space. Glenn had no problems eating. "As long as the food is solid you can hold onto it and can get it into your mouth, and from that point on there appears to be no problem. It's all positive action. Your tongue forces it back in the throat and you swallow normally and it's all a positive displacement machine all the way through," he told reporters afterward.[6] From there, Finkelstein made rapid progress. Later that same year, astronaut Wally Schirra not only squoodged tube food but consumed juice, coffee, and brownie bites. Finkelstein encapsulated the baked goods in hydroxy-propyl methyl cellulose skins and wrapped them in polyethylene so they would remain unspoiled and crumb-free for up to six months.

The US Army produced two major space-food nutrition-ists. Mary Klicka got her start designing rations, and eventually earned the army's highest civil-service award. Doris Calloway, a divorced mother of two, discovered that broccoli helped guard against cancer; for that work, the army named her Man of the Year in 1959. She displayed the plaque proudly, amused by its gendered terminology, for the rest of her career. Calloway transitioned into space-focused work at Menlo Park, where she freeze-dried orange juice and developed food packaging. However, her real specialty was precise measurement of exactly what nutrients people needed, undertaken in a famous series of nutrition studies in a UC Berkeley campus apartment called the "Penthouse," after she became a nutrition professor there. (In its past life, the Penthouse had been the home management apartment.) Because every pound cost pennies, NASA could afford to send up only a narrow range of foods. They had to satisfy all the astronauts' nutritional needs, and "if we have forgotten anything, we don't have a chance to go back and add it, or for them to get out somewhere en route and pick it up on their own," Calloway told a reporter in Boston's *Science Reporter*, one of the first science TV shows, which interviewed Klicka and her in their labs.[7]

To create workable, nourishing rations that astronauts would actually eat, Klicka, Calloway, and Finkelstein left no technique unturned, including freeze-drying; irradiation with gamma rays, electrons, or X-rays; freezing; "spray-drying, drum-drying, vacuum-drying, hot-air-drying, and foam-mat-drying"; compression; and flexible pouch packaging, which was lighter and more compressible than cans. These advances soon made it to supermarket shelves as corporations capitalized on both the research and the glory that reflected off the space program like the sun's rays off the moon. Freeze-drying created the now-familiar dried mixes for things like instant mashed potatoes, packaged soup, noodle casserole, and instant nonfat milk. Flour and tropical fruit began to be irradiated. Pouches became commercial boil-in-a-bag rice and, way down the line, Capri Sun and toddler food dispensers. (It just so happened that some initial freeze-drying research was done by a graduate student named Karen Johnson, who later oversaw the Pillsbury Doughboy mascot before becoming Borden's first woman vice president.) When Stouffer's provided frozen dishes for the *Apollo 11* post-splashdown quarantine period, it capitalized on the contract with an ad campaign that proclaimed, "Everyone who's been to the moon is eating Stouffer's." The corporation bragged in a press release that "ease of preparation, purity, quality and variety were the main reasons frozen convenience foods were selected. . . . The scientists looking for signs of alien organisms have demanded assurance that diet will cause no illness that might mistakenly be attributed to hostile bacteria."[8] Black newspapers picked up the Stouffer's story as well, writing about African American recipe developer Julie Stewart and quality-control supervisor Sara Thompson.

The most famous space food, incidentally, came from neither NASA nor a rations-making home economist. A male chemist, William A. Mitchell, developed an orange-flavored, vitamin-packed beverage powder from flavoring, vitamins, sweetener, and consistency agents for General Foods in the late 1950s as a convenience product for busy moms—Tang. When mothers didn't buy it, General Foods, which already provided some military food, sold the powder to NASA, which packaged it in a vacuum-sealed pouch to be injected with water and slurped. Mitchell later invented quick-set Jell-O, Cool Whip, and Pop Rocks. Truly, an age of discovery had opened. "Man's compelling urge to explore and develop the unknown has been whetted. What lies ahead?" Finkelstein asked.[9]

Military food wasn't the only World War II product getting a high-gloss makeover. A humble magazine was, too. For more than fifteen years after World War II, J. C. Penney's continued *Fashions and Fabrics* as a focused publication for home economics teachers. It promoted Penney's patterns and cloth by teaching sewing. That was pretty much it. Its educational director Edna Bryte Bishop specialized in fit—today's sewing blogs would love her. If a skirt hiked up in front, the cause was "heavy figure below waistline due to large hips or abdomen," she wrote in the magazine.[10] The quick fix was to let out the side seams; next time the sewer should redraw the lower hem. When Penney's home economics coordinator Mary Omen visited stores to teach the Bishop method, she was mobbed. Still, undeniably no one could call the magazine forward thinking. Bishop did not give patterns for trousers. In all those years, the magazine depicted one nonwhite person. Only when Omen retired in 1959 did *Fashions and Fabrics* catch up with the times enough even to profile business home economists at work—at the magazine's few advertisers, of course.

At the same time, Penney's hired Satenig Sahjian St. Marie. Born in 1927 in Massachusetts, walking one and a half miles to and from school every day, St. Marie dreamed of having a career and doing something big. She went to the private women's college Simmons, because that was the alma mater of the only college student in her neighborhood. She then worked as an extension home economist before Penney's hired her in 1959, the same year she earned a master's degree from Columbia and married a dentist. Where Omen and Bishop looked mumsy, St. Marie, a dark-haired woman with an aquiline nose, was modern. A 1961 photo shows her presenting before a racially integrated audience of Detroit teachers, wearing a black sheath dress with elbow sleeves, two strands of graduated beads, and a pouf of a hat. And from the moment she took over *Fashions and Fabrics* in 1963, everything at Penney's home economics changed.

St. Marie was a managerial genius and a business visionary who made the company a leader in home economics. She didn't just put out a magazine: she created a complete, cohesive teacher-education program. The twice-annual *Fashions and Fabrics* had a set of matching classroom aids—games and activities—plus a showcase event that her team presented live to home economics teachers in major markets. The tools built on each other, year after year. The 1965 classroom kit "How to Furnish a First Home" included large riveted oak-tag paper dolls—think Flat Stanley—representing several couples, in an envelope that looked like a house. The following year's "Trends in Home Furnishings" added floor plans for those imaginary couples and pictures of furniture for students to arrange. The 1967 "Financing a New Partnership" kit added a new household of two single roommates, Liz and Barbara, and taught students to budget via a Game of Life–like series of event cards and surprises.

"Sat" had sharp elbows. She was tactful, and she cared about her team of young women employees, but she wasn't warm.[11] How could she be, when she had to be so carefully and perfectly professional? Every morning she left her split-level ranch home in Westport and boarded the train for her ninety-minute commute, dressed in hat and gloves, one of the few women on the 6:23 a.m. train to New York. She gritted her teeth when, in 1962, a twenty-two-year-old boy leapfrogged over her, a thirty-five-year-old educational consultant, to run the Penney's consumer services department. That was a turning point. "I decided to let him sink or swim on his own with only a minimum of help from me, and I prayed hard for a miracle," she said.[12] The miracle happened. Six months later the kid was called up for military service, and St. Marie became the boss. No new title at this time and no raise, but she got to run the show.

To support her vision, St. Marie looped in the professional groups. Already past president of the Connecticut Home Economics Association, she arranged for Penney's to make the first direct corporate contribution to the American Home Economics Association, prominently at the organization's conference. She quoted Ellen Richards in *Fashions and Fabrics* and collaborated with the federal extension service to create a training program for 4-H leaders.

Penney's home economics staffers found dealing with the store managers to be a headache. They were independent men used to having their own way who didn't necessarily support directives from headquarters. For smaller markets, where it didn't make sense to send a field home economist, St. Marie created a step-by-step guide for managers to present the latest teaching unit themselves. The guides included invitations, lists of materials to request from HQ, a script complete with jokes, responses to expected audience questions, and all-caps hospitality reminders: "YOUR GUESTS ARE WOMEN AND THEY WILL NOTICE DETAILS OF REFRESHMENT SERVICE. KEEP IT SIMPLE, REFRESHMENT DAINTY, AND COLOR OF TABLE APPOINTMENTS CO-ORDINATED."[13] St. Marie knew that she could reach home economics teachers only if they didn't feel like they were watching a commercial. Though the live presentations showcased only Penney's merchandise, store managers must not identify fabrics, give prices, or mention that the store employed home-décor consultants during the program, she warned. That said, they were free to mention the consultants in private conversations with attendees afterward . . . and all the answers to sample audience questions ended with a suggestion that the questioner talk later to store staff.

Nonetheless, St. Marie did not ignore the bottom line. *Fashions and Fabrics* included perforated consumer guides on how to buy everything from run-resistant hosiery to smoke detectors. And building relationships with local home economics teachers and establishing Penney's as a disinterested source of reliable information did pay. "The resulting sales increases justify and highly recommend the programs," the house outlet *Penney News* reported. A store in Barstow, California, for instance, increased sewing-pattern sales by 41 percent "in great part due to a close relationship with the school home economics department. We have furnished them with all our educational materials—and the head of the department is in the store at least once a week," the Barstow manager said. By the end of 1964, St. Marie's first full year in charge, more than 1,500 Penney's stores had participated in her outreach initiative. She claimed they reached thirty to thirty-five thousand of the forty thousand home-ec teachers in the nation, who in turn taught more than three million schoolgirls.[14]

The sales support helped smooth the waves as St. Marie began to express the tenor of the times. No, she was ahead of it. St. Marie used African American models and interviewed African American experts in *Fashions and Fabrics*. She commissioned philosophical articles questioning consumption, theorizing about how home economics might change with the times, asking how Americans could use their leisure fruitfully, untangling the psychology of impulse buying, and expressing unease over whether "we have allowed technology to run ahead of our concern for a meaningful life," as an author she published wrote. Any home improvement should be "for the enhancement of meaning and human worth." Imagine trying to sell curtains to that! You *could* sell curtains to the 1967 home-décor unit "At Home with Color," for which St. Marie hired prominent designer Milo Baughman. One wonders if the company earned a dime considering the cost of public relations, Baughman's design fee, and the props and travel to present Baughman's vision around the country. The following year, the field home economists' presentation included an audio recording that "emphasized the generation gap, alternating parents' confused and distressed comments with teen age rock music," the *Milwaukee Journal-Sentinel* reported. The presenters told midwestern teachers that Paul Simon and the Beatles were "the poets of today": "Why not use them as teaching supplements during class discussions about values?" The *Journal-Sentinel* headlined its story "Educators Urged to Be 'With It.'"[15]

St. Marie succeeded not only because of her innovations but because she was a consummate politician who knew how to work the system. She cultivated the men on the fast track "and planted my ideas with them," she said. She thought that field staff didn't understand company politics: "They did not know how to get the boss to do what they wanted done. They did not understand how to analyze the political hierarchy in the company, how to determine the power structure, or how to feed an idea into the system so that it was eventually presented by someone in a position of power as his."[16] (Or at least, that's how she saw it. Maybe her women staff wanted to get the credit themselves.) The chairman of the board, William Batten, believed in St. Marie's vision and that of James Cash Penney. The long-retired but still-living founder set the philosophy that his store managers should be a positive force in the community and not just try to sell as much as possible. His initial customer-education program consisted of his personal religious teacher giving lectures on morality. And Penney's was changing—modernizing—too: adding appliances, furniture, and ready-to-wear clothing; piloting a catalog; de-emphasizing its fabric line; and selling its Advance sewing-patterns division.

In 1966, the men in charge finally gave St. Marie the official title of "manager." The following year, having thoroughly outgrown *Fashions and Fabrics*, St. Marie unveiled a new name for the magazine, *Forum*. It referenced the Roman concept in perfect home economics fashion: a physical place that fostered dialogue to benefit society. After almost two decades of work, St. Marie had found her groove. She was writing a textbook on the weekends, entitled *Homes Are for People*. The book was "a philosophical statement about home and its importance in shaping human lives," expressing her beliefs that the purpose of décor and architecture was to develop "the creative soul." She was motoring ahead—up to a point: "I knew that I could never become the CEO."[17]

At the same time that designers like Milo Baughman were creating futuristic-looking furniture and St. Marie was pondering the home as inner space, the future was entering the household in other ways as a handful of people took the first steps into merging it entirely with a promising new technology: the computer. Home economists were enthusiastic. Their visions ran more along the 1962 utopian case of Rosie the Robot and Jane Jetson than Ray Bradbury's 1950 apocalypse where a house continues turning on lights and reciting poetry despite the death of its residents via nuclear blast. As early as 1961, the *Journal of Home Economics* began reporting on the promise of computers to calculate cafeteria workflow, improve social-science analysis, and control washing machine cycles. "Computers in Homes Not So Distant," the journal announced in June 1966, describing a General Electric project that put computer access into twenty Arizona homes. In an amazingly contemporary move, "the experiment was made possible by means of a procedure called 'time-sharing,' that is, a technique that allows many people to use the same computer at the same time, even though the computer itself may be located miles away."[18] Wives adjusted recipe quantities and designed drapes; kids played blackjack and tic-tac-toe; and men, alas, brought home work from the office.

In one home, computers weren't distant at all. Six weeks earlier, on April 16, 1966, Westinghouse engineer Jim Sutherland flipped the switch on his hobby project, the "Electronic Computing Home Operator," or ECHO IV, the first computer to run a home. Perhaps it's relevant that his wife, Ruth Sutherland, worked as a home economist before motherhood. The ECHO IV was an eight-hundred-pound behemoth that did the family finances, stored messages, and automatically adjusted the television antenna to get the strongest signal for the family's favorite shows. It could schedule events a year into the future. The family entered commands through a keyboard that Sutherland cobbled together from a Selectric typewriter and a telex machine; the family's cat enjoyed snoozing on it, the first of countless laptop cats. The possibilities were really extraordinary. Sutherland planned to modify his kitchen cupboards so the computer could automatically track inventory. ECHO IV would be able to change the interior temperature and humidity in response to the weather. Sutherland was going to connect it to the family TV so that the kids would have to answer questions on a school night (perhaps a homework quiz?) before being allowed to watch.

Clearly this was Ellen Richards's dream, and the American Home Economics Association was on it, inviting the Sutherlands to speak at the 1967 conference. Ruth Sutherland confessed to a little anxiety at first: "I thought it really might replace me!" But she had become excited about the computer's potential to help her children, free up time for her hobbies, and teach her to program. "What a sense of accomplishment it will be to me to answer, 'I wrote a new menu and shopping list program,' when Jim asks the question that every man asks his wife when getting home from work, 'And what did you do today?'" she said.[19]

Most of the new ideas came from appliance companies. Westinghouse in 1960 designed a remote "phone home" system that let people turn the stove on or off by dial telephone: you picked one digit to choose which appliance to control remotely, then a second digit to indicate off or on. For the 1964–65 World's Fair, Whirlpool imagined a 1985 home equipped with "menumatic control" that "will order foods from storage and deliver them to the food preparation center when she needs them, ready for the microwave oven which will cook them from the frozen state to delicious doneness in seconds."[20] (For all the changes Whirlpool imagined, the company was not far enough advanced to envision a male homemaker.) The microwave oven, incidentally, already existed, discovered by accident from World War II technology. It began to be popular only in 1967 when the first relatively affordable, relatively small model came out. The device would create lots of work for home economics recipe-writers.

St. Marie celebrated this transformation of the home. The fall/winter 1966 *Fashions and Fabrics* focused on technology, including computers. St. Marie commissioned Marjorie East to write an enthusiastic tribute to cybernetics. As usual, the magazine took the philosophical long view.

> Yes, there is talk of matchmaking by computers. But no one suggests you will be *required* to marry a man who looks like an IBM card. Yes, there is evidence that many present jobs will be eliminated by automation. But wouldn't you rather sun yourself on a lazy beach than to work in a fish factory packing sardines in cans? Some even say that school children will learn all their facts and many of their skills in programmed and computerized booths. But wouldn't you welcome the chance to work with youngsters who already have the knowledge and look to you to help them integrate it into a value system which builds toward a free and joyous life?[21]

Who would want to argue the other side? Two years later, the Penney's home economists told teachers about an end-of-the-century home that featured not only computers but a version of Find My iPhone and 3D printing. In this house of the future, which the Delco Ford Research Corporation was test-modeling, a computer prepared meals; lasers opened cans and vaporized garbage; mothers sewed metal tags in their children's clothes, then tracked the kids via radar; and a device made dishes from powdered plastic. After dinner, the easily bored resident could put the dishes back into the machine, which would break them down and produce a new set in a different color.

But would the computer be a doorway to growth and freedom as East and St. Marie (and Ellen Richards) hoped, or a frivolous luxury item? In 1969, Neiman-Marcus featured the Honeywell Kitchen Computer in its famously extravagant holiday catalog, enthusing, "No hostess can claim to have the 'mostest' unless she has this marvelous mini-computer to help her plan menus for her family and for dinner guests." Under the hood it was the Honeywell 316, with its big black cabinet redesigned into a sleek, Dansk-like pedestal table with built-in cutting board. Primarily, the computer stored recipes. It could build a complete menu around a chosen entrée, then turn the meal plan into a shopping list. Or the homemaker could enter the ingredients she had on hand and the computer would spit out a recipe. According to the press release, it could also be "programmed as an 'appliance' to handle such home management chores as budgeting, checkbook balancing, and children's homework." The computer came with a two-week programming course, which was fortunate, considering that its display showed data in binary—zeros and ones. It had no input device—you had to plug in a Teletype machine. For an extra fee, one could order the computer pre-fed with one thousand recipes created by Neiman-Marcus home economist and restaurant director Helen Corbitt. (Perhaps it included "Texas Caviar," a black-eyed pea salad that Corbitt is credited with creating.) Rich ladies needed the Honeywell because they were careless and extravagant, Neiman-Marcus implied. "If she pales at reckoning her lunch tab, she can program it to balance the family checkbook," the catalog cooed. The item bore the charming tag line, "If she can only cook as well as Honeywell can compute."[22] But apparently no one was profligate enough to pay more than $70,000 in today's dollars to buy the Honeywell Kitchen Computer. There is only one extant version, at the Computer History Museum. The curators think none was ever sold.

By 1968, home economics had emerged from its struggles and was booming. The number of home economists had gone up to almost ninety thousand. The integrated Future Homemakers had well over half a million members. Seven thousand people attended the 1968 American Home Economics Association conference, the most ever. The association broke ground on a new headquarters in 1969 with more than $3.5 million in today's dollars already pledged.[23]

Home economists had even converted the man sent to destroy them. Almost a decade had elapsed since that powerful land-grant university president pettishly called for a study of the field's viability. First home economists dragged their feet (understandably), and then it took until 1964 to find a foundation to fund the study. That foundation hired former US education commissioner Earl McGrath to lead the work. McGrath admitted that he came in a skeptic. When he presented his findings, home economists' hearts must have been in their mouths. So what an enormous relief to hear that after surveying almost 1,700 home economists, he had seen the light. The field had an important role to play in a changing world, he said. Yes, they needed to update, but "the demand for home economists will increase indefinitely." McGrath didn't say anything that home economists didn't know and weren't already doing or starting. It was the affirmation from a powerful male education leader that mattered. Home economics' "central mission has been and must continue to be that of *family service*," he said.[24] They needed to play a bigger role in social change, and shift focus from the white rural middle-class to the Black urban poor. Teachers needed more training in pedagogy.

The establishment celebrated McGrath's endorsement. "The long-awaited McGrath report emphasizes that the time has never been more right for home economics," American Home

Economics Association director Doris Hanson exulted.[25] They would no longer have to defend the profession.

So why is it that home economists ended the decade as anxious about the field's future as they were at the start? "Home Economics is in one of the most challenging times in its history. It is a booming business," a Columbia University Teachers College professor wrote in a 1965 *Fashions and Fabrics*, neatly capturing the contradiction. At the same conference meeting that feted the McGrath report, a Michigan State professor fretted about the turmoil in her field: confusion over its purpose and relevance, embarrassment and guilt over its drab image, "a frantic search for identity and status." Maybe they were just feeling the agitation of the times? East, for one, was sick of it. "Home economics in its recent history of self-examination does rather remind one of an adolescent endlessly absorbed with her mirror image," she wrote.[26] McGrath said that the constant fretting over the strength of their leadership made men doubt the strength of their leadership.

More concretely, fifteen-plus years after Marjorie Child Husted gave managers a talking-to, the business world still didn't use home economists to their capacity. Betty Crocker called its test-kitchen workers "the girls in the kitchens."[27] By the late 1960s, those test kitchens were open to visitors. Each kitchen had unique décor, like a stage set, and the "girls" had to wear aprons to match: Barbara Jo Davis, for instance, had a pink apron with black curlicues to evoke wrought iron in the "New Orleans" kitchen, in which she worked on the rather un– New Orleanian Hamburger Helper product (it derived from Minnesota hotdish casserole). On top of their jobs, they had to bake treats for company events and Christmas fruitcakes for the board of directors. Davis once tripped and threw a pan of muffins at the gawkers. It was an accident, but, boy, did she enjoy it.

Home economics leaders also got tangled in education philosophies. The year before McGrath called for pedagogy reform, the American Home Economics Association published *Concepts and Generalizations*, the results of a committee that had been reimagining curriculum since Beatrice Paolucci called for less time teaching skills and more on management and executive thinking. That group diagnosed the problems that needed to be fixed in high school home economics classes not as dumbed-down content or gender stereotypes or vapid beauty tips or outdated techniques. No, they said that students should draw *generalizations* from each element of the curriculum that illustrated *concepts* about the world. The suggested concepts were so mind-numbingly obvious as to be meaningless—such as "creativity is the capacity to innovate, invent, or reorganize elements in ways new to the individual."[28] In a field whose concreteness had always been a strength, *Concepts and Generalizations* was so fuzzy that even St. Marie and her team had trouble wrapping their minds around the, well, concept. Home economics was failing to find a way to be more meaningful, evidently not seeing that the technology and poverty work was already succeeding in that regard.

And home economics had not won back its old prestige. Some people in the field began wondering whether a rose by a different name would get more respect. By 1963, about ten colleges had stopped using the name "home economics." Often retrenchment accompanied the name change. West Virginia University appointed a home economics skeptic as president; he turned home ec into a division of "home and family studies" and hired a man to lead it. The University of Wisconsin divided and rearranged the home economics department, assigning some specialties elsewhere with new resources, renaming the rest the School of Family Resources and Consumer Sciences— and hiring the West Virginia dean. Penn State undertook a similar dissection and reconstitution, adding specialties like criminal justice that attracted men after Dean Grace Henderson retired. (First the university put together a committee on its future that included no one from the home economics college—a bad sign.) Less than ten years later, the share of women on the faculty of the Department Formerly Known As Home Economics had fallen from 78 to 51 percent.[29] Though nine of ten home economics university programs did not have changes, many of the changes that did happen were high profile. The most devastating takeover happened at the mothership, Cornell. Again a powerful dean, Helen Canoyer, neared retirement. Again administrators appointed a mostly male committee to determine the future of the program that employed by far the most women faculty at the university. Again the committee came up with conveniently denigrating findings—in the case of Cornell, that home economics students were not as smart as women in liberal arts or agriculture. Again a new male dean, lots more money, lots of new students (many male), cascading retirements among women faculty, and a name change, to the College of Human Ecology. Higher-ups told Canoyer that the changes were inevitable.

The home economists' unexpected new champion, Earl McGrath, opposed a name change. After collecting alternatives, "some of which were rather bizarre," he concluded that changing the name "home economics" risked significant loss of identity for no real gain.[30] To get respect, fix the underlying problems, he said. That said, some home economics leaders approved. Kittrell recommended to Howard administrators in 1970 that they change her college's name to Human Ecology to help the public better understand its activities. St. Marie was beginning to think of herself not as a home economist but as a consumer-relations expert. She and Paolucci applauded

Michigan State's 1970 name change to the College of Human Ecology. Home economics, they said, *had* to move forward.

But were they opening the door to a better tomorrow, or getting smacked by the door on their way out? A woman pushing for a better future was about to answer that question.

CHAPTER 13

Addressing the Enemy

"As a radical feminist, I am here addressing the enemy," Robin Morgan told the home economists who crowded the Denver convention center.[1] She smiled. The air went out of the room.

After early celebrity as a child actress, Morgan had turned to politics. By the time of her AHEA appearance, she had organized civil rights rallies, written a scathing denunciation of sexist leftist men, founded Women Inspired to Commit Herstory (aka WITCH), and co-organized the Miss America protest that got feminists permanently labeled "bra-burners" even though no bras were actually burned. Morgan's feminist colleagues thought she was wasting her time at the American Home Economics Association conference, speaking to those hopelessly retrograde instruments of the oppressor. But Morgan figured that you couldn't build a movement by preaching to the choir. Besides, it drove her crazy when people said that feminists were anti-family: she was a mother. In fact, motherhood was a radicalizing experience for the seasoned activist, she wrote in the anthology she edited, the first of the newly reawakened feminist movement, *Sisterhood Is Powerful*. When her son was born, cultural assumptions wrapped around him with the blue hospital blanket. Morgan experienced the inadequacy of childcare as she traveled, wrote, protested, and was hauled to jail. She was hassled for breastfeeding in public, and pressured to try infant formula that put money in corporations' pockets. Officially her husband shared the work, but in reality she was "sharing" more than he was. Before setting off on a work trip she'd load the freezer with food; she'd return to a mess, which she would clean. Her initial title for the anthology was *The Hand That Cradles the Rock*, but when the book was sent out for reviews, the publisher received a letter from lawyers for humorist S. J. Perelman, who had written a short story by that name, that indicated that he did not have a sense of humor about her using the title.

The American Home Economics Association members attending Morgan's panel discussion that June morning in 1971 knew that she represented the women's liberation movement. Even so, they were certainly not expecting to be called the *enemy*, especially not by a beloved former child star. After all, they empowered women. Morgan's panel included an African American home economics dean and the first woman to be appointed vice president of the US Civil Service Commission. The association had had Betty Friedan speak in 1963, though its magazine never published her statements, merely running a photo with the caption that she "excited much comment from the audience." That same year, the association praised the Equal Pay Act, which prohibited gender wage discrimination between men and women doing the same job at the same workplace. At the 1970 conference, a presenter called out the hypocrisy of the (male) National Council on Family Relations experts who gave women's-liberationists the side-eye when they, invited to speak to the NCFR, brought their children and even nursed in public. The very week that Morgan lambasted the AHEA, its members approved resolutions supporting the repeal of anti-abortion laws and the end of discrimination against women. In 1969 Cornell's home economics college held the first conference in what would become women's studies. Which made sense: What field besides home economics spent so much time taking women seriously? Besides, Cornell's home economics college employed as much as three-quarters of the university's women faculty, whereas there were departments that had never hired a woman professor and were proud of the fact.[2]

Apparently the association members didn't notice the *Journal of Home Economics* steel wool ad that depicted a young man and woman kneeling in front of a car with the headline, "She'll clean the whitewalls while the fellows do the rest." That morning in Denver, Morgan showed how her feminist colleagues saw home economics: as conservatives and hypocrites. It was ugly.

"You do have immense power, psychological and economic, because every young woman in our culture at one time or another passes through your tutelage," she said. "And very frequently that is the final icing on the cake, the nail in the coffin, after which she is a limp, jabbering mass of jelly waiting for marriage."

For what sort of life were they readying these young women? The average US housewife walked five miles a day inside her home, washed seven thousand glasses per year, and worked 99.6 hours per week for no pay at a job society disdained, Morgan said. If home economists really wanted to help women, "you can quit your jobs," she announced. If they didn't quit, they should stay in the profession "with one aim in mind which is not to further reinforce the mores of society but to change them." They could lobby for home ec not to be required for girls—or also to be required for boys, to break down the idea that parenting and homemaking were women's work. Home economists could tell the truth about women dying from illegal abortions, about economic discrimination. They could deal with their own oppression as women. All those activities would benefit not only society but home economics itself, she said. Because family, marriage, and consumerism were all dying, and home ec would crumble with them. "You run the risk of being obsolete," she said. And concluded, "I hope that you will join us—but we're going to win in any event."[3]

Immediately afterward, attendees were not just polite but warm, Morgan recalled. Nobody booed. Teachers came up to say they had tried to include boys but hit brick walls with school administrators. They were on her side. "It was kind of like this is what they were waiting to hear," she said.[4] But they were pretty well stunned. Morgan had hit her target. The threat of obsolescence was something home economists sensed and feared—it was probably their worst nightmare. On the association side, the invitation seemed to go down as an epic blunder. The *Journal of Home Economics* printed the other two panelists' words in its fall issues, leaving Morgan's out. The AHEA public relations consultant wrote Morgan with the tension of a PR person who knows she screwed up. "I guess my major frustration is that I feel I didn't really communicate very effectively on what home economics really is," she wrote. She quoted Richards—"an extraordinary woman."[5]

In fact, Morgan's speech was crucial. It triggered an overdue and absolutely necessary revolution from within. One and a half years later, the *Journal of Home Economics* printed her speech in full, with the headline "What Robin Morgan Said at Denver." Alongside, it ran a discussion by the association's new work group on "women's roles." Its members were shocked to realize how much they had missed. Maybe because they had created a (comparatively) feminist world, where women had (some) power. Beatrice Paolucci taught Betty Friedan and Simone de Beauvoir in the 1960s to girls whose parents pushed them into home ec to prepare for lives as housewives. In a breast-beating exchange, the work group agreed that they had been wrong. They had been perpetuating the patriarchy. They had been hypocritical: "We teach one lifestyle and we ourselves practice another." Perhaps they had contributed to the guilt working mothers felt. "We've really had our heads in the sand and haven't been listening," said Virginia Trotter, who was about to become the first woman to run the federal education office.[6]

With remarkable speed, all things considered, home economists made a U-turn and began overtly fighting sexism. They must have been hungry for the old, macro vision of home economics they now revived: the one that nested the family in a larger society, that talked about changing the world. Over the next few years, the *Journal of Home Economics* examined the field's internal sexism and offered policies to render economic justice to divorced homemakers. In an article titled "Now That Women Are Liberated," Iowa State's home economics dean called on her peers to run for public office. (The dean hadn't waited: in 1966, she became the first woman to win a seat on the Ames City Council. She married at the age of sixty and enjoyed knitting and reading about Catherine the Great.) "We have been teaching women that both careers and child care–homemaking, two full-time jobs, are *their* jobs, and if they cannot do both well, they are failures," a (male) professor wrote. "We do not teach men the same things and neither does anyone else."[7] Even the ads changed. "Liberate Your Home Economics

Curriculum," the publisher McGraw-Hill said. The steel wool company's new ad showed a girl in a mortarboard.

The American Home Economics Association endorsed the Equal Rights Amendment. It redefined "family" in a broad, inclusive way, as "a unit of interacting and interdependent personalities who have a common theme and goals, have a commitment over time and share human and material resources." Title IX, the 1972 law that brought us women's basketball, permanently (well, officially) ended the practice of shuttling boys to shop and girls to home ec. In fact, the federal Department of Health, Education, and Welfare called out home economics by name in the Title IX regulations. The first home economics faculty member became president of a major university: Lorene Lane Rogers at the University of Texas. Called a "red-headed dynamo," the biochemist joined the university in 1962 as a nutrition professor after the chemistry department told her, "We've never had a woman in our department, and we never will."[8] On the negative side, at least one former Cornell home economics faculty member was among the "Cornell Eleven" who filed (and eventually lost) a federal lawsuit against the university citing sex discrimination in tenure.

Home-ec authors seemed practically to break loose from a corset. In the 1976 college textbook *Families: Developing Relationships*, Mollie Stevens Smart and her daughter, sociologist Laura Smart, explicitly eschewed the prescriptive, patriarchal marriage course, whose books Laura had read and hated. Their new textbook discussed discrimination and inequality, and stated up front that it would not routinely refer to a person of unspecified gender as "he." It emphasized the value of the unpaid labor in the home usually performed by women. It was everything progressive that Mollie's fifties high school textbook had not been. The photos depicted families of all races and backgrounds, including men playing with their children and a white hippie family soaking together in a bathtub.

Home economists tried to modernize in other domains as well. They pitched home ec as vocational education for hotel managers, diet counselors, and fashion designers. Future Homemakers created a new vocational program, HERO, for "Home Economics–Related Occupations." Right away, two of HERO's three national student-board representatives were boys. The American Home Economics Association elected its first Black president in 1975 and hired Gladys Gary Vaughn as its first African American professional staff member. When Beatrice Paolucci chaired the organization's Committee on Committees, she insisted that there be at least one person of color on each of the many committees. The association also called for the purposeful recruitment of "minority group members," though that did not move quickly: a Black teacher criticized the association in 1979, saying the field had only "a token representation of minorities," just 6 percent.[9]

The burgeoning environmental movement made an impact as well, and not just because Cornell had changed its home economics school's name to "human ecology." In the 1890s, Ellen Richards briefly suggested the term "oekology" for her "science of right living." Given her work on water quality, the extent to which that chimes with our term "ecology" has been debated ever since, with at least one environmentalist claiming her as foremother. Now Paolucci drew on environmentalism to formulate her core philosophy, writing, "The rapid depletion of essential resources and the necessity to maintain man's humanness has forced us to reconsider the interdependence of man and his environment." She concluded that the family was an ecosystem—"a life support system" that interacted with the world—and the work of home economists was to study and help with how families managed that interaction.[10] (Urie

Bronfenbrenner, a psychologist at Cornell's home economics school, is the more famous exponent of the theory envisioning the person as embedded in and interacting with the environment. He published his book on "ecological systems" in 1979.)

Morgan rapidly moved on to a million other meetings, the editorship of Ms., global activism, and twenty-plus books. More than forty-five years later, she was pleased to hear of the reaction to her speech. "I had no idea the speech was this seismic," she said. "I'm glad that they took it that seriously." She admitted that she had not researched the roots of home economics—as a working child actor, she had never taken home ec herself. If she had, she would not have told them to quit their jobs. "I would have said, 'Lo, how the mighty have fallen.'"[11] She would have told home economists to go back to their roots.

And she recalled an instance from about ten years after she spoke in Denver. In an attempt to quit smoking, she took up knitting to occupy her hands. Keynoting a conference in Tokyo and faced with a table lined with ashtrays, she pulled out her project. The next day, every newspaper in the city trumpeted about it. They couldn't focus on anything else. A feminist, knitting in public!

Among the institutions that Morgan criticized was "consumerism, which you may euphemistically call consumer protection . . . the incredible manipulation of women as consumers."[12] Satenig St. Marie did not agree with Morgan's negative formulation. Consumer protection was becoming the heart of her work.

Corporate America was struggling. Worst off were the utility companies, steamrolled by the energy crisis. Columbia Gas was one of many that put a moratorium on new hookups because they didn't have enough supply to fill orders. They didn't need Betty Newton to sell gas when there was no gas to sell. In 1973, Newton "retired." In addition, the consumer-rights movement had revived—the movement that had started with the Progressives' clean-food laws, Richards testing wallpaper for arsenic, and home economists warning about the dangers of adulterated food. President Kennedy laid out a "consumer bill of rights," Ralph Nader published *Unsafe at Any Speed*, and Congress passed the Consumer Credit Protection Act and then created the Consumer Product Safety Commission in 1968 and 1972. Activists clamored for a consumer-protection agency with broader powers.

St. Marie believed in Kennedy's four consumer rights: "the right to safety, the right to be informed, the right to choose and the right to be heard, including redress."[13] Her team created a new publication, *Insights into Consumerism*. They continued to produce an enormous variety of buying guides in English and Spanish covering everything from smoke detectors and pocket calculators to hairpieces, strollers, and chainsaws. In 1971, St. Marie began an annual weeklong consumer-education workshop in New York, with attendees coming from all over the country. She sought out university cosponsorship to underline the workshop's educational purpose. The first installment started, grandly, in the New York Stock Exchange board room, before proceeding to the Penney's merchandise testing center, Consumers Union, and Best Foods, among other sites.

Though Home Economists in Business (ex-HEWIB) members had from the start been seen as consumer representatives, St. Marie redefined home economics *as* consumer affairs. As others had done with family-life education, she used consumerism to embrace, reframe, and refocus her entire slate of work. She saw herself as someone who had trained as a home economist but worked in business. Even when she created an in-store sewing school, she saw it as an opportunity to extend the reputation of Penney's as a community leader in consumer education. After all, crafts were back in vogue; retired football star Rosey Grier put out a "needlepoint for men" book depicting him stitching in aviator glasses. The Penney's sewing classes ran for a good five years, quietly selling the stores' fabric and sewing machines while remaining overtly nonpromotional. However, when the economy tanked, enrollment fell. (Also, sewing students didn't enjoy working on tables left sticky by the stores' cake-decorating classes.) Penney's discontinued the program.

As St. Marie spun home economics education, women's traditional power base in business, into a program of consumerism, she was canny enough to play both sides. She pitched her new activities to the Penney's board as a way to control the train that threatened to hit them. Serving the customer, and educating teachers about how companies worked, served Penney's, she said. When the summer workshop participants judged actual consumer problems, they learned "that consumers are not always reasonable, that they do not always articulate their problems, and that sometimes their problems really are caused by themselves," St. Marie wrote in a report afterward. Consumer confidence in business was dropping precipitously, she told the board. If corporations didn't do something to regain trust, the government would intervene, and Penney's wouldn't like the results. "In other words the consumer dagger is pointed to the very heart of business."[14]

In 1973, St. Marie reached perhaps the apex of her career. She got her department renamed Consumer Affairs, was promoted to be its director, and became president of the American Home Economics Association. Penney's knew how valuable that role was: it covered her expenses for her pre-presidency and presidency years, which included $45,000 in today's dollars for her travel alone.

As AHEA president, St. Marie was upbeat and optimistic.

Enough of anxiously accepting the judgments of outside crit-
ics! she told the members. The association had reached an all-
time high of fifty-two thousand members and was one of the
twenty largest professional groups in the country. They had to
start talking about what was *right* with home economics, a field
that combined the scientific and the human. "Ours is a noble
profession. We have much to contribute to our changing world.
You know it and I know it. Somehow we must get rid of our
old stereotypes and help the rest of the world know it, too," she
said in her acceptance speech. She offered a new, modern definition of home economics, adopted from a Frenchman: "the art
and the science of relating families to progress."[15]

So whose side was St. Marie on—business or consumer?
Was the work to make consumers feel understood a sop to
get them to buy? St. Marie believed, absolutely, that she supported the consumer. "My role in the company was to represent the consumer's perspective," she wrote. However, that
position required careful, tactful influencing. The consumer
affairs director had to "'meet' management where *they are*" and
"not try to achieve utopia overnight." And again, Penney's did
genuinely include community service in its mission. "We have
a responsibility to contribute to the social and physical environment of the communities in which we do business," wrote
board chairman William Batten, St. Marie's most important
ally at the company. "Our educational program, which focuses
on consumer education, is one of the ways we feel we are helping educators, who are an important segment of each community, in their efforts to help individual consumers achieve a
fuller, richer life."[16]

A memo that St. Marie wrote outlining the tasks she could
and could not delegate during her presidency shows how
hard she worked. Someone else could respond to two-thirds
of the 150 letters she received per week, handle the summer

workshop, liaise with external-relations staff and national groups, meet with the educators who simply showed up at the New York office, and write scripts for small stores to put on the twice-yearly home-ec presentations (yes, they were still happening). St. Marie had a much more substantial list of matters she had to handle herself. They included supervising her home economists and clerical staff; expanding field programs in seventy-two cities; critiquing all publications and teaching aids; developing the sewing school, which she was expanding into knitting; supervising the budget; and dealing with national issues. It all made rather a joke of her prediction to the AHEA of a thirty-two-hour, four-day workweek.

Those Penney's publications she oversaw continued to burgeon. The educational kits that Penney's stores loaned to teachers grew ever more elaborate: boxed sets that packaged worksheets, readings, classroom activities, games, film strips, and audio tapes on a single theme with cutting-edge graphic design. They covered all the cultural issues that home economics came to embrace in the seventies. In "Who's Who?," students evaluated whether male or female characters made major decisions or reflected stereotypes in television shows and stories they made up themselves. The kit "Ethnic Heritage: A Living Mosaic" addressed racial diversity. "Your Space and Mine," packaged in a box printed with trees, transformed the traditional interior design unit into a philosophical discussion of personal space, ecology, and the impact of environments on people, with sections titled "Proxemics" and "Environmessages."[17] If that sounds like Paolucci, there's a reason. St. Marie brought her in as a close collaborator, frequently commissioning work from her. Together the two women made a complete sphere: the businesswoman and the philosopher, embracing modernity, pushing the future.

Especially Paolucci made near-incessant appearances in the

jewel in St. Marie's crown, *Forum* magazine, the new generation of what once had been *Fashions and Fabrics*. *Forum*, too, dealt with all the trends: singledom, economic uncertainty, futurism, the new vision of the good life as one in which one was fully self-actualized. The fall/winter 1974 issue, which coincided with the publication of St. Marie's own long-worked-on book *Homes Are for People*, reframed interior design as "human environments." Judging from *Forum*, St. Marie was very big on "values clarification," a method of self-examination. Indeed, *Forum* could go positively hippie-dippy. It ran articles on "The Creative Potential Within" and "Attitudes, Behavior and Human Potential." A 1975 issue, "The Future as Transition," suggested that readers write a cinquain poem to focus their thoughts. Humanistic psychology star Carl Rogers contributed an article entitled "To Be Fully Alive." Though St. Marie included contrarian views, the weight was always on the liberal side.

It could also be quite rarefied. The bulk of the 1974 issues came from two symposia of experts, including Paolucci, who met at a two-hundred-year-old tavern in Connecticut. "Windows on two sides opened to the Old Mill pond where wild ducks paddled back and forth in newly falling snow," St. Marie wrote. "The fire crackled companionably nearby." Plus it was abstract. It's hard to see how home economics teachers might apply, for instance, the advice of educational philosopher Martin Haberman when he wrote, "Schools can contribute most fully if they cease the teaching and reward of restricted self-image, restricted areas of learning, restricted recreational and life pursuits, restricted occupational goals, and restricted modeling by teachers and administrators."[18] Were families really going to conduct an exercise entitled "Appraising Role Shifts"? Yet home economists loved *Forum*. As of 1976, the company printed forty-five thousand copies, five times a year, beautifully designed on heavy, glossy paper. It "was a piece of educational literature to die for. It carried *the* most innovative information," Gladys Gary Vaughn remembered. "People waited for *Forum* to come out. That's how good it was. And it was so different."[19]

Abstraction was in, as was futurism, as was self-exploration. In the seventies the field had no fewer than three major self-examination events: an eleventh Lake Placid conference, a second *New Directions* statement, and a 1979 paper the American Home Economics Association commissioned from Paolucci and home economics deep-thinker Marjorie Brown: "Home Economics: A Definition." Paolucci was considered the approachable author. The sixty-page document started by defining the word "definition" and was so dense that Penn State's home-ec department convened a multimonth reading group to understand its implications. "While brevity may be the soul of wit, it is seldom the soul of understanding," Brown and Paolucci wrote. They said . . . more or less . . . that the mission of home economics was to empower families to help their members grow and to use "enlightened, cooperative participation in the critique and formulation of social goals and means for accomplishing them." Penn State home-ec dean Marjorie East translated that as "We are to lead families to reform society."[20]

East's reaction was one of more than a dozen responses the association requested to accompany the statement in a monograph. All the respondents found the paper stunning, an intellectual tour de force. But many thought that it didn't solve any problems. Some thought that Brown and Paolucci unnecessarily complicated matters, and did not define home economics at all—there was no single-sentence takeaway. They thought that home economists should cut the philosophizing and get on with the work, that the profession needed not redefinition but power. A textile scientist thought Brown and Paolucci downplayed both physical sciences and fine arts. East thought that not only would no one consult a home economist to "help them define their highest aspirations for society" but that Brown and Paolucci's mission statement did not capture what made their profession unique: the expertise in helping people work out problems in the home, which is "the cradle and the haven for creating good people." She suggested a simpler definition: "that profession which applies rational thought to home life for improving that matrix for human development."[21]

The paper now known as "Brown and Paolucci" did, however, have a much longer life than another bid to futurism. In the 1970s, home economists jumped feet (or meter) first into a renewed effort to convert the US to the metric system.

Metric was nothing new—it was one of Melvil Dewey's pet causes, and as early as the nineteenth century, "the United States first began to inch its way toward the metric system," two home economists wrote, making what one can only hope was a purposeful pun.[22] The new push started in the 1960s, as the international metric authorities simplified the system and Britain began to switch over. The American Home Economics Association seems to have started actively advocating for the metric system in 1967. Metric was easier, faster, and more logical. Yes, it was hard to change habits of daily life. But what else were home economists all about? Studies showed that the more people knew about metric, the easier they thought the transition would be. Home economics leaders agreed that they, as change agents, had to lead the way with an intensive education program. The American Home Economics Association testified before Congress, became a charter member of the American National Metric Council, began using metric in its research journal, and passed a resolution advocating for a swift transition. The *Journal of Home Economics* advertised metric guides from a flurry of entities, from the Government Printing Office to Butterick to Union Carbide. Of course St. Marie got on board, creating an educational kit featuring an original folk song on cassette, "The Metric Song," which was the hit of the Uniontown, Pennsylvania, Penney's store.

Seen in the rearview mirror, this endeavor looks somewhere between quixotic and goofy. Before we giggle at the earnest home economists, we should remember that the country's leading science and defense entities also thought that metric conversion was imminent. NASA switched its reports to metric in 1970. The CIA endorsed decimation. "The Intelligence Community should begin using the metric system almost immediately after enactment of the metric conversion legislation," the US Intelligence Board wrote in 1974. "The Intelligence Community should prepare now."[23]

In fact, there was a new kind of measurement on the horizon. But home economists weren't going to like it.

CHAPTER 14

Home Economics at Risk

On the whole, home economists work until they physically can't anymore. Fabiola de Baca moved to a nursing home in Albuquerque after being diagnosed with dementia in 1984. She died in 1991 at age 97 and was buried on the family ranch under a gravestone she had made herself from local rock. After Flemmie Kittrell retired from Howard in the mid-seventies, she kept busier than ever. Though she moved out to a country community of Black intellectuals, she seems to have hardly been home. She spent two years at Cornell as a visiting professor and continued traveling in Australia, New Zealand, China, the Philippines, and India, the last to mark the twenty-fifth anniversary of the University of Baroda's College of Home Science. She was attending a Howard University meeting in 1980, with a Fulbright application to return to Baroda under consideration, when she had a heart attack and died. The Fulbright would have been approved despite her age, the administrator said, "because of who she was."[1]

Louisan Mamer stayed strong at the Rural Electrification Administration through the 1970s. When she gave speeches, she projected her voice as if it had to reach the back of a tent. In DC, she still strode down the office hallway as if she was harrowing a field, heels clicking rapidly on the granite down to her private office. Her husband had retired, though most people didn't know she even had a husband, let alone that he had been a fellow REA employee. Her boss didn't like working women, but Mamer shrugged him off: he was the director of public affairs, "but she was famous," her colleague Kathryn Vanzant remembered. Like St. Marie, like Kittrell, Mamer wasn't cozy at work; she didn't lunch with Vanzant or the two other young women writing about energy conservation. "You just didn't buddy up to Louisan Mamer," Vanzant said. "She was an entity unto herself."[2] Mamer finally retired in 1981, aged seventy, after forty-five years at her job. President Ronald Reagan sent her a congratulatory letter and her colleagues made scrapbooks calling her "The First Lady of the REA." Mamer continued to attend DC home economics association meetings and chair a national association for women in utilities.

One of our heroines, however, died well before her time, and the impact of that loss lingered. In 1982, Beatrice Paolucci was diagnosed with colon cancer. As she went through treatment, she never missed a class, lecturing with tape on the back of her hands from the hospital needles. As late as the spring of 1983, she spent two weeks as a visiting professor in Utah. On her last Saturday night in Lansing, at the end of that semester, she went to church with a friend and then out for ice cream. The next day she went to live with her sisters in Illinois, where she continued to talk with students, receive friends, and write recommendation letters. Near the end, when her niece bid her farewell until the next weekend, she would say, "I hope not, Katie. I hope I won't be here." She died on October 1, 1983, just sixty-three years old. To this day, home economics leaders speak reverently of Paolucci. To this day, Satenig St. Marie continues to believe that Paolucci could have made all the difference if only she had lived longer. "There weren't enough people out in front. And the people in the back needed to be pulled, [because] when someone speaks to a person who's interested in cooking and sewing about Maslow's hierarchy of needs, it falls flat," St. Marie said in 2019. They were trying to sprout some seeds. But Paolucci "passed away too young. So that never took place."[3]

In 1984, St. Marie bid farewell to *Forum*'s readers, saying she was retiring. The company was moving its headquarters to Texas. New management didn't understand St. Marie or how her program benefited stores—*Forum* was focusing on distinctly anti-commercial topics such as "voluntary simplicity." And Penney's had closed its fabrics and kitchen appliances departments. Soon after St. Marie's departure, after forty-five years, the company ended its consumer/home economics educational program. Penney's replaced it with broader youth-development outreach, releasing after-school-special-esque videos for classroom and community use on issues such as drug addiction, with acid-washed jeans and melodramatic titles such as *Not Me!* and *Has Anybody Seen Phil?* The company also undertook initiatives in its new Texas community, such as United Way. St. Marie became the founding executive director of the Antiques Dealers' Association of America, a job she held for twenty years until retiring for real in her eighties.

Something else happened the year of Paolucci's death that cast a chill on home economics: *A Nation at Risk*. The presidential National Commission on Excellence's landmark report came out in April 1983, and it opened with a ringing declaration: "The educational foundations of our society are presently being eroded by a rising tide of mediocrity that threatens our very future as a nation and as a people." The US was falling behind the rest of the world educationally in a way that would, if not stanched, inevitably end its global preeminence, the report said. The country had committed "unthinking, unilateral educational disarmament"—words that packed a punch when the threat of the Soviets still loomed large. If another nation had forced the US to follow the current education system, "we might well have viewed it as an act of war."[4] It was like Sputnik without *Sputnik*.

America had to raise its educational standards, the commission said. Schools should run for seven or eight hours a day, not six, and educate students for 220 days per year, not 180. The commission called for higher teacher salaries (and qualifications) and "far more homework" in high school. And most important for home economists, schools should quit spending so much time on "physical and health education, work experience outside the school, remedial English and mathematics, and personal service and development courses, such as training for adulthood and marriage," and double down on academics, especially critical thinking, science, computers, and languages. "In many schools, the time spent learning how to cook and drive counts as much toward a high school diploma as the time spent studying mathematics, English, chemistry, U.S. history, or biology," the report exclaimed.[5]

It stung. The dismissal of home ec as "learning how to cook"—so narrow, so insignificant, such a waste of time—was particularly devastating given how much work home economists had done in recent years to change their reputation. The threat was clear. "If the public perceives home economics education programs to be unnecessary, lacking in academic rigor, and taught by incompetent instructors, then the public will support program elimination and reductions," Emporia State home economics chair Virginia Munson Moxley wrote. "This perception is widespread."[6]

This time, unlike their one-pronged response to *Sputnik*, home economists pulled out every counterargument they had. University of Illinois home economics professor Hazel Taylor Spitze took the lead on them all. Spitze edited the influential journal *Illinois Teacher of Home Economics*, which had 5,500 subscribers and as many readers in California as in Illinois. Over several articles in *ITHE* and the *Journal of Home Economics*, Spitze argued that a society needed all kinds. Not everyone was going to be a scientist, but every child grew up to be a homemaker, consumer, family member, and citizen. The commission missed the real problems, she wrote. Our nation *was* at risk: from suicide, alcoholism, racism, sexism, child abuse, infants born addicted to drugs, people raped and murdered by assailants they knew, absent parents, war, the loss of pride in work, smoking, the high cost of health care, and pollution, just to name a few. Two more years of science alone wouldn't solve those problems or teach children to make good choices as adults, Spitze wrote, and quoted Shirley Chisholm, the first African American congresswoman: "If you don't accept others who are different, it means nothing that you've learned calculus."[7] You know what would address those problems? Home economics.

She also argued for her field's intellectual value. Spitze was proud of being a home economist. In an article, "Helping Students Learn to Think, or The Purpose of the Muffin Lesson," she contrasted the wrong and right ways to teach what she called "the inevitable muffin lesson." The wrong way was rote and routine: the teacher demonstrated making a muffin, and the students learned nothing more than how to copy her. When

Spitze asked students in such a class why they were studying muffins, one girl answered, "Because it's a quick bread," that is, one leavened with baking soda or baking powder, not yeast. "Is there a law," Spitze retorted, "which says that all home economics girls must learn to make quick breads?"[8] In the better lesson, the teacher chose a student ahead of time who needed a little extra attention, and taught them how to make muffins. After several rounds of practice, the student demonstrated muffin-making for the class. While the treats baked, the teacher led a complex conversation. What nutrients did muffins provide? The ingredient lists for muffins and biscuits differed in several ways—what was the impact? Could you be a good family member without knowing how to make muffins?[9] Could skill at making muffins lead to a job, or help a person serve the community?

Everyone in home economics could agree, generally, on those points. Not so on another possible tactical response. The call went up again to rename the profession. Here, Spitze was in the opposition, arguably the reactionary group, a position to which she was not accustomed. Spitze was progressive. Almost a decade earlier, she had written that "as home economists, we accept societal and attitudinal change as inevitable."[10] She supported the ACLU and volunteered for Planned Parenthood. She had grown up in small-town Arkansas, the oldest of four, with a strong mother who cultivated a huge garden, bartered for what the family needed, taught the kids to play bridge, and moved the family in the middle of the Depression so that her children could attend college—and fixed up an abandoned house for them to live in. In her thirties, with two children, Spitze went back to school to earn her doctorate, and then successfully overcame the University of Illinois's anti-nepotism policy, getting hired even though her husband already taught at the agriculture school.

So Spitze most emphatically supported progress. She just opposed changing the field's name. At best, it was meaningless window-dressing, she said. University departments calling themselves "human sciences" or "human ecology" diluted the discipline and confused prospective recruits without fixing whatever was at the root of home economics' declining popularity, she wrote in one of her characteristically opinionated articles, titled "A Rose by Any Other Name Would Not Be a Rose." If high school home economics was badly taught, fix the teaching. Would a college chemistry department rename itself "elemental ecology" to differentiate itself from high school courses whose teachers made baking-soda volcanoes? And as for the lingering idea that men refused to take "home economics," it was "absolutely silly . . . to think that a seventy-five-year-old profession should change its name to attract males," she wrote.[11] She ran a graphic in the March/April 1985 *Illinois Teacher*: "Changing the name of our profession may gain next to nothing. Making our profession worthy of the name HOME ECONOMICS may gain everything we need."

Retired University of Nevada dean Marilyn Horn echoed the point in a 1989 letter to the *Journal of Home Economics*. "We must all now be 'scientists' if we are to command respect on a university campus," Horn wrote. "Suppose dental schools decided that 'dentist' was old-fashioned, and they now wished to be known as 'tooth scientists.'"[12]

A Nation at Risk got plenty of things wrong. Its charge that test scores were falling overlooked the fact that far more students were participating in high school and college and taking those tests, not just the elite; the best in the US continued to be the best in the world. It barely mentioned early-childhood, elementary, or middle schools. It certainly didn't mention poverty, racism, or other societal influences on how children learn. Nonetheless, it scared the daylights out of educators like nothing since *Sputnik*, and it changed US education like putting a man on the moon. Asking for measurable results meant adding measures and accountability—that is, standardized tests—leading directly, twenty years later, to No Child Left Behind. Forty years later, the standardized testing of core academic subjects remains at the heart of US schools.

It's impossible to overstate the hit home economics took from *A Nation at Risk*. Just when the field had gotten back on its feet, the rug got pulled out from under it. It didn't help that the political and industrial support so essential to the Lake Placid founders had ebbed—unlike with, say, welding. There was no federally funded national research center for home economics as there was for vocational education as a whole. Nor could home economists make themselves part of the conversation with the new wave of working moms, because to most progressives, home economics still seemed irrelevant, stodgy, and sexist. Never mind that in the 1980s the Future Homemakers of America elected its first male president, Thomas Lucas, a West Virginia defensive tackle who had seen *Rambo* three times. "People have had a hard time understanding how a guy could be president of FHA and still retain the masculinity they envision for a male," Lucas wrote in *Seventeen* in 1987, below an ad for press-on nails. The "snickers, stares, comments, and questions" made him redefine what it meant to be a man, he said. (He also got to meet a lot of girls in FHA, he admitted.)[13] Home economics was too conservative for liberals who held on to their old assumptions. And to arch-conservatives, who had paid attention to the changes in the field, it was now too liberal.

In 1980, the religious right drafted home economics into the culture wars. The Heritage Foundation published a booklet attacking the American Home Economics Association for its new, broader definition of "family" and for encouraging students to make their own choices, which religious conservatives saw as endorsing moral relativism. "The struggle is between the Judeo-Christian ethic, based on God-given eternal law, and the secular humanist orthodoxy that rejects God and traditional values," author Onalee McGraw wrote.[14] Moreover, she said, people in the *soi-disant* helping professions were simply well-connected people sucking on the federal teat to advance their own careers. The American Home Economics Association took the booklet seriously. In an extended review, two staffers called it a must-read. The book would anger home economists, they wrote, but they had to know what they were up against so they could defend and explain the field's beliefs. For instance, home economists advocated for high-quality day care, not pushing women back into the home; while families might teach sexual restraint, a teacher seeking to reduce teen pregnancy ought to give information, not advocate chastity. McGraw railed against gender equity, contraception, sex education, abortion rights, and family research, "all areas in which the American Home Economics Association has made supportive commitment through policy resolutions over the past 10 years," the AHEA reviewers wrote. "Perhaps some of the values McGraw discusses do need recapturing, but can they be legislated? This is a dangerous course, and an incongruent one for those advocating removal of government from family life."[15]

Still, even they might not have expected that the family values movement would literally put home economics on trial.

It happened in 1986 in Alabama federal court. Though the class-action suit, *Smith v. Board of School Commissioners of Mobile County*, challenged forty-four textbooks, the five home-ec books took center stage—they were the worst, a prosecutor said. (That initially boggled one of the attorneys, a man who knew nothing of home ec except the stereotypes. What were they talking about, profane recipes?) The case was national from the start. Phyllis Schlafly's Eagle Forum brought the textbooks to the attention of Alabama conservative-education activists, one of whom was on the state's textbook-authorization committee. The National Legal Foundation funded the prosecution; it was founded by televangelist Pat Robertson, who was at that time seeking the Republican presidential nomination. In response, the ACLU and the liberal People for the American Way funded a defense team to argue alongside the Alabama school board's attorney. The judge W. Brevard Hand was already, as the *New York Times* put it, a "hero" of the religious right for favoring Christian prayer in schools.[16]

The plaintiffs charged that the books unconstitutionally established a religion: secular humanism. Secular humanism, the plaintiffs said, "espouses that there are no moral absolutes and that humans are strictly a result of some biological process and nothing more." It gave no reason to believe in God. The humanist psychological view said that humans were essentially good. That was inconsistent with a theistic religion and would "cripple" children, the plaintiffs said, because they wouldn't need divine salvation or their parents.[17]

The textbooks indoctrinated captive students in humanism in many ways, the experts contended. Take a passage saying that students were in charge of their own lives, that nothing was predestined, and that they could plan and work for what they wanted. That was "anti-theistic." A sentence that said parents sometimes made mistakes was "anti-family." Telling students that "the foundation for integrity has to come from within" improperly promoted "personal and subjective values." The books prioritized happiness above all else, which was hedonistic. They attacked St. Marie's old favorite, *values clarification*.

And what the heck were these home economists doing in this domain anyway? "It takes an awful long time to get to sewing and cooking in those textbooks," an expert complained.[18] They weren't qualified to teach morals and values—what were they, ethicists? Philosophers?

The defense attorneys did not take up the American Home Economics Association's offer to help, preferring to focus on the religious-liberty claims rather than the teaching of home economics. To bolster its case, the defense lined up Christian witnesses, such as a Mobile teacher who said that young people needed an open place to talk about values. She would never teach secular humanism, she added. One witness, who most likely was author Verdene Ryder, a Lutheran grandmother from Texas, told the court that her book, the most thoroughly challenged in the case, "complements Christianity in building strengths of families."[19]

The plaintiffs and experts misquoted some passages and took others out of context. For that matter, many of the academic experts on both sides admitted that they had not read the books, their children had not taken home economics, and they had not seen a home economics class. Even so, the decision was a foregone conclusion. It didn't help that Judge Hand not only brought in his own expert witness, a religious conservative who had praised his previous rulings, but took that witness out for dinner and picked up the check.[20] In a lengthy opinion, Judge Hand ruled on March 4, 1987, that secular humanism was a religion, and that the textbooks unconstitutionally promoted it. They must be removed from the classroom immediately. The next day, the news showed teachers taking textbooks out of students' desks.

Judge Hand's decision held for only a few months. The state school board voted by a single person to appeal the case, despite the opposition of Alabama governor Guy Hunt. The appellate court swiftly overturned the verdict, ruling that the books taught "independent thought, tolerance of diverse views, self-respect, maturity, self-reliance and logical decision making," all of which were entirely "appropriate" for a public school. Moreover, many of the books noted that "religion is one source of moral values," and none told students to ignore religious teachings.[21] No home economics association submitted an amicus brief to the appellate court, and the *Journal of Home Economics* barely mentioned the case.

Despite the appeals ruling, the case had a chilling effect. Publishers reexamined home economics textbooks to avoid offending Christian fundamentalists and had authors soften or remove some passages or add explicit references to religion. In particular, the next editions of the books targeted in the trial deleted the word "values," substituting the word "priorities." (One imagines that Paolucci would have been indignant.) One of the authors shrugged and didn't think the terminology mattered, saying, "Home economists are good communicators and we know not to use words that offend the listener."[22] Even edited, one of the textbooks drew hours of criticism from Eagle Forum members in front of the Alabama school board because two sentences that suggested yoga and meditation as options for managing stress promoted, the Forum members said, an Eastern religion. Surveying Alabama teachers, a researcher found that one quarter changed what they taught after the case, either censoring themselves or omitting hot-button subjects. One-tenth did not realize the ban had been overturned. Some felt threatened by what they saw as a change in public attitudes toward home economics. None agreed with Judge Hand's decision. One of the authors felt proud of her testimony, saying, "In my estimation, no one can teach family life education better than home economics. That's why we must continue to be on the forefront of this matter."[23]

But were they?

The American Home Economics Association started the 1980s with fifty thousand members. A dozen years later, it had fewer than twenty-five thousand. New college graduates called themselves family counselors, gerontologists, nutritionists, commercial interior designers, fashion designers, and teachers, not home economists. And they joined the professional groups that matched their specialties instead of the AHEA. In 1990, the Bureau of Labor Statistics stopped reporting the job title "home economist" in its *Occupational Outlook Handbook*. In 1991, *Illinois Teacher* folded. Its circulation had fallen below two thousand. Two years after that, its publisher, the University of Illinois, began phasing out its undergraduate home economics education degree, one of the oldest and most significant home economics programs in the country. The money was gone, and so were the faculty. "I'm the dinosaur," said *Illinois Teacher's* last editor, Mildred Barnes Griggs, the pioneer—she had been the university's first African American dean.[24]

Meanwhile, the business home economists had their own problems. Mrs. Housewife had become Ms. Working Mom, with no time for home visits. Companies weren't hiring "home economists" anymore. They did still hire in marketing, communications, test kitchens, and consumer affairs, and the business home economists who had already risen through the ranks, who had experience and savvy and connections, adapted. They called themselves "marketing consultants" or "communications specialists" or "consumer leads" and kept working. As of 1992, Home Economists in Business had 2,500 members.[25] They could easily raise the modern equivalent of $600,000 in sponsorships for the annual meeting from their employers. Former director Marlisa Bannister recalled an epic Land O'Lakes–sponsored salad bar. Connie Cahill rode in a limo with Olympic star Peggy Fleming and feted the winners of an M&M's contest in a trip that included a Disney ballroom filled with beach sand and a closed-down Tomorrowland peopled by candy sculptures. Another HEIB promoted natural gas wearing pantyhose with a pattern of blue flames running up the leg. Even Betty Newton, like so many retired home economists, kept working. Customers loved her too much to let go. They still called asking for her help, and the remaining Columbia Gas employees who had been Betty Newtons continued to give advice. One former Betty was still taking calls in the 1990s.

HEIB was at once cohesive and diverse: all its members had home economics college degrees, but they worked in a range of consumer industries. (And there were a few African American members now, including Chicago food writer Charla Draper and Indianapolis power company powerhouse Queen Bowman.) As businesses trimmed home economics departments in the 1980s, the organization grew even more important as a networking group for consultant gigs. Its member directory was a lifeline. Food consultant Dee Munson joined in 1958 after landing her first job, as an assistant editor at *Better Homes and Gardens*. Looking at the members over the decades, she marveled over how much they had accomplished—and how close they were. As women, "we had to stick together because there wasn't anyone else who was going to help us," Munson said.[26] Members vacationed together. The top women in the field mentored newcomers. Friendships spanned entire careers. However, HEIB was aging. There simply were no new, young business home economists for companies to hire. Universities stopped teaching business home economics. It didn't seem central to their mission, and women students had other options.

Some went the newly popular culinary-school route. Others went to business school, where they were finally welcome—they no longer had to enter companies through the kitchen door like Gilbreth. The former didn't have business or science coursework and the latter didn't know anything about textiles or food. Nor did the group feel like the mother association valued them. When the newly computerized American Home Economics Association screwed up HEIB's directory in the late eighties, Munson was ready for HEIB to go off on its own right then and there.

Across the field's specialties, the signs were clear: home economists had to do something. They had tried and tried, for three decades, to change their reputation. It was time—some said long past time—to rebrand. To change their name. But what to replace "home economics" with? That was the kicker. Like Ellen Richards and Annie Dewey almost a century before, they decided to call a meeting and choose a name. Close to a hundred home economists met, for the last time as "home economists," in sunbaked Scottsdale, Arizona, in October 1993. They had less than three days to make a decision for another century.

Though the organizers consciously compared the Scottsdale meeting to Lake Placid, in several key ways it was quite different. Ellen Richards, Melvil Dewey, and the rest of the Lake Placid Eleven were optimistic, shaping a new field, driving the train. The Scottsdale team was the time-worn, battle-scarred caboose. Whereas the brash founders shrugged, cut the red tape, and renamed their profession from "domestic science" to "home economics" in a practically empty room, their heiresses were considerately, mind-numbingly thorough. They aimed to ensure scrupulously fair representation of every element of their constituency. There were five organizations at the helm, who carefully chose conference attendees to reflect regional, professional, ethnic, gender, and age diversity. They had college administrators, extension workers, businesspeople. The organizers hired consultants, held twenty-two "creative input" pre-sessions, created eleven work groups and a joint writing team, commissioned papers from eleven leaders on the potential name change (presented with authors' names removed so as not to let reputation or professional considerations influence voters), and published a monograph.[27]

The Scottsdale meeting was intense and exhausting. On the surface the atmosphere was collegial, but everyone knew the stakes. As water beaded on the surface of the hotel water glasses, attendees worked into the wee hours, desperately seeking consensus. The ninety-six participants shared their takes on every single draft of the vision paper the joint writing team produced. There were multiple rounds of voting on names: "human ecology" versus "human environmental sciences" versus "human development," more than thirty-five options in all. In the end, the best they could do was "family and consumer sciences"—a name one-quarter of the group, including Spitze, rejected. It was too bad, the Finnish attendee lamented, that the English language did not have the right words to fully express the founders' complex and extraordinary idea. (Perhaps that person thought the Finnish *kotitalousoppi*, "philosophy of the household," did a better job.) They also developed a four-hundred-plus-word, thirty-bullet-point "conceptual framework" listing the profession's concerns, foci, fundamental beliefs, desired outcomes, and so on. For instance, family and consumer science practitioners "use a systems approach in professional practices." For shorthand there was a six-word "sound bite" version of what they did: "empowering individuals, strengthening families, enabling communities."[28] If it looked like a multisyllabic, focus-grouped effort, well, it was. (Nor, after all those years, did it actually define what home economists did. Though Horn had given a good suggestion in her 1989 letter to the editor: "improve the quality of life for families.")

Though the "perfect harmony" of Lake Placid did not prevail, the Scottsdale meeting ended in apparent unity. Standing on the hotel pool deck, the participants lit candles and floated them in the water to symbolize the profession's enduring strength. Afterward, everyone received a specially commissioned piece of art entitled "Spirit Rising," on handmade paper touched with gold and sky blue, inscribed with a swirly design that practically served as a Rorschach blot, letting you see whatever you wanted in it.[29]

Some of the participants did feel celebratory. A few did not come along: Spitze decided that she had given all she could to home economics, and turned to serving other public-spirited groups in her retirement. Many were simply relieved that they had finally reached a conclusion. Now they could get on with the work.

CHAPTER 15

What Would Ellen Do?

The conference emcee opened with politics. It was June 2018, and Central American children dominated the news, sobbing as they were pulled from their parents at the Mexico-US border. The core mission of the American Association of Family and Consumer Sciences—*née* the American Home Economics Association—was "creating healthy and sustainable families," according to its website. Yet speaking out against President Donald Trump's family-separation policies could be controversial, potentially alienating some supporters. Fortunately, the audience had an infallible guide for right action. "WWED—what would Ellen do?" the emcee asked. Understanding chuckles and "uh-huhs" echoed in the hotel ballroom. The answer was clear to all: AAFCS must condemn family separation at the border. "Ellen Richards would be having, as we say in the South, a sho'-nuff hissy fit right now," the emcee said. "Our nation needs us."

To be sure, the nation didn't necessarily know that it needed them. The years since Scottsdale have been tough on home economics. That is, on family and consumer sciences, though even within the discipline the new name has not completely taken over. The Future Homemakers of America held on to its old name until 1999, when it became Family, Career and Community Leaders of America (FCCLA). The federal education statistics office continued to use "home economics" for a number of years. Other countries and many university departments did not adopt the new name at all. Nor did the name reunify the profession around the ecological view that its specialties meant more together than apart. At the Western Michigan University Department of Family and Consumer Sciences, for instance, fashion students didn't understand why they were part of the same department as cooking. An interior design professor told me that her team focused not on homes but on commercial spaces, and that its placement in the Family and Consumer Sciences department was "vestigial. . . . We've come a *long* way."[1] As for an acronym, some say "FACS," pronounced "facks," and some say "FCS," eff-cee-ess.

And "people *still* think we sit around baking brownies all day," Kansas Education Department administrator Gayla Randel said.[2]

Contrary to public impression, home ec is not dead. As of last count, 2010–12, states reported that 3.5 million public school students took family and consumer sciences in the US, taught by more than twenty-seven thousand teachers. Some states didn't track middle school enrollment, so the real number was higher. You can still major in the subject: 786 US universities awarded more than thirty-eight thousand degrees in family and consumer sciences in 2017–18, according to federal data.

On top of that, colleges awarded close to twenty-five thousand degrees in the related fields of dietetics, fashion, hospitality, and interior design. However, that secondary school enrollment figure is a significant drop from 2002–3, when 5.5 million students took home ec—a similar percentage of the student body from 1959, with much better gender equity.[3] The enrollment researcher, Purdue professor Carol Werhan, attributed the decline partly to No Child Left Behind, which punished schools for low test scores and graduation rates, and to the continued dissolution of university home economics departments. When a Cornell panel recommended changing the name of the College of Human Ecology to the College of Public Policy, it wasn't clear what would happen to the textile, nutrition, and environmental design programs. The textile department chair criticized the process, saying it was purposely limited in a way that made the recommendations a foregone conclusion. Sound familiar?

Both popular culture and large scale efforts to promote nutrition have passed family and consumer sciences by. Even Rachael Ray, who got her start in the used-to-be-home-economics job of supermarket food demonstration, lamented in 2019 that no one taught home ec anymore. Her team heard the small Twitter outcry, through the AAFCS's preferred attention-raising hashtag #sayyestofcs, and brought on an adorably bow-tied man to promote the field and lead a knife skills demo, consciously using sound to increase interest as a fifties tel-a-structor would have. That was a victory. On the other side, then–First Lady Michelle Obama partnered with more than two hundred corporations, the Food Network, the Produce Marketing Association, the nutrition team in the government's agriculture department, and *Sesame Street* for Let's Move, the biggest child fitness and nutrition initiative of the last thirty years. But she did not respond to the American Association of Family and Consumer Sciences in 2010 when they wrote a letter informing her about their work combating obesity and about Ellen Richards's pioneering role in school lunch, a letter that concluded, "[We] look forward to collaborating with you." Nor did she respond to the AAFCS-directed Alliance for Family and Consumer Sciences in 2014, when they sent a twenty-three-page information packet fronted by a letter pleading to help. When the FCCLA asked her to dance her "Gimme 5" Let's Move routine on the Capitol lawn with three thousand earnest teenagers for the group's seventieth anniversary in 2015, she turned them down. They danced without her.[4]

Neglect breeds neglect. As colleges shutter home economics educator programs, there are fewer FCS teachers, which gives school districts a reason to cut the class, which narrows the pipeline of young people entering the field. Job cuts have also made it harder to track home ec in schools. There's no longer an Edna Amidon in the federal Education Department, and many state education departments have eliminated their home economics specialists. Bureaucratic inattention has real consequences. In Louisiana, where I live, the academic standards that are supposed to govern family and consumer sciences are so old that they refer to the Future Homemakers of America. They don't cover hospitality and tourism, a major part of the state economy. That class does exist—in fact, it's one of the state's career-technical education pathways that qualify a student for professional credentials. But it might be taught by a business teacher or, for that matter, a sports coach. And it's not in the 2017–18 list of family and consumer sciences courses that the state sent me, which means the students in those classes wouldn't be counted in Werhan's analysis.[5] No wonder the home economics professional groups fought so hard to make sure that the latest iteration of the Perkins Act, the federal vocational education law, included family and consumer sciences.

The federal government provides only a small amount of the overall funding for career education, but it drives the agenda.

As for business home economics, it has essentially vanished. Soon after Scottsdale, Home Economists in Business bowed to the mother organization's request that it cease holding a separate, two-day pre-conference and instead mingle all its events within the main conference. Things quickly broke down from there. The HEIBs held that pre-conference not only to focus on consumer trends, and maybe attract a person or two who would be turned off by the term "home economics," but because many of them had to work through the actual conference staffing exhibition tables. After a few years, HEIB spun off entirely. It renamed itself Consumer Science Business Professionals, then Consumer Trends Forum International, and continued holding an annual conference.[6] However, attendance did not recover, because companies were a lot less willing to pay to send employees to a conference when they weren't also going to promote the business as exhibitors. Members shifted their focus to groups such as the American Dietetic Association's business unit, the International Textile and Apparel Association, or the International Association of Culinary Professionals. After a decade, the group formerly known as HEIB shut down entirely.

The American Association of Family and Consumer Sciences would give its lifetime supply of silicone food replicas to draw the five thousand attendees of the 1985 American Home Economics Association convention, which featured Geraldine Ferraro not long off the vice-presidential trail. In 2018 and 2019, before the COVID pandemic, the AAFCS drew a little more than one-tenth of that. Once all the consumer-magazine food editors came to this conference, but when I checked in, no one could find an ID ribbon for "press." What was easy to find were the ribbons and cloth flowers that identified their wearers

as Legends or 50-Year Members. One could see the preponderance of retirees as depressing. One could also see it as an
admirable, enduring commitment. When Louisan Mamer died
in 2006, she had been an American Home Economics Association member for seventy-six years.[7]

The conference did still have a sewing machine competition and an old-school cookware demo, where business home
economist Betty Hahn kept up a running patter while sautéing,
shredding, and shuffling pans. "Folks, we're saving energy. But
you know what we're really saving? Money," she said into a
headset mic. "Save yourself some money, make your own fresh
coleslaw." And there were lots of college students—including,
most noticeably, a young white man with pink cheeks and a
sweet smile, wearing a suit and an AAFCS tie pin, who seemed
to be everywhere. He stood on the dais and urged people to
contribute to Habitat for Humanity. When the AAFCS public
relations person realized that they were about to have an all-
female quilting race, he gamely joined even though sewing was
his weak point. Joshua Eddinger-Lucero found his place in the
world through family and consumer sciences, and he wanted
everyone to be able to do the same.

Joshua Eddinger-Lucero didn't get dealt the world's easiest
hand. His father was not in the picture, his mother left high
school one credit short of a diploma, and the family didn't have
a lot of money, though his mother always told him and his little
sister, "Others have it worse." The three of them lived with her
parents in small-town Arkansas, and Eddinger-Lucero started
hanging out in the kitchen with his grandmother when he
was too short to reach the counter. His grandfather handled
most of the housekeeping and told stories about his time in
the navy over dinner. When his grandfather died in 2010, the

eighth-grader stepped up to give more support. He had to. His mother began having terrifying episodes of syncope and was hospitalized, the start of a wearying battle with autoimmune disease. But there was a bright spot in that dark time: Eddinger-Lucero had begun taking home economics. It immediately became his favorite class, and he a star student. His teacher bragged about his skills and encouraged him to join FCCLA.

Any parent would worry less about their teenager if they were involved in FCCLA. Even when its members aren't dancing on the Capitol lawn, it is an incredibly wholesome organization: the most popular after-hours pursuit at the national conference is trying to collect a full complement of state pins. Though its official boxy red blazer remains stuck in 1982, the organization has changed a lot. Students of color make up a large minority, 48 percent, and 27 percent of members are male. It has 181,000 members—in fact, membership is up.[8] At the 2020 Mississippi state convention, teenagers, some so nervous they had to stop to wipe away tears or fan themselves, presented reports on time-consuming, community-improving projects: a nutrition plan for an injured basketball player, a town celebration to teach kids about blues music, makeup kits for teenagers in foster care, an affordable marriage for a couple from church.

Eddinger-Lucero and two teammates put together an FCCLA project on preventing obesity, which included dressing up as a football player, a carrot, and a banana to give a workshop for elementary-school students. They won the local competition, then the state, and he took his first plane flight to present at the national competition in Anaheim. The judging panel gave the team a silver award (despite being somewhat nonplussed by the banana). But strangely, almost immediately, Eddinger-Lucero's teacher stopped encouraging him and became extremely critical of his class performance, as well as of him personally.

Despite her opposition, he kept taking family and consumer sciences. He felt at home in the classroom, a converted apartment with scratched floors and 1970s harvest-gold ovens, stocked with eggbeaters because the district had no money for mixers. He could smell when his classmates had oversalted their brownies. He ran to become treasurer of the Arkansas FCCLA board, and won. That was the start of a love of leadership for the shy teen. He went to board meetings, his hair sharply parted and slicked to the side. He stood up and spoke up and volunteered and made his voice heard, and the national home economics people began to know who he was. He became co-chair of the AAFCS student unit. He said the women he met in the national group were "powerhouse women. They may not sit in these corner offices . . . but they're having a lasting impact."[9] Becoming a home economist was a little intimidating—after all, he was no Ellen Richards, he thought. But he was determined to become a leader in the field. "I want to be that support network for a student just like me," he said. By his senior year of college at the University of Central Arkansas, he was student government president, with a myriad of commitments, who somehow still found time to call his mother several times a day and exercise his emotional-support dog Aiden Scout, a German shepherd who hadn't fully grown into his ears and needed some emotional support of his own.

Bonnie Eddinger wasn't initially a fan of her son's career decision, given the conflicts with his high-school teacher. But she teared up at a 2019 university luncheon to watch him receive the Outstanding FACS Student of the Year award. Home economics faculty "just saw the potential in him," she said. They "treated him like a person, and not the kid his mother wouldn't shut up and leave alone." People came up to her on campus and said, "We just love Josh—he's going places." Where he was going, to start with, was a teaching job. Even

with the enrollment drop in public school family and consumer sciences, college home economics teacher-training programs report exceptionally high placement rates. It was one
of the things that encouraged his interest in the field, he said,
unknowingly echoing Louisan Mamer from ninety years earlier: "I don't have to worry about finding a job."[10]

The most innovative teachers aren't necessarily the youngest.
The second the small blonde girl walked into Angela DeHart's
classroom in Virginia's largest middle school, she pulled me
over. "Welcome to the most *amazing* class," she said. DeHart
was named a Virginia Lottery Super Teacher in 2017, and her
students had indeed hit the jackpot.

A tall, African American woman, DeHart joked with her students but respectfully called them "lady" and "sir." She went
back to school in her forties to become a teacher, and commuted
forty-five minutes each way to Glasgow Middle School because
she wanted to educate children of color. DeHart had spent years
in dead-end jobs, crafting on the side. When she discovered family and consumer sciences, she had a personality-shaking revelation: "I am an engineer," she said. "I'm an engineer because I
craft." The problem-solving, the physical manipulation of material, the technology—this was a way into science, especially for
girls, who often see science as a male subject. DeHart's father
was an engineer, but he didn't recognize the same skills in his
daughter. ("I believe men wouldn't have succeeded at hunting
if the place hadn't been *full* of animals," DeHart said during
lunch duty. "They can't find their *socks*.") Nobody had framed
engineering in a way she could understand, she said; if they
had, "that would have changed my life." The discovery inextri-
cably tied home economics to science and technology for her.
"The first computer was the weaving machine," she said. And it

needed a reboot. Forget learning how to write a check. DeHart wanted to set up a classroom bitcoin economy. She branched into STEM education, running the Glasgow robotics and technology clubs as well as FCCLA, and stocked her classroom with both circuit kits and felt.

And home economics wasn't just science. DeHart made connections for her students to life skills and careers. Like most home economics school kitchens, Glasgow Middle has a room with several home-kitchen-style pods, as if kids were playing house at Ikea. DeHart thought it should be set up like a professional catering kitchen, with central metal prep tables and pots hung on the walls. She taught students not how to follow a recipe but how to write one: that's what chefs do. However, whether or not one ever entered a professional kitchen, she thought that everyone needed to learn how to cook. "If we don't teach our children how to cook, we turn them over to the machine that makes food," she said. And again, the science led the way: "You're a chemistry experiment walking around, and what you feed yourself matters." She envisioned using the *Cook's Illustrated* food science cookbook as a textbook.

Over and over, DeHart reworked home economics tropes into activities that hit multiple domains at once. Instead of having her class machine-sew quilted pillows, she created her own unit in which students learned about the role of the sewing machine in capitalism; researched quilt patterns; collaboratively designed quilts that felt meaningful to their own lives; "shopped" from "Bank of d'Heart" paying $25 in (imaginary) class cash if they lost a needle; and hand-sewed a quilt top, which proud parents viewed at a Quilt Exhibition Party. Below the fun, it was Hazel Taylor Spitze's ideal muffin lesson. Along with fine motor skills and the practical ability to mend torn clothes, the quilting project taught public speaking, history, problem-solving, and how to work as a team, an experience so frustrating at times it prompted one girl to exclaim, "Democracy is insane!"

DeHart taught Japanese rice-bran composting and the life cycle of a cotton T-shirt. Kids researched apartment rental options in metro DC, learning firsthand how important it was to get an education and a decently paid job. If she ran the world—and with her energy, she could—her class would grow food for the cafeteria. Home economics "would be alive! We would have bees! We would know stuff!" she said. What would Ellen Richards do today? She would teach like Angela DeHart.

Yet despite the American Association of Family and Consumer Sciences conference workshops on emotional wellness and cultural competence, and even earning the incredibly tough teaching award of middle-schoolers' rapt attention, DeHart felt quite alone. Curriculum changes forced her to end several of her most innovative units, including quilting. The maintenance team mowed down her mint. The day I visited, sixth-grade textiles consisted of assembling pieces of felt into a daisy whose petals represented the different areas of students' lives. "You've got a lot of entrenched people," DeHart said. "There's no creativity, there's no invention."[11]

Though DeHart chafed under the old ways, some teachers are drawn to family and consumer sciences precisely for its lo-fi elements—like Eddinger-Lucero's college classmate Leah Welch. The mother of grown children, she brought bunny-shaped wooden gift baskets to thank faculty for all their help. Her son made the baskets, and Welch stocked them with snacks tagged with notes such as "Thanks for 'pudding' up with me" and "Your friendship has 'mentos' so much."

"I think kids need good hobbies, wholesome hobbies," Welch said. She thought home economics should be as focused on life as on careers. Kids need to learn to be good neighbors, friends, digital citizens. They need to learn skills that can save them money as an adult—"go anywhere and try to do a kid's birthday party," she said, rolling her eyes. She wanted her classroom to be a place where kids would have to interact with one another instead of using screens.

However, even when a teacher is less innovative than DeHart—and let's face it, most are—home economics classes have a lot to offer. Beth Elms of Mayflower High in Arkansas kept a closet full of prom dresses that any student could borrow, and snack cubbies so anyone hungry could eat. Her walls had vision boards and inspirational quotes from Jimmy Carter, Winston Churchill, and 1 Corinthians 10:31, "Do all to the glory of God." A "Take What You Need" board offered slips of paper printed with reassuring words for peace, confidence, happiness, courage, and self-control. Elms was the only home economics teacher in a rural high school with fewer than four hundred kids, so her workload had a lot of variety. One spring day included a granola-bar lab; Introduction to Teaching, whose students were about to earn their paraprofessional certification, qualifying them for immediate, reliable, and meaningful, if low paid, employment; a project where kids interviewed their parents about what it was like to parent at different stages of their children's lives; preparation for Elms's popular Cupcake Wars competition; and Sewing II, which was taking a break from complicated jackets and curved seams to quilt.

Elms's students in their track pants, leggings, and baggy shirts said her class mattered. The granola-bar makers analyzed what they did wrong when the oats wouldn't hold together. Sure, you could buy granola bars at the store, but "you can make them yourself and make them much better," a boy told me. The sewing students talked of the accomplishment and savings of repairing their clothes. Homemade gifts are better. Making a tote bag is better than spending your time on social media. It relieves stress (well, except when you screw something up in your sewing project, they said, and then it *causes* stress).

Home economics "is really important," one of the juniors said. She spoke of the parenting mistakes she had seen, and of her older sister, who had a baby earlier than she'd planned but was making it work. "I think it should be mandatory."[12]

And it could look many different ways, Welch said. She thought that DeHart's class sounded great. She was excited about her own plans too. "It takes all of us to make the world go 'round."[13]

Where is home economics now? Hidden, beleaguered, burgeoning, changing, and still here.

After negative feedback from students, faculty, and alumni, Cornell ditched the proposal to reconfigure the College of Human Ecology into a public policy school, opting instead to create a separate, new college and leave the college formerly known as home economics as is.

Even with the business home economics organization likely gone for good, its pursuits remain, former chair Roberta Duyff said. "I think that it's found a new route," she said. "The terminology is lost but the profession is still there." People still work on consumer safety for the government, teach community nutrition, and design space food and nanotextiles. "Maybe what needs to be celebrated is the fact that we've graduated."[14]

Angela DeHart retired in early 2020, when she turned sixty. After a dozen years, "the fight was too much," she said. "They didn't get it. They're fighting for sewing machines." She was worn out. Working endlessly after hours to do the innovative things she wanted, pushing against her bosses, being the isolated rabble-rouser, stepping on toes, reaching out but never getting reached out to. "I heard rumors of people talking about me but they never talked *to* me," she said. "If I had been white, I think that would have been a huge difference."[15] She has continued to intensively mentor two cohorts of teenage girls of color, the STEM Impressionists, in science and technology. When they all graduate from college, she might write a book sharing her home economics resources, she said. She still sees home ec everywhere. In the doctor's office. In "makerspaces," the new cool hands-on tech lab for schools—cool and not considered home economics because men had claimed it, she said. The appropriation irritated her deeply.

Joshua Eddinger-Lucero got a teaching job, in a brand-new building, in the middle of a pandemic and the worst recession since the 1930s. He and his mother were packing up to move to Hot Springs, bringing his dog, Aiden Scout. In fact, there were more FCS teacher openings in Arkansas than anyone could remember before, more than two dozen—a bunch of teachers retired when they had to switch to online classes, he said. Simultaneously he enrolled in a distance master's program so he could work in policy, maybe in politics, later on. But first he wanted to teach. The COVID-19 pandemic might make a difference, he said. It showed people why home economics mattered: "All of the skills that everyone needs stuck at home are skills that we teach."

But the field had to hold up its end of the bargain and keep up with society, "to make sure that we don't slide into this abyss of irrelevance," he said. "If we don't come out of it and change the narrative, it will disappear."[16]

How to Bring Back Home Ec

I wasn't a home economics true believer when I began research-
ing this book. I had spent five years covering charter schools
in Louisiana, where double blocks of time for reading and
math were the norm due to a history of educational failure and
a tightly enforced set of academic-renewal standards. School
leaders had a hard time justifying *recess*, let alone a hands-on
subject such as home economics that doesn't count on the state
report card. For that matter, I'm not constitutionally inclined
to come down on one side or the other of a tendentious issue.
But a funny thing happened when I mentioned I was writing
The Secret History of Home Economics to, by now, hundreds if not
thousands of people. Almost every time, they have the same
reaction: *We should bring that back.*

I have never heard that level of consensus about anything
else I have covered, ever. People want home economics.

And yet the field continues to flounder. Why the disconnect? At American Association of Family and Consumer Sciences conferences, I heard panel after panel talk urgently about how to revive the field, how to show decision-makers that they matter. I could fill fifty pages with quotes from hand-wringing home economics leaders. The unfortunate instinct of those earnest and well-meaning organizers is to form committees and reexamine the accreditation standards. To borrow a metaphor from Beatrice Paolucci, how can we hitch the booster rocket of public demand to the home economics spaceship to make it take off again? I have several suggestions.

1. Change the name back to "home economics."

The only people I meet who know the term "family and consumer sciences" are middle-school teachers or married to them. The 1993 name change failed. Hazel Spitze was right: rather than shift the public perception of home economics, it rendered the field invisible. People in the US think that home economics no longer exists because children no longer take a class by that name. Besides, the name "home economics" has never fully disappeared, in that family and consumer science professionals constantly find themselves explaining their jobs by saying, "It used to be home economics." So change the name back!

For that matter, to the extent that anyone pays attention to the connotations of the two terms, I would contend that the word "home" is more inclusive than the word "family." No matter how broadly the field defines it—"You and your dog are a family," International Federation for Home Economics president Gwendolyn Hustvedt told me—the fact is that "family" is not a happy term for everyone. It's also not always relevant to our daily personal caretaking. If you live alone, as 14 percent of Americans do, is family relevant to your decisions about clothing, home environment, and what you have for dinner?[1] I think not. But everyone who has a home thinks about what they're going to put on their plate for dinner, what detergent to wash that plate with, and how they're going to pay for the food and the cleaning supplies.

2. Make home economics mandatory.

There are good reasons to make home economics part of the middle- or high school day, even if they don't include Catharine Beecher's contention that teachers are better qualified to teach the subject than parents, even focusing on practical skills and not ecological analysis. For 180 years, men in power have argued that kids can just learn that stuff at home. But whom does that serve? Every institution or person that benefits when housekeeping and caretaking are invisible. If we needed any further evidence of this invisibility, take the prevailing and disastrous conclusion among political decision-makers and most employers that parents quarantining against COVID-19 in 2020 could simply work their paid jobs from home without school supervision or childcare—as if kids aren't work.

Besides, who has the time to teach home economics at home? A single parent, or one working two jobs, or working twelve-hour days and still on call after the kids go to bed, or supervising virtual schooling, or spending the hours after school shuttling a kid to sports or music practice with the hope that the child will earn a college scholarship and not have decades of debt? Does a teenager working after school or doing hours of homework have time to learn the many practical skills of housekeeping? Parents have more than enough to do without also having to be the sole trainers in cooking, cleaning, financial literacy, and relationship skills. Teaching a child to cook takes far longer and creates far more mess than doing it yourself. As Catharine Beecher observed, "Almost every woman knows, that it is easier to do the work, herself, than it is to teach an awkward and careless novice; and the great majority of women, in this Country, are obliged to do almost every thing in the shortest and easiest way."[2]

Besides, we often default to gendered expectations. Boys spend less time on chores than girls; heterosexual, partnered women do more of the housework than men. That is why, Robin Morgan told me, she now considers home economics crucial for gender equality. She gave an impromptu 2018 postscript to her explosive 1971 keynote speech: "Home economics definitely should exist. And it should flourish. And it should be for males—*only*."[3] While we're at it, let's go back to Ellen Richards and require home economics to include light carpentry so that everyone can install closet shelves at their favored height.

Finally, thanks to the strength of the historical connection between girls and domesticity, when home economics is elective, fewer boys take it. Purdue professor Carol Werhan found that home economics courses were evenly divided by gender in middle school in 2010–12, and had a 65 percent female majority in high school. Yet during the last three years, I have never seen a home-ec class at any level that was not majority, and typically a good 75 percent, female. The FCCLA youth organization is 73 percent female.[4]

If you want kids to learn home economics, and maybe even liberate future adult women from unequal housework, make the class mandatory. In many places, home economics could fulfill existing requirements: as of February 2020, twenty-one states required high school students to take a personal finance course, an increase of four states since 2018.[5] Such a decision would also pressure universities to expand the home economics teacher-training programs that they have been cutting for years. Speaking of which . . .

3. Diversify the profession.

Yes, it's obvious, and it's part of a broader problem in teaching and social services. While professional organizations have been working on this issue for a while, the fact is that home economists are still, overwhelmingly, older white women. "I don't think we value diversity as much as we preach it," new teacher Joshua Eddinger-Lucero said. With all due respect to older white women, "when those are the people leading our field . . . you're not changing the conversation." And it's hard to shift the stereotypes of a field when its face remains the same.

There are ways to recruit people who are not white and not women. They include adjusting the content of the field to emphasize science and technology, and appealing to career-changers from professions that have more men, such as restaurant chefs. Home economics, or nutrition at least, still has a home at many historically Black universities, including Prairie View A&M, where Margaret Murray Washington could have taught; Tuskegee University, where she did; Florida A&M, Gladys Gary Vaughn's alma mater; and Southern University, home of Pinkie Thrift. The National Coalition for Black Development in Family and Consumer Sciences works on recruiting and retaining Black home economists through mentoring and scholarships. Finally, making home economics mandatory in K–12 would encourage more young people to join the profession: no one prepares for a job they don't know exists.

4. Embrace life skills as well as career preparation.

Home economics has clung for decades to its place in vocational education, for both the funding mandates and the respect. The recent revival of career-tech increases the incentive for that partnership. Preprofessional cooking classes and their like should absolutely remain in place: they matter, and they provide a quick entrée into careers. However, the public wants home economics to also teach life skills. You don't need to become a banker. You do need to know how not to get scammed by credit-card companies. Home economics should not have to defend its worth solely as job preparation, especially because the current framework for vocational education is a lousy fit. The 2018 Perkins Career and Technical Education Act lists sixteen "career clusters."[6] Due to its interdisciplinary nature, home economics cuts across several of them, which means it tends to get overlooked.

The emphasis on careers has a second problem that stems from the undervaluation of what has traditionally been women's work: educators emphasize well-paid vocational tracks, and many home economics–related jobs pay badly. That's especially true with professions that public-school career-technical education targets, those that require more training than a high school diploma but less than a four-year college degree. Daycare staff earn less than welders. Of course, if we seriously valued this work that makes our lives much easier, that in some cases makes it possible for people to work outside the home as (for instance) welders, we might improve the pay of the people who do it.

5. Advance the progressive, scientific, ecological view within home economics.

The people who talk to me want home economics to teach life skills so that kids can be better-functioning adults (and teenagers!). They don't give the broader answer given by Ellen Swallow Richards: *"so we can change the world."*

Sewing can be soothing, and life skills do matter. The public may be happy with "stitching and stirring." But reporting this book made it vividly clear to me that the vision of home economics that has real impact is the one shared by Ellen Swallow

Richards, Beatrice Paolucci, and Angela DeHart. Home economics has to be rigorous and challenging as well as fun—not just a brain break— or there's no place for it in today's schools. "I need to be the norm and not the aberration," DeHart said. I agree. Home economics is, can, and should be an interdisciplinary, ecological field that explores the connections between our homes and the world with an eye to addressing the root causes of problems such as hunger, homelessness, isolation, and environmental devastation.

This focus means getting pragmatic about what classes *don't* need to include, as Paolucci said sixty (*sixty!*) years ago. We don't need to teach every kid to use a sewing machine, and we especially don't need to quiz teenagers on naming a sewing machine's parts, as I heard one teacher-in-training plan. Instead, we should teach how the technology of the sewing machine changed the world. Students should learn about the labor problems of Southeast Asian sweatshops and the urban gig economy; the beauty and significance of the quilts made by formerly enslaved African Americans; the electrical engineering behind e-textiles; ways to limit the pollution caused by fabric dyes and create nontoxic alternatives. Which means training teachers to lead sophisticated discussions, translate between sciences and hands-on projects, and make connections. Home economics teachers should be as comfortable with 3D printers as they have been with rotary cutters. DeHart advocates bringing together a multifaceted group to reinvent curriculum—including innovators, traditionalists, representatives of the careers into which home economics feeds, and teachers of academic subjects so home ec can support their work. I want to see home economists "using all the resources of modern science," as Richards put it, to tackle adaptation to climate change from every angle of their 360-degree perspective: redesigning homes and clothes to keep us comfortable in more heat using less energy; preserving community ties when entire towns have to relocate away from sea-level rise; helping people find resources to lower their power bills—to name a few possibilities. They might also make our lives happier by solving lesser problems. For instance, speaking selfishly as a knitter, there's got to be a way that home economists can cut the Gordian knot to produce yarn that preserves local traditions and heritage species, pays farmers and manufacturers a living wage, doesn't pollute waterways, and doesn't cost a fortune. Right?

Part of finding those solutions will entail bringing the science work that used to be home economics back into the fold, infusing it with a socially responsible ethos. Without that, flavor scientists create new varieties of Mountain Dew and textile innovators put out those 1990s T-shirts that changed color with body temperature. Which are fun, but the possibilities are far greater. (Besides, a Mississippi FCCLA member warned me solemnly that Hot Cheetos—a miracle of food science if ever I saw one—burn the digestive tract.) Cornell College of Human Ecology fiber-science professors still think like their home economist predecessors. They're working on everything from making fashion supply chains more sustainable to creating safer suits for firefighters to engineering fabric at the molecular level through nanotechnology to embedding solar cells and making better medical personal protective equipment.

These solutions have to go beyond individual actions to advocating for policy change. If we could fix problems as enduring as poverty and racism through individual effort, they would have been fixed long ago. Home economics tells us to pair the American reflex of bootstrapping with structural solutions. If the ironing board is a home economics tool, so is the zoning board. Hazel Spitze replaced broken zippers in her family's clothing, because she could, and she valued saving money and not throwing away something fixable. She also said, "I wonder if it isn't about time someone invented a better zipper!"[7] Day care, the economic value of housework, consumer protection, the freedom to achieve regardless of race or gender—all these have been and must continue to be home economics issues. The field is inherently feminist, which is, as writer Marie Shear defined it, "the radical notion that women are people." (If the profession dedicated to upholding the home and family embraces feminism, then who can argue against it?) When home ec hasn't harnessed politics, it's been taken over by people in power for their own uses, as the ugly history of segregated classes for Blacks and Latinas shows. The home may be a refuge, but it is also political and economic, and it always has been. People affect and are affected by everything outside their walls. As Paolucci said, it's ecological.

As I write this halfway through 2020, people are more aware than ever of the permeability of those four walls as we stay inside, entertain outside, and wonder whether sanitizing the groceries makes us safer or risks bleach poisoning. We may be cleaning supermarket shelves of flour, cooking from the back of the pantry or from a food pantry, or sewing masks. We are trying to find ways to connect. After years of agita from the remaining home-ec establishment and of valuing homemade things as a trendy luxury, we are thinking about home economics more than we have in a long, long time. I hope this book has made you realize that its possibilities go far deeper than a jar of homemade jam in a pretty Mason jar with a bow. As Ellen Richards said, we all should "keep thinking."

(Even after the rush of people making cloth masks to protect against COVID-19, DeHart still thought sewing machines were worthless. As usual, she preferred ingenuity and made masks by adapting a bra, reorienting the straps into ear loops, by hand. Added benefit: "I made two of them, because it's a bra," she said.)

Satenig St. Marie, now in her nineties, still lives in her elegant split-level ranch in Westport. The nightmare of coronavirus "offers a golden opportunity for Home Economics to integrate its image of cooking and sewing into broader needs of society," she wrote in an email. "I sound like a preacher, but I do believe that, with enlightened leadership, the profession could play a significant role in shaping what is probably going to be a changing world."[8]

Is the field up to the challenge? Can it persuade the many people who are committing home economics in sheep's clothing—the cool purveyors of farm-to-table food, the architects of smart doorbells, the designers of nanotextiles—to join them? Can it convince the people in charge of schools, and workplaces, and state houses? It has to.

We have an opportunity to bring back home ec. Let's not waste it. Home economists hate waste.

ACKNOWLEDGMENTS

Thank you to my agent, Jen Marshall of Aevitas Creative Management, for seeing what this book could be, and to my editor, Amy Cherry, for never wanting it to be anything else. To Bee Holekamp, Zarina Patwa, and Huneeya Siddiqui for answering my innumerable questions; Stephanie Romeo for help with photos; publicist Erin Sinesky Lovett and marketer Michelle Waters for reaching the people who reach the readers; Susan Sanfrey, Anna Oler, and Sarahmay Wilkinson, who guided the book through its kitschless design and production; and Norton and ACM's rights staff, for their midwifery. Terri Simon provided sarcasm and late-breaking insensitivity feedback.

I could not have written this book without the financial, temporal, and emotional support (and free seltzer) of the Knight-Wallace Journalism Fellowship. Thank you to Lynette Clemetson, Birgit Rieck, Rob Yoon, John Godfrey, June Howard, the rest of the staff, the board, my fellow fellows, and the KWF alumni community for your tireless cheerleading. I'm so happy to make you proud.

The Robert B. Silvers Foundation supported this book financially at a crucial time, and Purdue and Southern Methodist universities funded my visits to their invaluable archives.

The staff and board members of the American Association of Family and Consumer Sciences; Family, Career and Community Leaders of America; and Kappa Omicron Nu were unfailingly helpful, especially Nancy Bock, Jacqueline Holland,

Carolyn Jackson, Gwynn Mason, and Janet Ryder. Geraldine Luepke and Deb Zwiefelhofer of Twin Cities HEIB/FCS Professionals sent me stacks from their archives, as did Satenig St. Marie.

Thank you to the many librarians and archivists who guided my research. Jan Barnes at the New Orleans Public Library fielded a gajillion obscure ILL requests, and the Mid-City Library branch staff were always excited by them. Nancy Brown-Martinez at the University of New Mexico let me hear Fabiola de Baca's voice. Dana Chandler at Tuskegee went beyond above and beyond. Sarah Edwards at Winthrop University and Valerie Stenner at the University of Delaware found documents pertaining to the integration of Southern American Home Economics Association chapters. The archives staff at Columbia University opened up Annie Dewey's world. Elaine Engst, Eileen Keating, and Eisha Neely held the string through Cornell's labyrinthine archives. Robert Garrett at the Archives of Michigan and Donzella Maupin at Hampton searched through files so I didn't have to. Joan Gosnell at Southern Methodist University filled in all the necessary gaps about J. C. Penney's. Reinette Jones at the University of Kentucky got the only extant library set of the New Homemakers of America magazine scanned. Emily Marsh at the National Agricultural Library put together an exceptionally helpful exhibit and tracked down obscure facts. Juli McLoone at the University of Michigan started me on the way. Franklin Robinson Jr. at the Smithsonian National Museum of American History is the archivist for everyone's favorite spark plug, Louisan Mamer. Stephanie Schmitz at Purdue University not only found files but took me to buy groceries. Additional thanks to the staff at the AMEDD Museum, Eastern Illinois University, the Iowa Women's Archives, the MIT Museum, the U.S. Air Force Research Laboratory, and the U.S. Army Heritage and Education Center for tracking down photos. Librarians rule.

As a long-enduring academic and government discipline, home economics produced reams of dissertations and reports over the decades—you would never believe how many. These scholars' meticulous research made this book possible. Among the living, I am particularly indebted to Amy Sue Bix (technology), Megan Elias (Miss Van Rose), Carolyn Goldstein, Virginia Railsback Gunn (early land-grant colleges), Sheena Harris (Washington), Alison Horrocks (Kittrell), Erika Janik (radio), Mire Koikari (Okinawa), Linda Rochell Lane (Washington), Susan Levine (school lunch), Sharon Nickols, Merrihelen Ponce (de Baca), Penny Ralston, Lori Rohlk (radio), Margaret W. Rossiter, Laura Shapiro, William Shurtleff and Akiko Aoyagi (Cooper), Kathryn Kish Sklar (Beecher), Sarah Stage, Virginia Vincenti, and Carol Werhan. Ralston and Werhan additionally contributed invaluable feedback on my first draft. Elias is the author of the only large-scale history of home economics to predate mine; although it is different in approach and timeline, I nonetheless waited to read it until I was almost done with this book to avoid unintentional duplication

I send my deepest appreciation to the sources who sat with me for hours. Never before have I interviewed three nonagenarians for a project. Thank you, among others, to Evelyn Birkby, Connie Cahill, Angela DeHart, Doris Hanson, Gayla Randel, Laura Smart, Glenna Spitze, Satenig St. Marie, Gladys Gary Vaughn, Virginia Vincenti, and especially Joshua Eddinger-Lucero, who shared his toughest experiences in the faith that home economics matters. And thank you to the many AAFCS members who continue to enlighten me.

Thank you to the Education Writers Association and the edu journalism community, especially Sarah Carr, Caroline Hendrie, Katherine Reynolds Lewis, Emily Richmond, Greg Toppo, and Liz Willen. To the editors who have made my work better, particularly Drew Broach, Marcia Dick, Bill Friskics-Warren, and Sarah Garland. To the Blue House in New Orleans, led by Aron Chang and Gilad Meron, for financial, professional, and mental health support, and for giving me a break from Alexander the Action Cat. To the Boston musicians-etc. who believed in my writing from way back: Flynn Cohen, Elio DeLuca, Mark Erelli, Matt Parish, Evan Sicuranza, Matt Smith, Ryan Walsh. To the Metairie Nissan dealership shuttle driver who lit up when I told her about Margaret Murray Washington. Thank you to my writers-in-crime Alison Fensterstock, Matt Higgins, Marisa Meltzer, Azi Paybarah, John Pendygraft, Tanya Shaffer, triply Kate Schapira, and Patrick Wall. To Heidi Nieland Hall, gone too soon. To the dharma bums, the Ladies' Email Auxiliary, the Old Buggaz Martini Club, the Olde Mouldy, and Piehxle. To my family, including my cats Eva, Alexander the Action Cat, and John Hearn, because Gwendolyn Hustvedt of the International Federation of Home Economics told me, "You and your dog are a family." To Chris Cromwell, my biggest fan; the feeling is mutual. To Lindsay and Harper, for endless enthusiasm. To my dad, who thinks I'm funny. Cathy Lewis Dreilinger is the original writing home economist in my life. Linda Lewis Grigg, I wish you could read this.

NOTES

Preface: Everything You Know about Home Economics Is Wrong

1. Caroline Louisa Hunt, *The Life of Ellen H. Richards* (Boston: Whitcomb & Barrows, 1912).
2. Gladys Gary Vaughn, interview by author, June 24, 2019.
3. Sandra Stansbery Buckland, Catherine Amoroso Leslie, and Teena Jennings-Rentenaar, "Needlearts in the Journal of Family & Consumer Sciences: A 100-Year Retrospective," *Journal of Family and Consumer Sciences* 101, no. 2 (Spring 2009): 33–37, Judy Rollins, "Secondary Home Economics Curricula Perpetuate a Stereotype," *Journal of Home Economics* 73, no. 1 (Spring 1981): 24–26.
4. Ellen Swallow Richards, "Ten Years of the Lake Placid Conference on Home Economics: Its History and Aims" (Lake Placid Conference on Home Economics, 10th Annual Meeting, Chautauqua, NY, July 6, 1908).
5. National Center for Education Statistics, Digest of Education Statistics, "Table 322.10. Bachelor's Degrees Conferred by Postsecondary Institutions, by Field of Study: Selected Years, 1970–71 through 2016–17," 2018.
6. Carol R. Werhan, "Family and Consumer Sciences Secondary School Programs: National Survey Shows Continued Demand for FCS Teachers," *Journal of Family and Consumer Sciences* 105, no. 4 (2013): 41–45.

Chapter 1: The Road to Home Economics

1. Marion Talbot, *The Education of Women* (Chicago: University of Chicago Press, 1910); Thomas D. Snyder, *120 Years of American Education: A Statistical Portrait* (Washington, DC: National Center for Education Statistics, January 1993).
2. Martha Bacon, "Miss Beecher in Hell," *American Heritage*, December 1962.
3. Catharine Esther Beecher, *Suggestions Respecting Improvements in Education, Presented to the Trustees of the Hartford Female Seminary, and Published at Their Request* (Hartford, CT: Packard & Butler, 1829).

4. Kathryn Kish Sklar, *Catharine Beecher: A Study in American Domesticity* (New York: W. W. Norton, 1973).

5. Catharine E. Beecher, *A Treatise on Domestic Economy*, 2nd ed. (New York: Harper & Brothers, 1842).

6. Caroline Louisa Hunt, *The Life of Ellen H. Richards* (Boston: Whitcomb & Barrows, 1912); Pamela Curtis Swallow, *The Remarkable Life and Career of Ellen Swallow Richards: Pioneer in Science and Technology* (Hoboken, NJ: Wiley, 2014).

7. Hunt, *The Life of Ellen H. Richards*; Swallow, *The Remarkable Life and Career of Ellen Swallow Richards*.

8. Hunt.

9. Hunt.

10. Sheena Harris, "A Female Reformer in the Age of Booker T. Washington: The Life and Times of Margaret Murray Washington" (PhD diss., University of Memphis, 2012). Fisk listed Murray's birth year as 1864. As Harris discusses, no one has gotten to the bottom of this. Another unsettled matter is her height. Some biographers, as well as rangers at the US Park Service Tuskegee Institute National Historic Site, say she was short, pointing to the unusually low bannister in her home. However, the *Fisk Herald* graduation issue (as per Lane, below) gives it as five foot seven, and photos show her about the same height as her husband.

11. Emmett J. Scott, "Mrs. Booker T. Washington's Part in Her Husband's Work," *Ladies' Home Journal*, Philadelphia, May 1907. The name is sometimes listed as "Saunders" but MMW corrected it herself in Scott's draft, which is preserved at Tuskegee.

12. Linda Rochell Lane, *A Documentary of Mrs. Booker T. Washington* (Edwin Mellen Press, 2001).

13. Booker T. Washington and Edith Shehee papers at Tuskegee (BTW).

14. BTW.

15. BTW.

16. Amy Bix, "Chemistry of Cooking, Chemistry in War: Women in Nineteenth and Twentieth-Century Land-Grant Science and Engineering," *Bulletin for the History of Chemistry* 38, no. 2 (2013): 132–39; Virginia B. Vincenti, "Chronology of Events and Movements Which Have Defined and Shaped Home Economics," in *Rethinking Home Economics: Women and the History of a Profession*, ed. Sarah Stage and Virginia B. Vincenti (Ithaca, NY: Cornell University Press, 1997), 321–30; Richard Gordon Moores, *Fields of Rich Toil: The Development of the University of Illinois, College of Agriculture* (Champaign: University of Illinois Press, 1970); Virginia Railsback Gunn, "Industrialists Not Butterflies: Women's Higher Education

at Kansas State Agricultural College, 1873–1882," *Kansas History*, Spring 1995; *Catalogue of the Hampton Normal and Agricultural Institute, Hampton, Va., for the Academical Year 1870–71*, 1871.

17. W. E. B. Du Bois, *The Souls of Black Folk* (Chicago: A. C. McClurg, 1903); Sarah Stage and Virginia B. Vincenti, eds., *Rethinking Home Economics: Women and the History of a Profession* (Ithaca, NY: Cornell University Press, 1997).

18. Gunn, "Industrialists Not Butterflies."

19. Maggie J. Murray, "Training Our Girls for the Responsibilities of Life," *Fisk Herald*, June 1890; Booker T. Washington, "'Atlanta Compromise' Speech" (Cotton States and International Exposition, Atlanta, GA, September 18, 1895).

20. Margaret Murray Washington, "Helping the Mothers," in *Working with the Hands* (New York: Doubleday, Page, 1904), 119–34.

21. Margaret James Murray Washington (Mrs. B. T. Washington), *Work for the Colored Women of the South* (Tuskegee, AL: Tuskegee Normal School Press, 1894).

22. Washington, *Work for the Colored Women of the South*; "Kicks on Pictures of 'Aunt Jemima': Mrs. Booker T. Washington Addresses Colored Club Women," *Nashville Tennessean and the Nashville American*, June 13, 1913; Margaret James Murray Washington, "We Must Have a Cleaner Social Morality" (Old Bethel AME Church, Charleston, SC, September 12, 1898).

23. Virginia Church, "The Servant Question" (Hampton, VA: Press of the Hampton Normal and Agricultural Institute, 1911); "Editorial: The Servant Question," *Southern Workman*, July 1911.

24. Harris, "A Female Reformer in the Age of Booker T. Washington."

25. "Cry from the Colored Women," *Chicago Daily Tribune*, September 23, 1895.

26. "National Federation," *Boston Daily Globe*, August 2, 1895; *Historical Records of Conventions of 1895–96 of the Colored Women of America*, Washington, DC: National Association of Colored Women, 1902.

27. Hunt.

28. Swallow, *The Remarkable Life and Career of Ellen Swallow Richards*. Richards's partner in the water study was the aptly named Dr. Drown.

29. Hunt.

30. Ellen Henrietta Swallow Richards, ed., *Plain Words about Food: The Rumford Kitchen Leaflets* (Boston: Rockwell and Churchill Press, 1899); Massachusetts Board of Managers, 1893 World's Fair, *Report of the Massachusetts Board of World's Fair Managers* (Boston: Wright & Potter Printing Company, State Printers, 1894).

31. Box 42, AAFCS archives, Cornell University.

Chapter 2: The Lake Placid Conference

1. Ellen H. Richards, "Housekeeping in the Twentieth Century," *American Kitchen Magazine*, March 1900.

2. Deweys' biographical material largely from Melvil Dewey Papers, Columbia University; Wayne. A. Wiegand, *Irrepressible Reformer: A Biography of Melvil Dewey* (Chicago: American Library Association, 1996); George Grosvenor Dawe, *Melvil Dewey, Seer, Inspirer, Doer, 1851–1931* (Lake Placid, NY: Lake Placid Club, 1932); "Obituary Articles for Annie Dewey," *Journal of Home Economics*, July 1923. The Dawe "biografy" is in simplified spelling.

3. Melvil Dewey Papers. Quotations from letters to and from Annie Dewey are from here unless otherwise noted.

4. *Lake Placid Conference on Home Economics Proceedings, Vols. 1–10*, Lake Placid Conference on Home Economics, 1899–1908. Quotes from Lake Placid conferences from this document unless otherwise noted.

5. Flora Rose, "Pioneers in Home Economics," *Practical Home Economics*, 1948.

6. *Lake Placid Conference on Home Economics Proceedings, Vols. 1–10*.

7. Melvil Dewey Papers.

8. Helen Dodd and Ellen Henrietta Swallow Richards, *The Healthful Farmhouse* (Boston: Whitcomb & Barrows, 1912).

9. Caroline Louisa Hunt, *The Life of Ellen H. Richards* (Boston: Whitcomb & Barrows, 1912). Hunt did not identify the conference where Richards made that stirring retort.

10. Ellen S. Richards to Annie Dewey, May 25, 1900, in Melvil Dewey Papers.

11. Wiegand, *Irrepressible Reformer*; Melvil Dewey Papers.

12. Anne Ford, "Bringing Harassment out of the History Books," *American Libraries*, June 1, 2018, https://americanlibrariesmagazine.org/2018/06/01/melvil-dewey-bringing-harassment-out-of-the-history-books/; Wiegand, *Irrepressible Reformer*.

13. Melvil Dewey Papers.

14. Emmett J. Scott, "Mrs. Booker T. Washington's Part in Her Husband's Work," *Ladies' Home Journal*, May 1907; Edited draft of *Ladies' Home Journal* article, Papers of Booker T. Washington (1887–1915): The Tuskegee Collection.

15. Wiegand, *Irrepressible Reformer*; Dawe, *Melvil Dewey*; Elizabeth Izzo, "Controversial Founder of Lake Placid Club, Melville Dewey, Taken off Top Library Award," *Adirondack Daily Enterprise*, July 11, 2019, https://www.adirondackdailyenterprise.com/news/local-news/2019/07/controversial-founder-of-lake-placid-club-melville-dewey-taken-off-top-library

-award/; Ford, "Bringing Harassment out of the History Books"; "Model Home. Atlanta University," *American Kitchen Magazine*, May 1900.

16. Sheena Harris, "A Female Reformer in the Age of Booker T. Washington: The Life and Times of Margaret Murray Washington" (PhD diss., University of Memphis, 2012); Booker T. Washington, *Up from Slavery: An Autobiography* (New York: Doubleday, Page, 1901).

17. Linda Rochell Lane, *A Documentary of Mrs. Booker T. Washington* (Lewiston, NY: Edwin Mellen Press, 2001).

18. Harris, "A Female Reformer in the Age of Booker T. Washington."

19. Mrs. Booker T. Washington, "The Advancement of Colored Women," *American Missionary*, March 1905; Mrs. Booker T. Washington, "II.—The Gain in the Life of Negro Women," *Outlook*, January 30, 1904.

20. Ford, "Bringing Harassment out of the History Books."

21. *Lake Placid Conference on Home Economics Proceedings, Vols. 1–10.*

22. Melvil Dewey Papers.

23. *Bulletin of the American Home Economics Association* (Washington, DC: American Home Economics Association, 1912–1930).

Chapter 3: Food Will Win the War

1. Grace MacLeod, "Reminiscences of Ellen H. Richards," *Journal of Home Economics* 34, no. 10 (December 1942).

2. Melvil Dewey Papers, n.d., Columbia University; Pamela Curtis Swallow, *The Remarkable Life and Career of Ellen Swallow Richards: Pioneer in Science and Technology* (Hoboken, NJ: Wiley, 2014). Swallow, a descendent of Richards and a school librarian who has written about Dewey, writes, "It seems that not everything was returned to the Richards and Swallow families." Hunt died of illness unexpectedly and her papers were not archived. Dewey's papers are at Columbia University and do not include that mythical vanished trunk. Robert Richards outlived Hunt and Dewey, dying at one hundred in 1945. He did not quote from his late wife's letters or diaries in his tedious autobiography.

3. Marie T. Spethmann, "Institutions in the United States Giving Instruction in Home Economics," *Journal of Home Economics*, June 1911.

4. Flora Rose and Esther Stocks, *A Growing College: Home Economics at Cornell University* (Ithaca, NY: Cornell University, 1969).

5. "Comfort for Country Homes," *American Kitchen Magazine*, July 1901; Rose and Stocks, *A Growing College*.

6. Rose and Stocks; New York State College of Home Economics Records, 1875–1979, Cornell University.

7. Megan Elias, "'Model Mamas': The Domestic Partnership of Home

Economics Pioneers Flora Rose and Martha Van Rensselaer," *Journal of the History of Sexuality* 15, no. 1 (January 2006): 65–88; New York State College of Home Economics Records, 1875–1979.

8. Marjorie East, *Caroline Hunt: Philosopher for Home Economics* (State College: Pennsylvania State University, 1982); Rose and Stocks, *A Growing College*.

9. Elizabeth G. Holt, "Negro Industrial Training in the Public Schools of Augusta, Ga.," *Journal of Home Economics* 4, no. 4 (October 1912): 315–23.

10. US Office of Indian Affairs, "Outline Lessons in Housekeeping, Including Cooking, Laundering, Dairying, and Nursing: For Use in Indian Schools" (Washington, DC: Government Printing Office, 1911); US Office of Indian Affairs, "Some Things That Girls Should Know How to Do: And Hence Should Learn How to Do When in School" (Washington, DC: Government Printing Office, 1911); Maxine Seller, "The Education of the Immigrant Woman, 1900 to 1935," *Journal of Urban History* 4, no. 3 (May 1, 1978): 307–30.

11. David Torres-Rouff, "Becoming Mexican: Segregated Schools and Social Scientists in Southern California, 1913–1946," *Southern California Quarterly* 94, no. 1 (Spring 2012): 91–127; Gilbert G. Gonzalez, "Segregation of Mexican Children in a Southern California City," *Western Historical Quarterly* 16, no. 1 (January 1985): 55–76.

12. Raymond A. Mohl, "Schools, Politics, and Riots: The Gary Plan in New York City, 1914–1917," *Paedagogica Historica* 15, no. 1 (January 1975): 39–72; Seller, "The Education of the Immigrant Woman."

13. Mrs. Annie L. Hansen, "Two Years as a Domestic Educator in Buffalo, New York," *Journal of Home Economics*, December 1913: 433–37; Mary L. Schapiro, "Jewish Dietary Problems," *Journal of Home Economics* 11, no. 2 (February 1919): 47–59.

14. *Lake Placid Conference on Home Economics Proceedings, Vols. 1–10.*

15. Lenna Frances Cooper, "Serving the New Vegetables," *Good Health*, August 1916: 448–50.

16. Booker T. Washington, "An Address on the Negro Race at the First National Conference on Race Betterment" (Battle Creek, MI, January 8, 1914).

17. "Graduating Exercises at the Sanitarium," *Battle Creek Idea*, July 1914; Melvil Dewey Papers.

18. Ellen Henrietta Swallow Richards, *Euthenics, the Science of Controllable Environment* (Boston: Whitcomb & Barrows, 1910); Dr. Irving Fisher, "A Report on National Vitality, Its Wastes and Conservation," Report of the National Conservation Commission (Washington, DC: Government Printing Office, 1909).

19. "Battle Creek College Bulletin, 1924–1925," (Battle Creek, MI: Battle Creek College, 1924); John Harvey Kellogg Collection, Archives of Michigan.

20. Logan, the wife of the Tuskegee Institute treasurer, had been suffering from severe depression. In addition, her husband was rumored to be having an affair. Logan went to the Battle Creek Sanitarium for treatment but had been there for only a month when she was called back to campus for the president's funeral. See Adele Logan Alexander, "A Granddaughter's Story," *Sage* 1, no. 2 (Fall 1984): 32–33; Daria J. Williams, *The Life and Times of Adella Hunt Logan: Educator, Mother, Wife, and Suffragist, 1863–1915* (Tallahassee: Florida State University, Fall 2012).

21. New York State College of Home Economics Records, 1875–1979, box 249.

22. Rose and Stocks, *A Growing College*; "New York State College of Home Economics Records, 1875–1979."

23. Maude A. Perry, "[Experiences during the War]," Presentation given at the American Dietetics Association Second Annual Convention, September 9, 1919, Cincinnati, as published in the conference proceedings book.

24. New York State College of Home Economics Records, 1875–1979, box 249.

25. New York State College of Home Economics Records, 1875–1979, box 249.

26. New York State College of Home Economics Records, 1875–1979, box 249.

27. New York State College of Home Economics Records, 1875–1979, box 249.

28. Joan L. Sullivan, "In Pursuit of Legitimacy: Home Economists and the Hoover Apron in World War I," *Dress* 26, no. 1 (January 1, 1999): 31–46; "[Chicago Schools]," *School Life: Official Journal of the U.S. Office of Education* 1, no. 3 (September 1, 1918): 10; "Women's War Work Reviewed by Former Dietitian of Army," *Cincinnati Enquirer*, September 9, 1919.

29. "Mid Winter Meeting with the N. E. A.," *Bulletin of the American Home Economics Association* 6, no. 3–4 (December 1920): 1–2.

Chapter 4: Perhaps It Wasn't Really a Man's Job After All

1. Mrs. Booker T. Washington, "Club Work among Negro Women," in *The Progress of a Race* (Washington, DC: J. L. Nichols, 1920); "Mrs. Booker T. Washington Dead," *Southern Letter*, July 1925.

2. "Dr. Washington's Home," *New Journal and Guide*, August 8, 1925; "Mrs. Booker T. Washington Leaves Estate of $50,000.00," *Philadelphia Tribune*,

July 11, 1925; "News from the Field: Margaret Murray Washington," *Journal of Home Economics*, November 1925.

3. Sheena Harris, "A Female Reformer in the Age of Booker T. Washington: The Life and Times of Margaret Murray Washington" (PhD diss., University of Memphis, 2012).

4. US Department of Agriculture, "Women Confer on Plans for Bureau of Home Economics," *Official Record of the United States Department of Agriculture*, December 26, 1923; Carolyn M. Goldstein, *Creating Consumers: Home Economists in Twentieth-Century America* (Chapel Hill: University of North Carolina Press, 2012); Louise Stanley, "Plans for the Bureau of Home Economics," *Journal of Home Economics* 15, no. 12 (December 1923): 679–83.

5. Michael Waters, "The Government Taste Testers Who Reshaped America's Diet," *Smithsonian*, August 9, 2019, https://www.smithsonianmag .com/history/government-taste-testers-who-reshaped-americas-diet -180972823/; US Bureau of Home Economics, *Publications of the Bureau of Home Economics, U.S. Department of Agriculture, July, 1923–January, 1930* (Washington, DC: US Department of Agriculture, January 1930).

6. Goldstein, *Creating Consumers*.

7. Marie Sellers, "Home Economics Women in Business," *Journal of Home Economics* 15, no. 6 (June 1923); Goldstein, 153.

8. Amy Bix, "Creating 'Chicks Who Fix': Women, Tool Knowledge, and Home Repair, 1920–2007," *WSQ: Women's Studies Quarterly* 37, no. 1 (2009): 38–60; Arthur G. Woolf, "The Residential Adoption of Electricity in Early Twentieth-Century America," *Energy Journal* 8, no. 2 (April 1987): 19–30.

9. Melvil Dewey Papers, East letter of April 4, 1917.

10. Lillian M. Gilbreth, "Johnson & Johnson Market Research Report and Correspondence," 1926–1927, box 78, folder 4, MSP 8—Gilbreth Library of Management Research and Professional Papers, Archives and Special Collections, Purdue University Libraries.

11. Lillian Moller Gilbreth, *As I Remember: An Autobiography* (Norcross, GA: Engineering & Management Press, 1998).

12. Frank B. Gilbreth Jr. and Ernestine Gilbreth Carey, *Belles on Their Toes* (New York: Thomas Y. Crowell, 1950).

13. Christine (McGaffey) Frederick, *Household Engineering: Scientific Management in the Home* (Chicago: American School of Home Economics, 1919); Goldstein, *Creating Consumers*.

14. "[words missing] Wants to Know—Can I Have a Family without Sacrificing My Career?" *World Magazine*, May 16, 1926, box 27, Frank and

Lillian Gilbreth Papers, Archives and Special Collections, Purdue University Libraries; Lillian M. Gilbreth, *The Home-maker and Her Job* (New York: D. Appleton, 1927).

15. Lillian M. Gilbreth, "Kitchen Practical: The Story of an Experiment" (Brooklyn Borough Gas Company, 1931), Smith College.

16. Gilbreth, "Johnson & Johnson Market Research Report and Correspondence."

17. Iveagh Sterry Lewis, "Eleven Children and a Career," *Children: The Parents' Magazine*, March 1928; George Currie, "As Applied to George, Roy and Donald," *Brooklyn Daily Eagle*, n.d., Weekly Book Review.

18. Susan Marks, *Finding Betty Crocker: The Secret Life of America's First Lady of Food* (New York: Simon & Schuster, 2005); Jane Lesley Lancaster, "'Wasn't She the Mother in Cheaper by the Dozen': A Life of Lillian Moller Gilbreth, 1878–1972" (PhD diss., Brown University, 1998).

19. Laura Shapiro, "And Here She Is . . . Your Betty Crocker!," *American Scholar* 73, no. 2 (2004): 87–99.

20. Lori Rohlk, "'Sisters of the Skillet': Radio Homemakers in Shenandoah, Iowa, 1920–1960" (master's thesis, University of Nebraska, 1997); "US Census Table 23: Families Having Radio Set" (Washington, DC: Government Printing Office, 1933).

21. Marks, *Finding Betty Crocker*.

22. Rohlk, "'Sisters of the Skillet'"; Marks.

23. US Bureau of Home Economics, "Katy Counts Her Calories" (US Department of Agriculture, Office of Information, Radio Service, October 17, 1927); "100 Stations to Broadcast News," *News-Democrat*, September 16, 1926.

24. Edward Bottone, "The Radio Homemaker," *Table Matters* (blog), March 2, 2016, http://tablematters.com/2016/03/02/the-radio-homemaker/.

25. Lucile Driftmier Verness, *The Story of an American Family* (Shenandoah, IA: Driftmier Publishing Co., 1950).

26. Evelyn Birkby, *Neighboring on the Air: Cooking with the KMA Radio Homemakers* (Iowa City: University of Iowa Press, 1991).

27. Verness, *The Story of an American Family*.

28. Anna Richardson, "Council Meetings: Standards of Home Economics in Colleges," *Bulletin of the American Home Economics Association* 9, no. 1 (October 1926): 23–24.

29. Megan Elias, "'Model Mamas': The Domestic Partnership of Home Economics Pioneers Flora Rose and Martha Van Rensselaer," *Journal of the History of Sexuality* 15, no. 1 (January 2006): 65–88.

30. *A Study of 952 Graduates of the New York State College of Home Economics,*

Cornell University, 1911 to 1930 (Ithaca, NY: New York State College of Home Economics, 1931); Elias, "'Model Mamas.'"

31. "Real Baby to Be 'Mothered' by Nebraska Girl Students in Home Economics Course," *Boston Daily Globe*, November 27, 1921; "Retreating Richard," *Cornell Countryman*, June 1921, New York State College of Home Economics records.

32. "Dr. Stanley Is Now Mother by Adoption," *Washington Post*, September 29, 1929, sec. O; "Real Baby to Be 'Mothered'"; "Thirty-Five Homes for Practice Baby," *Boston Daily Globe*, December 17, 1929; "'Practice Baby' Has Pick of 41 Homes to Hang Yule Stocking," *Boston Daily Globe*, December 22, 1929.

33. Jessaca B. Leinaweaver, "Practice Mothers," *Signs* 38, no. 2 (Winter 2013): 405–30; Elias, "'Model Mamas.'"

Chapter 5: It's Up to the Women

1. US Bureau of Home Economics, "The President's Low-Cost Dinner" (US Department of Agriculture, Office of Information, Radio Service, April 27, 1931).

2. Grace E. Frysinger, "Emergency Activities of the Home Economics Extension Service," *Journal of Home Economics* 24, no. 8 (August 1932); Katherine Lewis, "Red Cross Clothing Relief and Home Economists," *Journal of Home Economics* 25, no. 2 (February 1933): 128–29; "Coordination of Home Economics Agencies in the States (Editorial)," *Journal of Home Economics* 25, no. 6 (July 1933); Keturah E. Baldwin, *The AHEA Saga* (Washington, DC: American Home Economics Association, 1949); Keturah E. Baldwin, "Business Manager of the Journal," *Bulletin of the American Home Economics Association* 17, no. 1 (September 1934): 4–5.

3. New York State College of Home Economics Records, 1875–1979, n.d., Cornell University.

4. New York State College of Home Economics Records, 1875–1979.

5. Jane Ziegelman and Andrew Coe, *A Square Meal: A Culinary History of the Great Depression* (New York: HarperCollins, 2016); US Department of Agriculture Office of Experiment Stations, "Report on the Agricultural Experiment Stations, 1934" (Washington, DC: Government Printing Office, 1935), https://archive.org/details/CAT11088335035.

6. Jill Lepore, "Eleanor Roosevelt: 'Can a Woman Ever Be President of the United States?,'" *LitHub* (blog), April 27, 2017, https://lithub.com/eleanore-roosevelt-can-a-woman-ever-be-president-of-the-united-states/.

7. Eleanor Roosevelt, "My Day," The Eleanor Roosevelt Papers Digital Edition (2017), May 26, 1936, https://www2.gwu.edu/~erpapers/myday/displaydocedits.cfm?_y=1936&_f=md054340.

8. Ziegelman and Coe, *A Square Meal*; Ruth O'Brien, *Children's Body Measurements for Sizing Garments and Patterns: A Proposed Standard System Based on Height and Girth of Hips*, Miscellaneous Publication, No. 365 (Washington, DC: US Dept. of Agriculture, 1939); Ruth O'Brien and William C. Shelton, *Women's Measurements for Garment and Pattern Construction*, Miscellaneous Publication, No. 454 (Washington, DC: US Dept. of Agriculture, 1941).

9. Ira S. Wile, "School Lunch Progress in New York," *Journal of Home Economics* 6, no. 5 (December 1914): 442–47; Philadelphia School Lunch Committee, "Educational Need and Value of Lunches in Elementary Schools," *Journal of Home Economics* 5, no. 1 (February 1913): 55–57.

10. Louis Lyons, "Pork for Boston—Applesauce for Cambridge," *Boston Globe*, November 19, 1933; Janet Poppendieck, *Free for All: Fixing School Food in America* (Berkeley: University of California Press, 2010).

11. Doxey A. Wilkerson, "The Participation of Negroes in the Federally-Aided Program of Agricultural and Home Economics Extension," *Journal of Negro Education* 7, no. 3 (1938): 331–44; Margaret M. Edwards, "Cooperation with Southern Colored Home Economics Workers," *Bulletin of the American Home Economics Association* 18, no. 1 (September 1935); Edith Thomas, "Cooperation with Southern Colored Home Economics Workers," *Bulletin of the American Home Economics Association* 16, no. 1 (September 1933); Susan M. Burson, "Committee on Co-Operation with Southern Colored Home Economics Workers," *Bulletin of the American Home Economics Association* 21, no. 1 (September 1938); Lurline Collier and Katharine M. Ansley, "Report on Co-Operation with Southern Colored Home Economics Workers," *Bulletin of the American Home Economics Association* 20, no. 1 (September 1937).

12. Allison B. Horrocks, "Good Will Ambassador with a Cookbook: Flemmie Kittrell and the International Politics of Home Economics" (PhD diss., University of Connecticut, 2016); "Letters Fail to Satisfy," *The Pittsburgh Courier*, December 31, 1932; "Women Masters in Home Economics," *Chicago Defender*, March 11, 1933.

13. Flemmie Pansy Kittrell, interview, August 29, 1977, Schlesinger Library on the History of Women in America/Black Women Oral History Project, Harvard University.

14. Horrocks, "Good Will Ambassador with a Cookbook."

15. May Edwin Mann Burke, "The Contributions of Flemmie Pansy Kittrell to Education through Her Doctrines on Home Economics" (PhD diss., University of Maryland, 1988); Horrocks, "Good Will Ambassador with a Cookbook."

16. Burke, "The Contributions of Flemmie Pansy Kittrell."

17. Fabiola de Baca Gilbert, "New Mexican Diets," *Journal of Home Economics*, November 1942, 668–69.

18. Robert Martinez, email message to author, May 30, 2020; Pearl Idelia Ellis, *Americanization through Homemaking* (Los Angeles: Wetzel Publishing, 1929).

19. Merrihelen Ponce, "The Life and Works of Fabiola Cabeza de Baca, New Mexican Hispanic Woman Writer" (PhD diss., University of New Mexico, 1995); Virginia Scharff, "So Many Miles to a Person," in *Twenty Thousand Roads: Women, Movement, and the West* (Berkeley: University of California Press, 2002); Fabiola C. de Baca Gilbert, *We Fed Them Cactus*, 2nd ed. (Albuquerque: University of New Mexico Press, 1994).

20. Gilbert, "New Mexican Diets."

21. Scharff, "So Many Miles to a Person."

22. "LULAC News, Vol. 5 No. 9," December 1938; Adelina Ortiz de Hill, "My Memories of Fabiola C de Baca Gilbert," n.d., http://rancho.pancho .pagesperso-orange.fr/Fabiola.htm; Scharff, "So Many Miles to a Person." A few sources say no one they met ever actually heard de Baca speak those languages.

23. Gilbert, "New Mexican Diets"; Joan M. Jensen, "'I've Worked, I'm Not Afraid of Work': Farm Women in New Mexico, 1920–1940," *New Mexico Historical Review* 61, no. 1 (January 1, 1986): 27–52.

24. Ponce, "The Life and Works of Fabiola Cabeza de Baca"; Fabiola C. de Baca Gilbert, *Historic Cookery*, New Mexico Extension Circular 161, May 1946 (New Mexico College of Agriculture and Mechanic Arts, Agricultural Extension Service). Contrary to Wikipedia, there is no evidence that de Baca invented or even used the U-shaped, deep-fried, hard taco shell. Her taco recipe calls for the cook to fry the tortilla flat on a griddle and wrap it around the filling.

25. Franklin A. Robinson Jr., "Guide to the Louisan E. Mamer Rural Electrification Administration Papers" (Smithsonian National Museum of American History, December 2004).

26. Genevieve Jackson Boughner, *Women in Journalism* (New York: D. Appleton, 1926).

27. "President Sets Up Rural Power Unit," *New York Times*, May 12, 1935.

28. "REA Farm Equipment Tour," *Rural Electrification News*, December 1938.

29. Michelle Mock, "The Modernization of the American Home Kitchen, 1900–1960" (PhD diss., Carnegie Mellon University, 2011).

30. Baldwin, *The AHEA Saga*; Burson, "Committee on Co-Operation with Southern Colored Home Economics Workers."

31. Lillian M. Gilbreth, "[Passport]," 1946, box 108, Frank and Lillian Gil-breth Papers, Archives and Special Collections, Purdue University Libraries.

Chapter 6: Clothes Moths Work for Hitler

1. Caroline H. Wilson and Katherine L. Baker, "On to Convention," *Bulletin of the American Home Economics Association* 24, no. 2 (February 1942).

2. Carolyn M. Goldstein, *Creating Consumers: Home Economists in Twentieth-Century America* (Chapel Hill: University of North Carolina Press, 2012); "Rationing," National WWII Museum, n.d., https://www.nationalww2museum.org/war/articles/rationing.

3. "Mrs. Roosevelt Sponsors Preview of Snappy Togs for Girl Defense Corps," *Boston Daily Globe*, August 26, 1941; "Working Girl Can Keep Good Looks," *Washington Post*, August 26, 1941; US Department of Agriculture, Radio Service, "New Work Clothes for Women" (US Department of Agriculture, Office of Information, Radio Service, July 18, 1941); Clarice L. Scott, "Work Clothes for Women" (Washington, DC: US Dept. of Agriculture, 1942).

4. Susan Levine, *School Lunch Politics: The Surprising History of America's Favorite Welfare Program* (Princeton, NJ: Princeton University Press, 2008).

5. National Research Council Food and Nutrition Board, *Recommended Dietary Allowances: Protein, Calcium, Iron, Vitamin A, Vitamin B (Thiamin), Vitamin C (Ascorbic Acid), Riboflavin, Nicotinic Acid, Vitamin D* (Washington, DC: NRC FNB, 1941). Truly astonishing: the 2015–20 allowances for the various nutrients, at health.gov, assume that Americans weigh essentially the same as the original document assumed, 126 and 154 pounds. According to the CDC, in 2016 the average American woman and man weighed 171 and 198 pounds, respectively.

6. Levine, *School Lunch Politics*.

7. Rachel Ann Lusher, "Alums in the News," *Iowa Homemaker* 23, no. 3 (October 1943): 22–23.

8. Office for Emergency Management, *Women in Defense*, 1941, https://www.youtube.com/watch?v=tRH70pR_oCo.

9. Allison B. Horrocks, "Good Will Ambassador with a Cookbook: Flemmie Kittrell and the International Politics of Home Economics" (PhD diss., University of Connecticut, 2016).

10. Horrocks, "Good Will Ambassador with a Cookbook."

11. Mary I. Barber, *History of the American Dietetic Association, 1917–1959* (Philadelphia: J. B. Lippincott, 1959).

12. Lt. Col. Thelma A. Harman, "Professional Services of Dietitians, World

War II," in *Army Medical Specialist Corps* (Washington, DC: US Army Medical Department, Office of Military History, 1968).

13. Elizabeth M. Norman, *We Band of Angels: The Untold Story of the American Women Trapped on Bataan* (New York: Random House, 2011).

14. Norman, *We Band of Angels*.

15. Nursing Division, Office of the Surgeon General, "The Dietitian's Column," *Army Nurse*, April 1945.

16. Ann M. Ritchie Hartwick, *The Army Medical Specialist Corps: The 45th Anniversary* (Washington, DC: US Army Center of Military History, 1993).

17. Norman, *We Band of Angels*.

18. Hartwick, *The Army Medical Specialist Corps*.

19. Hartwick.

20. *Fashions and Fabrics*, Spring/Summer 1939.

21. *Fashions and Fabrics*, Spring/Summer 1939 and Fall/Winter 1939.

22. *Fashions and Fabrics*, Spring/Summer 1940, 1941, 1942; Fall/Winter 1940.

23. Alice L. Edwards to Alice Blood, "[Regarding AHEA Student Clubs]," January 3, 1935, box 145, AAFCS archives, Cornell University.

24. [Name cut off] to Dora S. Lewis, "[Future Homemakers Name]," May 12, 1945, box 145, AAFCS archives, Cornell University. The sender's name is cut off in the copy of the letter in the archives. It may have been from Gladys Wyckoff.

25. Edna P. Amidon to Dora S. Lewis, "[New Homemakers Board]," August 7, 1945, box 145, AAFCS archives, Cornell University.

26. Marie Clapp Moffitt, "The Growth and Development of the New Homemakers of America" (PhD diss., Walden University, 1977); Edna P. Amidon, "Contributions to Family Life Education by the Office of Education," *Marriage and Family Living* 20, no. 3 (August 1958): 282–88; Lorraine Corke Lacey, "The Future Homemakers of America as an Integral Part of the High School Home Economics Curriculum" (MS thesis, Kansas State University, 1949).

27. Janet Poppendieck, *Free for All: Fixing School Food in America* (Berkeley: University of California Press, 2010).

28. Margaret Rossiter, *Women Scientists in America: Before Affirmative Action, 1940–1972* (Baltimore: Johns Hopkins University Press, 1995).

Chapter 7: From Coveralls to Housecoats

1. Division of Vital Statistics, "Vital Statistics of the United States 1960 Volume III: Marriage and Divorce" (US Department of Health, Education, and Welfare, 1964); Howard N. Fullerton Jr., "Labor Force Participation: 75 Years of Change, 1950–98 and 1998–2025," *Monthly Labor Review*,

December 1999; Laura Shapiro, *Something from the Oven* (New York: Viking, 2004); Rebecca Lane Wiseman-Benner, "'Goodbye Mammy Hello Mom': Why Feminists Have a Responsibility to Reclaim Homemaking" (Denton, TX: Texas Woman's University, 2008).

2. Alexander A. Plateris, "100 Years of Marriage and Divorce Statistics, United States, 1867–1967," Vital and Health Statistics (US Department of Health, Education, and Welfare, December 1973); "Who Are Today's Families?," *Forum*, Spring/Summer 1969; Potomac Group, Home Economists in Homemaking, "Is Homemaking Important?," *Journal of Home Economics* 50, no. 2 (February 1958): 87–88; Richard S. Blaisdell, "More Women Are Working," *Journal of Home Economics* 50, no. 4 (April 1958): 261–65.

3. *Concepts and Generalizations: Their Place in High School Home Economics Curriculum Development* (Washington, DC: American Home Economics Association, 1967); M. D. Mobley, "A Review of Federal Vocational-Education Legislation 1862–1963," *Theory into Practice* 3, no. 5 (1964): 167–70; Pamela Ann Roby, "Toward Full Equality: More Job Education for Women," *School Review* 84, no. 2 (1976): 181–211; Lynn Stratton, *Opinion Building: A Public Relations Guide for Home Economists* (Washington, DC: American Home Economics Association, 1953).

4. "Home Economists," in *Occupational Outlook Handbook* (Washington, DC: US Department of Labor, Bureau of Labor Statistics, 1957), "Broader Education for Women Urged," *New York Times*, October 30, 1954; Potomac Group, Home Economists in Homemaking, "Is Homemaking Important?"

5. Penny A. Ralston, "Flemmie P. Kittrell: Her Views and Practices Regarding Home Economics in Higher Education," *Journal of Home Economics*, Spring 1994; Laura Shapiro, "And Here She Is . . . Your Betty Crocker!," *American Scholar* 73, no. 2 (2004): 87–99; "A Happy Home," *Chatter Box*, Fall 1957.

6. Paul Popenoe, "Heredity in Relation to the Family," *Family Living* 1, no. 2/3 (Spring and Summer 1939): 46; Paul Sayre, "The Work of the National Conference on Family Relations," *Living* 1, no. 2/3 (1939): 49–50.

7. Esther McGinnis, "AHEA Presents Program at Annual AAAS Meeting," *Journal of Home Economics* 43, no. 8 (September 1951).

8. American Home Economics Association, "Home Economics, New Directions: A Statement of Philosophy and Objectives," 1959.

9. Harold S. Freeman, *A Guide for Developing a Homemaking Curriculum in Junior and Senior High Schools of South Dakota* (Pierre, SD: Dept. of Public Instruction, Division of Vocational Education, 1950); "70 Years of Seventeen!," *Seventeen*, February 1, 2013, https://www.seventeen.com/fun/articles/65th-anniversary-cover-archive.

10. Edna Kraft James, Frieda Sloop, and Muriel W. Brown, "Boys and Girls

Study Homemaking and Family Living: Developing Courses for 11th- and 12th-Grade Pupils" (Washington, DC: US Office of Education, Federal Security Agency, 1951); Evelyn Millis Duvall, "Research Finds: Student Marriages," *Marriage and Family Living* 22, no. 1 (February 1960): 76–77.

11. Home Economics Curriculum Committee, *Home Economics Course of Study, Junior High Schools (Lakewood, Ohio)* (Lakewood, OH, 1952); *Concepts and Generalizations: Their Place in High School Home Economics Curriculum Development*; Mildred Weigley Wood, *Living Together in the Family* (Washington, DC: American Home Economics Association, 1946); Lawrence Downes, "Word for Word/Dr. Spock; Time to Change the Baby Advice: Evolution of a Child-Care Icon," *New York Times*, March 22, 1998, https://www.nytimes.com/1998/03/22/weekinreview/word-for-word-dr -spock-time-change-baby-advice-evolution-child-care-icon.html.

12. Mollie Stevens Smart, *Babe in a House* (New York: Scribner, 1950).

13. Mollie Stevens Smart and Russell Smart, *Living in Families*, 2nd ed. (Boston: Houghton Mifflin, 1965). The parents with the twin beds, incidentally, wanted their bedroom to have sitting-room furniture because they were ceding the living room to their teenagers.

14. Laura Smart, email message to author, May 2, 2020.

15. Beth L. Bailey, "Scientific Truth . . . and Love: The Marriage Education Movement in the United States," *Journal of Social History* 20, no. 4 (June 1, 1987): 711–32.

16. Evelyn Millis Duvall, "Growing Edges in Family Life Education," *Marriage and Family Living* 6, no. 2 (Spring 1944): 21–24.

17. Henry A. Bowman, *Marriage for Moderns*, 3rd ed. (New York: McGraw-Hill, 1954).

18. Evelyn Millis Duvall, "Evelyn Duvall's Life," *Marriage & Family Review* 32, no. 1–2 (May 8, 2002): 7–23; Robert O. Blood Jr., *Marriage* (Glencoe, IL: The Free Press of Glencoe, 1962); Bowman, *Marriage for Moderns*.

19. Henry A. Bowman, "Marriage Education in the Colleges," *Journal of Social Hygiene* 35, no. 9 (December 1949): 407–17.

20. Mary Schmich, "Whatever Happened to Baby David?," *Chicago Tribune*, August 19, 2007.

21. Margaret Mead, "Some Theoretical Considerations on the Problem of Mother-Child Separation," *American Journal of Orthopsychiatry* 24, no. 3 (1954): 471–83.

22. Bernice Milburn Moore and Dorothy M. Leahy, *You and Your Family* (Lexington, MA: D.C. Heath, 1948); Blood Jr., *Marriage*.

23. Sadye Pearl Young, "Looking at Home Economics for Negroes in Higher Education," *Negro Educational Review* 12, no. 3 (July 1, 1961): 96–107.

24. Druzilla Crary Kent, "Homemakers in the Defense Program: Implications for Education in Home Economics" (Federal Security Agency, Office of Education, Division of Vocational Education, 1951 or 1952).

Chapter 8: The Iron Fist in the Oven Mitt

1. Mary Hawkins, "Home Economists Plan for Defense," *Journal of Home Economics* 43, no. 5 (May 1951): 333–41.
2. Doris E. Hanson, "Pioneers in the Field of Home Economics Work Abroad," *Journal of Home Economics* 57, no. 4 (April 1965); William Safire, "The Cold War's Hot Kitchen," *New York Times*, July 23, 2009, Opinion; "The Kitchen Debate—Transcript," July 24, 1959, https://www.cia.gov/library/readingroom/docs/1959-07-24.pdf.
3. Flemmie P. Kittrell, "Some Observations on Life and Education in West Africa," *Journal of Negro Education* 17, no. 2 (1948): 192–94; May Edwin Mann Burke, "The Contributions of Flemmie Pansy Kittrell to Education through Her Doctrines on Home Economics" (PhD diss., University of Maryland, 1988).
4. Flemmie Kittrell, "A Preliminary Food and Nutrition Survey of Liberia, West Africa," *Faculty Reprints*, June 1, 1947, https://dh.howard.edu/reprints/230; Kittrell, "Some Observations on Life and Education in West Africa"; Allison B. Horrocks, "Good Will Ambassador with a Cookbook: Flemmie Kittrell and the International Politics of Home Economics" (PhD diss., University of Connecticut, 2016).
5. "University of Baroda Establishes Home Economics in Higher Education," *Journal of Home Economics* 44, no. 2 (February 1952): 97–100.
6. Horrocks, "Good Will Ambassador with a Cookbook."
7. "The Perpetual Career," *Peace Corps Sixth Annual Report*, June 30, 1967.
8. "What About Japan?," *Journal of Home Economics*, April 1947, 232.
9. "What About Japan?"
10. "What About Japan?"; Mire Koikari, "'The World Is Our Campus': Michigan State University and Cold-War Home Economics in US-Occupied Okinawa, 1945–1972," *Gender & History* 24, no. 1 (April 2012): 74–92.
11. Eleanor Densmore, "Home Economics in the Ryukyus," *Journal of Home Economics* 44, no. 5 (May 1952): 358–60.
12. Densmore, "Home Economics in the Ryukyus."
13. Rosemary Blackburn, "Kent County Women Adopt an Okinawan School," *Extension Service Review*, August 1955; So Mizoguchi, "Schooling for Democracy?: The Cultural Diplomacy of Education in Okinawa, 1945–1972" (PhD diss., Michigan State University, 2018).
14. Horrocks, "Good Will Ambassador with a Cookbook"; "Women Pioneers Wanted," *Journal of Home Economics* 42, no. 7 (September 1950): 521–23.

15. Florence W. Low, "Home Economists Observe Family Life Abroad," *Journal of Home Economics* 55, no. 9 (November 1963): 684–87.

16. Koikari, "'The World Is Our Campus'"; Dorothy L. Pillsbury, "UN Calls New Mexico's Fabiola Gilbert to Set Up Pilot Home Economics Project," *Christian Science Monitor*, March 17, 1952; "New Mexico News," *Journal of Home Economics* 44, no. 2 (February 1952).

17. Kittrell, "Some Observations on Life and Education in West Africa"; International Cooperation Administration and Federal Extension Service, US Dept. of Agriculture, "The Extension Home Economist around the World," 1957.

18. Merrihelen Ponce, "The Life and Works of Fabiola Cabeza de Baca, New Mexican Hispanic Woman Writer" (PhD diss., University of New Mexico, 1995); Fabiola C. de Baca Gilbert, *We Fed Them Cactus*, 2nd ed. (Albuquerque: University of New Mexico Press, 1994).

19. Kimiko Matsumoto, "Home Life in Japan and Homemaking Education," *Journal of Home Economics*, February 1953; Barbara E. Scott Fisher, "American Home Economist Anticipates Her Work with Japanese Educators," *Christian Science Monitor*, June 4, 1948.

20. Koikari, "'The World Is Our Campus'"; Eleanor Roosevelt, "As I Saw Them: Russia—The Country and the People," *Journal of Home Economics* 51, no. 7 (September 1959): 555–60.

21. Elena Tajima Creef, "Discovering My Mother as the Other in the Saturday Evening Post," *Qualitative Inquiry* 6, no. 4 (December 2000).

Chapter 9: Selling Mrs. Housewife

1. Barbara Lane, "Yogurt Recipes Featuring Knudsen Fruit Blended Yogurts," 1962.

2. Rossiter, *Women Scientists in America: Before Affirmative Action, 1940–1972* (Baltimore: Johns Hopkins University Press, 1995); "Income in 1965 of Families and Persons in the United States," Current Population Reports: Consumer Income, Series P-60 (Washington, DC: US Department of Commerce, Bureau of the Census, January 12, 1967).

3. Gladys Gary Vaughn, interview by author, June 24, 2019.

4. Sheila Castellarin, interview by author, May 11, 2018. All Castellarin quotes in chapter from 2018 interview unless otherwise noted.

5. Helen Hallbert et al., "Business Speaks to the Consumer through Home Economists," *Journal of Home Economics* 55, no. 6 (June 1963): 420–21.

6. Franklin A. Robinson Jr., "Guide to the Louisan E. Mamer Rural Electrification Administration Papers" (Smithsonian National Museum of American History, December 2004).

7. Columbia Gas of West Virginia, "Gaslight: Betty Newton's Notes," Pipe-
    line Accident Report, Report Number NTSB-PAR-74-4, December 2,
    1973, "Appendix: Ten 'Gaslight' Bill Stuffers Sent to Customers between
    April 1971 and October 1973"; Carolyn M. Goldstein, *Creating Consumers:
    Home Economists in Twentieth-Century America* (Chapel Hill: University of
    North Carolina Press, 2012); Harriett M. Grace, *More Favorite Honey Rec-
    ipes* (American Honey Institute, 1956).

8. Vera Falconer, "Classroom Screen," *Practical Home Economics*, September
    1962; Hallbert et al., "Business Speaks to the Consumer through Home
    Economists."

9. Dorothy Ellen Jones, "You Don't Use Commercial Aids? We Do," *Journal of
    Home Economics* 49, no. 6 (June 1957): 425.

10. Pinkie E. Thrift, "Taking Home the 44th Annual Meeting," *Journal of
    Home Economics* 45, no. 8 (October 1953).

11. Brian Ward, *Radio and the Struggle for Civil Rights in the South* (Gainesville:
    University Press of Florida, 2004).

12. Lori Rohlk, "'Sisters of the Skillet': Radio Homemakers in Shenandoah,
    Iowa, 1920–1960" (master's thesis, University of Nebraska, 1997); Evelyn
    Birkby, interview by author, September 27, 2018; Jane Stern and Michael
    Stern, "Neighboring," *New Yorker*, April 15, 1991.

13. Mary Brown Allgood, *Television Demonstration Techniques for Home Econo-
    mists* (State College: Pennsylvania State University, 1953). Allgood quotes
    from book unless otherwise noted.

14. Virginia F. Thomas, "An Opportunity for Home Economics Education
    through Television," *Journal of Home Economics* 51, no. 6 (June 1959):
    422–26.

Chapter 10: New Directions

1. Benjamin Fine, "Soviet Education Far Ahead of U.S. in Science Stress,"
    New York Times, November 11, 1957; William J. Jorden, "Soviet Fires
    Earth Satellite into Space," *New York Times*, October 5, 1957; Gladwin
    Hill, "Nixon Terms Bias a Curb on Science," *New York Times*, October 16,
    1957.

2. Eric Johnston, "Living with the Changes of the Space Age," *Journal of
    Home Economics* 50, no. 7 (September 1958): 495–98; "Washington News:
    AHEA President Asks Balanced Educational Program," *Journal of Home
    Economics* 50, no. 1 (January 1958): 8.

3. "Dr. Stanley: Nation's No. 1 Homemaker," *Washington Post and Times Her-
    ald*, July 16, 1954.

4. "Promotion Camera," *Gas Appliance Merchandising*, March 1956; Laura

Shapiro, "And Here She Is . . . Your Betty Crocker!," *American Scholar* 73, no. 2 (2004): 87–99.

5. Rossiter, *Women Scientists in America: Before Affirmative Action, 1940–1972* (Baltimore: Johns Hopkins University Press, 1995).

6. Judy Crawford, "Home? Career?," *Journal of Home Economics* 54, no. 1 (January 1962): 48–50; Janice Berg et al., "College Women Speak about Themselves and about Home Economics," *Journal of Home Economics* 57, no. 8 (October 1965); US Office of Education Division of Vocational Education, "Factors Influencing Enrollment in Home Economics" (Washington, DC: Office of Education, Division of Vocational and Technical Education, Home Economics Education Branch, 1957); Josephine Hemphill, "Home Economics Unlimited," *Journal of Home Economics* 47, no. 9 (November 1955): 653–60; Helen Canoyer, "The Thirty-First Annual Report of the New York State College of Home Economics at Cornell University" (Ithaca: New York State College of Home Economics, 1956).

7. Rossiter, *Women Scientists in America.*

8. Leah Jane Smith, "College Education Is for Women, Too!," *Journal of Home Economics* 50, no. 6 (June 1958): 436.

9. Marjorie Child Husted, "Public Relations Begins with You!," October 1948 (Minneapolis, MN: General Mills, Inc.); Marjorie Child Husted, "Would You Like More Recognition?" *Journal of Home Economics* 40, no. 8 (October 1948): 459–60.

10. Mary Kimball, "From Committees: AHEA Public Relations," *Journal of Home Economics* 50, no. 7 (September 1958): 547; Laura Lane, "You and Your Public Image," *Journal of Home Economics* 52, no. 7 (September 1960): 514–17.

11. Margaret M. Bubolz, ed., *Beatrice Paolucci: Shaping Destiny through Everyday Life* (East Lansing, MI: Kappa Omicron Nu Honor Society, 2002).

12. Bubolz, *Beatrice Paolucci.*

13. Beatrice Paolucci, "Reviewing Our Orbit," *Journal of Home Economics* 50, no. 7 (September 1958): 499–502.

14. American Home Economics Association, "Home Economics, New Directions: A Statement of Philosophy and Objectives," 1959.

Chapter 11: New Homemakers Build the Future

1. "Food for Young Families . . . Guide for Extension Home Economists" (Washington, DC: Government Printing Office, March 1966).

2. Helen S. Barney and Richard L. D. Morse, "Shopping Compared of Low-Income Homemakers and Students," *Journal of Home Economics* 59, no. 1

(January 1967): 48–50. One wonders how anyone could possibly think to improve a person's life and lot by depriving them of coffee.

3. June Stewart, "The Home Economist in Public Welfare," *Journal of Home Economics* 58, no. 6 (June 1964): 389–91; Marian M. Kira and Frank D. Alexander, "Home Economics Work with Low-Income People: July 1, 1961–June 30, 1967" (Ithaca, NY: Cornell University College of Home Economics, June 1969).

4. John Cassidy, "Relatively Deprived," *New Yorker*, March 27, 2006.

5. Mollie Orshansky, "Children of the Poor," *Social Security Bulletin*, July 1963, 3–13; Sewell Chan, "Mollie Orshansky, Statistician, Dies at 91," *New York Times*, April 17, 2007.

6. "[Various Letters and Memos Concerning AHEA and Head Start, Including UW–Stevens Point Application]," 1965, AAFCS archives, Cornell University; Charles Mohr, "'Head Start' Plan for Pupils Begun," *New York Times*, May 19, 1965, Late City Edition.

7. Allison B. Horrocks, "Good Will Ambassador with a Cookbook: Flemmie Kittrell and the International Politics of Home Economics" (PhD diss., University of Connecticut, 2016).

8. "[South Carolina Home Economics Association Correspondence Re. Negro Membership Applicants]," 1949–50, Louise Pettus Archives, Winthrop University.

9. Mildred B. Collier and Dorothy D. Scott, "Vocational Opportunities for Negro Home Economists," *Journal of Home Economics* 44, no. 2 (February 1952); Sadye Pearl Young, "Enrollment in Home Economics in Selected Negro Colleges," *Journal of Home Economics*, October 1960, 667–72. Howard University, under Kittrell, did not supply data for Young's study.

10. "4-H Club Integration up to Dixie—U.S. Official," *Afro-American*, August 11, 1956.

11. Carmen V. Harris, "States' Rights, Federal Bureaucrats, and Segregated 4-H Camps in the United States, 1927–1969," *The Journal of African American History* 93, no. 3 (Summer 2008): 362–88.

12. Marie Clapp Moffitt, "The Growth and Development of the New Homemakers of America" (PhD diss., Walden University, 1977).

13. "Florence Low Attends White House Meeting," *Journal of Home Economics* 55, no. 7 (September 1963): 486.

14. Moffitt, "The Growth and Development of the New Homemakers of America."

15. Moffitt; "1963–64 NHA Membership," *Chatter Box*, Fall 1964; "News Notes," *Chatter Box*, Spring 1965; Otelia R. Wyche, "Open House Set in Dinwiddie," *Progress-Index*, July 8, 1965; Francis Keppel to Edna P.

Amidon, "[Ordering Merger of FHA and NHA]," September 22, 1964, AAFCS archives, Cornell University.

16. Horrocks, "Good Will Ambassador with a Cookbook"; May Edwin Mann Burke, "The Contributions of Flemmie Pansy Kittrell to Education through Her Doctrines on Home Economics" (PhD diss., University of Maryland, 1988); Gladys Gary Vaughn, interview by author, June 24, 2019.

17. Horrocks.

18. Flemmie Pansy Kittrell, interview, August 29, 1977, Schlesinger Library on the History of Women in America/Black Women Oral History Project, Harvard University.

19. William L. Slayton, "Utilizing Your Strengths in Serving Urban Families," *Journal of Home Economics* 60, no. 8 (October 1968).

20. Dexter B. Wakefield, email message to author, June 1, 2018, and interview by author, August 28, 2020; Dexter Bernard Wakefield and B. Allen Talbert, "Exploring the Past of the New Farmers of America," Proceedings of the 27th National Agricultural Education Research Conference, December 6, 2000, 420–33.

21. *Wade v. Mississippi Cooperative Extension Service*, 372 F. Supp. 126 (N.D. Miss. 1974).

Chapter 12: Beyond Stitching and Stirring

1. Marjorie East, "Construction in the Hierarchy," *Illinois Teacher of Home Economics* 10, no. 6 (Spring 1967): 237–39; Penny A. Ralston, "Flemmie P. Kittrell: Her Views and Practices Regarding Home Economics in Higher Education," *Journal of Home Economics*, Spring 1994.

2. "The Mini (or, If You Prefer, Petite or Micro) Vacation," *Illinois Teacher of Home Economics* 10, no. 2 (Fall 1966): 45–52.

3. Richard Witkin, "Glenn's Orbiting Foiled by Clouds," *New York Times*, January 28, 1962; Mary Hoyt, *American Women of the Space Age* (New York: Atheneum, 1966).

4. Nadia Berenstein, "Eating at 100,000 Ft.: Man High and the Origins of Space Food," *Flavor Added* (blog), March 8, 2018, http://nadiaberenstein.com/blog/2018/3/8/eating-at-100000-ft-man-high-and-the-origins-of-space-food.

5. Hoyt, *American Women of the Space Age*.

6. "Transcript of Glenn's News Conference Relating His Experiences on Orbital Flight," *New York Times*, February 24, 1962.

7. "Food for Space Travelers," *MIT Science Reporter* (WGBH, 1966), https://infinitehistory.mit.edu/video/mit-science-reporter%E2%80%94food-space-travelers-1966; "Doris Howes Calloway, Nutrition: Berkeley," University

of California: In Memoriam, n.d., http://texts.cdlib.org/view?docId=hb9 87008v1;NAAN=13030&doc.view=content&chunk.id=div00008&toc depth=1..&brand=calisphere&anchor.id=0. Some sources say that Calloway's work on freeze-drying led to Tang. Former Kraft Foods archivist Becky Haglund Tousey confirmed that this is untrue. As we will see, Tang is not freeze dried juice.

8. Mary Klicka, "Convenience: Keynote of the Future," *Journal of Home Economics* 61, no. 9 (November 1969); Carol Moberg, "Isolation/Quarantine Foods for Apollo 11 Astronauts from Stouffer's," July 1969.

9. Beatrice Finkelstein, "Current Research for Space Travel Nutrition and Food Technology," *Journal of Home Economics* 54, no. 9 (November 1962): 755–59.

10. "Fitting Is No Problem," *Fashions and Fabrics*, Spring/Summer 1950.

11. Carol Pine, "The Real Betty Crocker Is One Tough Cookie," *Twin Cities*, November 1978.

12. Satenig St. Marie, "Reminiscences," in *Rethinking Home Economics: Women and the History of a Profession*, ed. Sarah Stage and Virginia B. Vincenti (Ithaca, NY: Cornell University Press, 1997).

13. Satenig St. Marie, "[Step by Step]," December 1969, JC Penney's Archives, Southern Methodist University (JCP).

14. "Teachers Acclaim Penney Program," *Penney News*, 1964, JCP.

15. Dorothy Lee, "Home Economics in a Changing World," *Penney's Fashion and Fabrics*, Spring/Summer 1964, JCP; Joy Krause, "Educators Urged to Be 'With It,'" *The Milwaukee Journal*, 1968, JCP.

16. St. Marie, "Reminiscences."

17. St. Marie; Satenig St. Marie, *Homes Are for People* (New York: John Wiley & Sons, 1973).

18. "Computers in Homes Not So Distant," *Journal of Home Economics* 58, no. 6 (June 1966).

19. Glenn Infield, "A Computer in the Basement?," *Popular Mechanics*, April 1968; Dag Spicer, "The ECHO IV Home Computer: 50 Years Later," *Computer History Museum* (blog), May 31, 2016, http://www.computerhistory.org/atchm/the-echo-iv-home-computer-50-years-later/.

20. Whirlpool, "7000 Tomorrows (1964–5 New York World's Fair Brochure)," 1964, http://www.nywf64.com/pavami13.shtml.

21. Marjorie East, "The Importance of Human Values—In the Age of Technology," *Fashions and Fabrics*, Fall/Winter 1966.

22. Dan Sweeney, "Press Release: The Age of Affluence May Include Computer for Mom in Kitchen," October 14, 1969; Kamla, *Honeywell's Kitchen Computer at Computer History Museum*, The Kamla Show, 2016, https://kamlashow

.com/2016/10/02/video-honeywells-kitchen-computer/; "Kitchen Computer," Computer Church, n.d., http://www.thecomputerchurch.org/cgi-bin/item-report-main.cgi?20131218c.

23. Helen Pundt, *AHEA: A History of Excellence* (Washington, DC: American Home Economics Association, 1980); Earl McGrath, "The Imperatives of Change for Home Economics," *Journal of Home Economics* 60, no. 7 (September 1968): 505–14; "History," FCCLA, 2019, https://fcclainc.org/about/history.

24. McGrath, "The Imperatives of Change"; Earl McGrath, "The Changing Mission of Home Economics," *Journal of Home Economics* 60, no. 2 (February 1968): 85–92.

25. McGrath, "The Imperatives of Change."

26. Anna K. Creekmore, "The Concept Basic to Home Economics," *Journal of Home Economics* 20, no. 2 (February 1968): 93–98; Arlene Otto, "[Inside Back Cover]," *Fashions and Fabrics*, Fall/Winter 1965; Marjorie East, "What Is Home Economics?," *Journal of Home Economics* 57, no. 5 (May 1965): 387.

27. Barbara Jo Davis, interview by Linda Cameron, September 17, 2002, Mill City Museum Test Kitchens Oral History Project.

28. *Concepts and Generalizations: Their Place in High School Home Economics Curriculum Development* (Washington, DC: American Home Economics Association, 1967).

29. Margaret W. Rossiter, "Protecting Home Economics, the Women's Field," in *Women Scientists in America: Before Affirmative Action, 1940–1972* (Baltimore: Johns Hopkins University Press, 1995).

30. McGrath, "The Imperatives of Change."

Chapter 13: Addressing the Enemy

1. Robin Morgan, "What Robin Morgan Said at Denver," *Journal of Home Economics* 65, no. 1 (January 1973): 13.

2. Velda V. Bricker, "AHEA Annual Meeting: The Pulse of Progress," *Journal of Home Economics* 55, no. 7 (September 1963): 501–6; Sheila Tobias, "New Feminism on a University Campus: From Job Equality to Female Studies" (Symposium on Feminism, September 23–24, 1970, University of Pittsburgh, proceedings published November 9, 1970).

3. Robin Morgan, "What Robin Morgan Said at Denver."

4. Robin Morgan, interview by author, August 10, 2018.

5. "Morgan, Robin, American Home Economics Correspondence," Robin Morgan Papers, David M. Rubenstein Rare Book & Manuscript Library, Duke University.

6. "The Roles of Women," *Journal of Home Economics*, January 1973, 9–22, 53.

7. William H. Marshall, "Issues Affecting the Future of Home Economics," *Journal of Home Economics*, September 1973.

8. Satenig St. Marie, "What's Right with Home Economics," JCP; Margaret W. Rossiter, *Women Scientists in America: Forging a New World since 1972* (Baltimore: Johns Hopkins University Press, 2012); "Lorene Lane Rogers," University of Texas, Office of the President, January 11, 2016, https://president.utexas.edu/past-presidents/lorene-lane-rogers. Anecdotally, Title IX did not end the practice of barring boys from home ec; a male acquaintance of mine tried to take the class in Louisiana twenty years ago, and his school wouldn't let him.

9. "FCCLA National Officers 1945–2020," FCCLA, January 23, 2020, https://fcclainc.org/sites/default/files/FCCLA%20National%20Officer%20history%201.23.20.pdf; Penny A. Ralston, "Black Participation in Home Economics: A Partial Account," *Journal of Home Economics*, Winter 1978; Mary P. Andrews, "Minority Members Enrich AHEA," *Journal of Home Economics* 76, no. 1 (Spring 1984): 41–44; Alyce M. Fanslow et al., "The 1979 AHEA Membership Survey: Process and Profile," *Journal of Home Economics*, Summer 1980.

10. Nancy C. Hook and Beatrice Paolucci, "The Family as an Ecosystem," *Journal of Home Economics* 62, no. 5 (May 1970). Emphasis in the original.

11. Morgan, interview.

12. Morgan, "What Robin Morgan Said at Denver."

13. Satenig St. Marie, "Consumer Affairs in J. C. Penney," JCP.

14. Satenig St. Marie, "Consumerism and Its Implications for the Penney Company," JCP.

15. Satenig St. Marie, "Thursday—President's Report"; Satenig St. Marie, "AHEA Acceptance," both JCP.

16. J. C. Penney, "[Flyer]," 1972–4?, JCP; Satenig St. Marie, "Consumer Affairs: Potentials for Professionalism," *Journal of Home Economics* 69, no. 10 (December 1977): 18–20; Satenig St. Marie, email message to author, July 14, 2020.

17. "Kit: Your Space and Mine" (J. C. Penney, 1975).

18. Satenig St. Marie, "Editor's Corner," *Forum*, Fall/Winter 1974; Martin Haberman, "What Are Your Own Experiences in Schools?," *Forum*, Spring/Summer 1973.

19. Gladys Gary Vaughn, interview by author, June 24, 2019.

20. Marjorie M. Brown and Beatrice Paolucci, *Home Economics: A Definition* (Washington, DC: American Home Economics Association, 1979); Marjorie East, "Comments on the Paper, *Home Economics: A Definition* by

Marjorie Brown and Beatrice Paolucci," in Brown and Paolucci, *Home Economics: A Definition*.

21. East, "Comments on the Paper."

22. Olive M. Batcher and Louise A. Young, "Metrication and the Home Economist," *Journal of Home Economics*, February 1974.

23. Executive Secretary, "Report of the U.S. Intelligence Board Metric Panel" (Washington, DC: Central Intelligence Agency, March 14, 1974).

Chapter 14: Home Economics at Risk

1. May Edwin Mann Burke, "The Contributions of Flemmie Pansy Kittrell to Education through Her Doctrines on Home Economics" (PhD diss., University of Maryland, 1988).

2. Kathryn Vanzant, interview by author, April 16, 2018.

3. Margaret M. Bubolz, ed., *Beatrice Paolucci: Shaping Destiny through Everyday Life* (East Lansing, MI: Kappa Omicron Nu Honor Society, 2002); Satenig St. Marie, interview by author, October 14, 2019.

4. David P. Gardner et al., *A Nation at Risk: The Imperative for Educational Reform. An Open Letter to the American People. A Report to the Nation and the Secretary of Education* (Washington, DC: Government Printing Office, April 1983).

5. Gardner et al., *A Nation at Risk*.

6. Virginia Munson Moxley, "Home Economics at Risk," *Illinois Teacher of Home Economics* 28, no. 2 (December 1984): 46–48.

7. "Did You Know . . . ," *Illinois Teacher of Home Economics* 17, no. 1 (September 1973): ii; Hazel Taylor Spitze, "Yes, Our Nation Is at Risk, But . . . ," *Journal of Home Economics* 76, no. 2 (Summer 1984): 50–52.

8. Hazel Taylor Spitze, "Helping Students Learn to Think, or The Purpose of the Muffin Lesson," *Illinois Teacher of Home Economics*, February 1986.

9. Yes.

10. Hazel Taylor Spitze, "Home Economics in the Future," *Journal of Home Economics* 68, no. 4 (September 1976): 5–8.

11. Hazel Taylor Spitze, "A Rose by Any Other Name Would Not Be a Rose," *Illinois Teacher of Home Economics*, October 1985.

12. Marilyn J. Horn, "College Programs Affect All AHEA Members," *Journal of Home Economics* 81, no. 3 (Fall 1989): 2.

13. Thomas Lucas, "Boys Are Victims of Sexism, Too," *Seventeen*, June 1987.

14. Onalee McGraw, "The Family, Feminism and the Therapeutic State," *Critical Issues* (The Heritage Foundation, 1980).

15. Wilma Hazen and Millie Riley, "Review: The Family, Feminism and the Therapeutic State," *Journal of Home Economics*, Winter 1981.

16. *Smith v. Board of School Commissioners of Mobile County*, No. 655 F. Supp. 939 (S.D. Ala. 1987); Deborah Tunstall Tippett, "An Analysis of *Smith v. Board of School Commissioners of Mobile County*: The Impact on Home Economics Curriculum" (University of North Carolina at Greensboro, 1991); Stuart Taylor Jr., "Judge Who Banned Textbooks: Hero of the Right," *New York Times*, March 7, 1987.

17. *Smith v. Board*; Tippett, "An Analysis of *Smith v. Board*."

18. *Smith v. Board*; Tippett.

19. Tippett. Tippett refers to trial participants by letters, not by names; triangulating with other sources, including the legal decision, it seems clear that "Author C" was Ryder.

20. Tippett.

21. *Smith v. Board*.

22. Tippett, "An Analysis of *Smith v. Board*."

23. Tippett.

24. Coby Simerly et al., "The Scottsdale Initiative: Positioning the Profession for the 21st Century," *Journal of Family and Consumer Sciences* 92, no. 1 (2000): 75–80; Ayoola White, "The Business of Home Economics, Then and Now," *Schlesinger Library Picks & Finds* (blog), November 21, 2019, https://www.radcliffe.harvard.edu/schlesinger library/blog/business-home-economics -then-and-now; Mildred Barnes Griggs, "Hello and So Long," *Illinois Teacher of Home Economics* 34, no. 5 (June 1991): 161; Ann Bielby, "Home Ec Updating Domestic Image," *Chicago Sun-Times*, September 23, 1993.

25. Jae-Bok Young, " 'Home Ec' Moves with the Times," *Christian Science Monitor*, December 7, 1992.

26. Dee Munson, email message to author, June 8, 2020.

27. Gwen Kay, "Changing Names, Keeping Identity," in *Remaking Home Economics* (Athens: University of Georgia Press, 2015).

28. "The Conceptual Framework for the 21st Century," *Journal of Family and Consumer Sciences*, Winter 1994, 38; Simerly et al., "The Scottsdale Initiative."

29. I personally think it looks like a buxom woman with arms akimbo wearing a robe.

Chapter 15: What Would Ellen Do?

1. Western Michigan University visit by author, February 1, 2018.

2. Gayla Randel, "Kansans Can: A Family and Consumer Sciences Model for Addressing Social, Emotional, and Life Success Skills as Part of the New Kansas Vision" (AAFCS, Atlanta, GA, June 25, 2018).

3. Carol R. Werhan, "Family and Consumer Sciences Secondary School

Programs: National Survey Shows Continued Demand for FCS Teachers," *Journal of Family and Consumer Sciences* 105, no. 4 (2013): 41–45; National Center for Education Statistics, Digest of Education Statistics, "Table 322.10. Bachelor's Degrees Conferred by Postsecondary Institutions, by Field of Study: Selected Years, 1970–71 through 2016–17," 2018.

4. "Yes, Home Economics Still Exists—But It's Called Consumer Sciences Now," *Rachael Ray Show*, September 10, 2019; Ahlishia J. Shipley, email message to author, July 16, 2018; Janet Ryder, email message to author, June 11, 2020. I did not get a response from several attempts to reach Mrs. Obama.

5. "Pathway: Hospitality, Tourism, Culinary and Retail," Louisiana Believes, October 3, 2017; Dinah Istre, email message to author, January 24, 2020; Louisiana Department of Education, "2017–18 Family and Consumer Science Course Enrollment by Site," October 21, 2018.

6. Annie Watts Cloncs, email message to author, March 4, 2020.

7. Shirley Baugher, "The Career and Times of a 70-Year Member," *Journal of Family and Consumer Sciences* 92, no. 1 (2000): 55–56; "Obituaries," *Washington Post*, January 20, 2006.

8. FCCLA, "Annual Membership Report, 2019–20," 2020, https://fcclainc .org/sites/default/files/2019-20%20Membership%20Report.pdf.

9. Joshua Eddinger-Lucero, interview by author, June 26, 2018. Additional interview dates and visits include April 15–19, 2019, and June 12, 2020.

10. Eddinger-Lucero, interview; Bonnie Eddinger, interview by author, April 19, 2019.

11. Glasgow Middle School visit, Lincolnia, VA, October 4, 2017; Angela DeHart, interviews by author, October 1, 2017, and June 11, 2020.

12. Mayflower High School visit, April 18, 2019.

13. Leah Welch, interviews by author, April 17, 2019, and June 16, 2020.

14. Roberta Duyff, interview by author, June 10, 2020.

15. Glasgow Middle School visit; DeHart, interview.

16. Eddinger-Lucero, interview.

Conclusion: How to Bring Back Home Ec

1. US Census Bureau, "Table B09021: Living Arrangements of Adults 18 Years and Over by Age," 2018: ACS 1-Year Estimates Detailed Tables, 2018.

2. Catharine E. Beecher, *A Treatise on Domestic Economy*, 2nd ed. (New York: Harper & Brothers, 1842).

3. Claire Cain Miller, "A 'Generationally Perpetuated' Pattern," *New York Times*, August 15, 2018; Claire Cain Miller, "Young Men Embrace Gender

Equality, but They Still Don't Vacuum," *New York Times,* February 11, 2020; Robin Morgan, interview with author, August 10, 2018.

4. FCCLA, "Annual Membership Report, 2019–20," 2020, https.//fcclainc .org/sites/default/files/2019-20%20Membership%20Report.pdf; Carol R. Werhan, "Family and Consumer Sciences Secondary School Programs: National Survey Shows Continued Demand for FCS Teachers," *Journal of Family and Consumer Sciences* 105, no. 4 (2013): 41–45.

5. Council for Economic Education, "Survey of the States 2020," February 5, 2020.

6. AdvanceCTE, "Career Clusters Pathways," 2020.

7. Hazel Taylor Spitze, "Pride and Prejudice," Presentation to ASA, 1989.

8. Satenig St. Marie, email message to author, April 29, 2020.

INDEX

THE SECRET
HISTORY OF
HOME ECONOMICS

Danielle Dreilinger

THE SECRET HISTORY OF HOME ECONOMICS

Danielle Dreilinger

DISCUSSION QUESTIONS

1. During the second half of the nineteenth century, more and different colleges were established and most college leaders supported a course in "domestic science" for women. Do you believe it was empowering or repressive to include housework in the curriculum for women? Do you think you would have chosen to study domestic science even after hearing it wasn't "a course of training for really intelligent women"? (p. 14) Why or why not?

2. Booker T. Washington said in his most famous speech, "No race can prosper till it learns that there is as much dignity in tilling a field as in writing a poem" (p. 15). Do you agree with Washington? How did Black women approach home economics differently than white women? How might white women and Black women have benefited from working together? What challenges did they share?

3. Ellen Richards and her colleagues at the Lake Placid Conference wanted to convince universities to embrace home science as a serious study in order to create "a new profession commanding adequate compensation" (p. 28). What made home economics "serious" to these pioneering women?

4. Eugenicists embraced home economics because they believed some heritable traits could be cured by right living.

Why do you think home economists were reluctant to reject eugenics? Do you think that a focus on "race betterment" helped or hurt home economists as they tried to secure support from white men in charge?

5. Betty Crocker, the fictional character who taught home economics in a radio program for General Mills, was not allowed to discuss her private life. Why do you think General Mills prevented its female influencer from sharing personal matters? How do you think women would respond to Betty Crocker or Aunt Sammy today?

6. In the 1920s, home economics departments began trying to teach students about parenthood with practice babies. Why do you think home economists embraced the "professionalization of parenthood"? (p. 82) What ethical questions did practice babies raise? What do you think of the practice yourself?

7. During the 1950s, a group of Maryland homemakers complained in *The Journal of Home Economics* that news coverage lionized working women and minimized the importance of homemaking. Which do you think is more important: paid work or homemaking?

8. Home economists made considerable contributions to progressive causes in the late 1960s, and yet they were uncertain about their purpose and future direction. What would you have advised home economists to do as they struggled for respect?

9. Robin Morgan went to the 1971 American Home Economics Association conference and declared, "As a radical feminist, I am here addressing the enemy" (p. 240). Why was Morgan so concerned about young women passing through home economics departments? What did she want home economists to do going forward? Did home

economists need radical feminists? Did radical feminists need home economists?

10. In 1980, the family values movement put home economics on trial. Why did Christian fundamentalists target home economists? Why didn't earlier home economists face the same scrutiny? Do you think home economics departments knew how to talk about family life at the end of the twentieth century? Why or why not?

11. Roberta Duyff believes that "the terminology [of home economics] is lost but the profession is still there" (p. 285). Do you agree with this assessment? Where are home economists working today? Have families paid a price as home economics programs have crumbled?

12. Danielle Dreilinger tells us how we might be able to revive home economics. Do you agree with her recommendations? Would you modify or add anything? Should home economics focus on life skills or career preparation? Personal improvement or societal change?

Meghan Kenny	*The Driest Season*
Nicole Krauss	*The History of Love*
Don Lee	*The Collective*
Amy Liptrot	*The Outrun: A Memoir*
Donna M. Lucey	*Sargent's Women*
Bernard MacLaverty	*Midwinter Break*
Maaza Mengiste	*Beneath the Lion's Gaze*
Claire Messud	*The Burning Girl*
	When the World Was Steady
Liz Moore	*Heft*
	The Unseen World
Neel Mukherjee	*The Lives of Others*
	A State of Freedom
Janice P. Nimura	*Daughters of the Samurai*
Rachel Pearson	*No Apparent Distress*
Richard Powers	*Orfeo*
Kirstin Valdez Quade	*Night at the Fiestas*
Jean Rhys	*Wide Sargasso Sea*
Mary Roach	*Packing for Mars*
Somini Sengupta	*The End of Karma*
Akhil Sharma	*Family Life*
	A Life of Adventure and Delight
Joan Silber	*Fools*
Johanna Skibsrud	*Quartet for the End of Time*
Mark Slouka	*Brewster*
Kate Southwood	*Evensong*
Manil Suri	*The City of Devi*
	The Age of Shiva
Madeleine Thien	*Do Not Say We Have Nothing*
	Dogs at the Perimeter
Vu Tran	*Dragonfish*
Rose Tremain	*The American Lover*
	The Gustav Sonata
Brady Udall	*The Lonely Polygamist*
Brad Watson	*Miss Jane*
Constance Fenimore Woolson	*Miss Grief and Other Stories*